New Perspectives on

Microsoft® Office Word 2003

Brief

S. Scott Zimmerman
Brigham Young University

Beverly B. Zimmerman
Brigham Young University

Ann Shaffer

THOMSON

COURSE TECHNOLOGY

Australia • Canada • Mexico • Singapore • Spain • United Kingdom • United States

New Perspectives on Microsoft® Office Word 2003—Brief

is published by Course Technology.

Managing Editor:
Rachel Goldberg

Senior Product Manager:
Kathy Finnegan

Senior Technology Product Manager:
Amanda Young Shelton

Product Manager:
Karen Stevens

Product Manager:
Brianna Germain

Editorial Assistant:
Abigail Z. Reider

Senior Marketing Manager:
Rachel Stephens

Associate Marketing Manager:
Caitlin Wight

Developmental Editor:
Pam Conrad

Senior Production Editor:
Elena Montillo

Composition:
GEX Publishing Services

Text Designer:
Steve Deschene

Cover Designer:
Nancy Goulet

Preface

Real, Thought-Provoking, Engaging, Dynamic, Interactive—these are just a few of the words that are used to describe the New Perspectives Series' approach to learning and building computer skills.

Without our critical-thinking and problem-solving methodology, computer skills could be learned but not retained. By teaching with a case-based approach, the New Perspectives Series challenges students to apply what they've learned to real-life situations.

Our ever-growing community of users understands why they're learning what they're learning. Now you can too!

See what instructors and students are saying about the best-selling New Perspectives Series:

"The New Perspectives format is a pleasure to use. The Quick Checks and the tutorial Review Assignments help students view topics from a real world perspective."
— Craig Shaw, Central Community College – Hastings

...and about New Perspectives on Microsoft Office Word 2003:

"The layout in this textbook is thoughtfully designed and organized. It is very easy to locate concepts and step-by-step instructions. The Case Problems provide different scenarios that cover material in the tutorial with plenty of exercises."
— Shui-lien Huang, Mt. San Antonio College

"New Perspectives Word 2003 is the most comprehensive text I've seen covering important word-processing skills. Not only does it cover the skills with easy-to-follow, step-by-step instructions using real-world examples, but also includes a thorough coverage of the conceptual material essential for students to fully understand word processing. The hands-on exercises and cases are excellent for helping students gain proficiency."
—Kathleen Bent, Cape Cod Community College

www.course.com/NewPerspectives

Why *New Perspectives* will work for you

Review

Apply

Reference Window

Task Reference

Reinforce

Context

Each tutorial begins with a problem presented in a "real-world" case that is meaningful to students. The case sets the scene to help students understand what they will do in the tutorial.

Hands-on Approach

Each tutorial is divided into manageable sessions that combine reading and hands-on, step-by-step work. Screenshots—now 20% larger for enhanced readability—help guide students through the steps. **Trouble?** tips anticipate common mistakes or problems to help students stay on track and continue with the tutorial.

Review

In New Perspectives, retention is a key component to learning. At the end of each session, a series of Quick Check questions helps students test their understanding of the concepts before moving on. And now each tutorial contains an end-of-tutorial summary and a list of key terms for further reinforcement.

Assessment

Engaging and challenging Review Assignments and Case Problems have always been a hallmark feature of the New Perspectives Series. Now we've added new features to make them more accessible! Colorful icons and brief descriptions accompany the exercises, making it easy to understand, at a glance, both the goal and level of challenge a particular assignment holds.

Reference

While contextual learning is excellent for retention, there are times when students will want a high-level understanding of how to accomplish a task. Within each tutorial, Reference Windows appear before a set of steps to provide a succinct summary and preview of how to perform a task. In addition, a complete Task Reference at the back of the book provides quick access to information on how to carry out common tasks. Finally, each book includes a combination Glossary/Index to promote easy reference of material.

Lab Assignments

Certain tutorials in this book contain Lab Assignments, which provide additional reinforcement of important skills in a simulated environment. These labs have been hailed by students and teachers alike for years as the most comprehensive and accurate on the market. Great for pre-work or remediation, the labs help students learn concepts and skills in a structured environment.

Student Online Companion

This book has an accompanying online companion Web site designed to enhance learning.
- All links have been completely updated for currency.
- The Web site acts as a gateway for all hands-on activities in each tutorial.
- Each page offers a list of additional Web sites for further exploration.

www.course.com/NewPerspectives

New Perspectives offers an entire system of instruction

The New Perspectives Series is more than just a handful of books. It's a complete system of offerings:

New Perspectives catalog
Our online catalog is never out of date! Go to the catalog link on our Web site to check out our available titles, request a desk copy, download a book preview, or locate online files.

Coverage to meet your needs!
Whether you're looking for just a small amount of coverage or enough to fill a semester-long class, we can provide you with a textbook that meets your needs.
- Brief books typically cover the essential skills in just 2 to 4 tutorials.
- Introductory books build and expand on those skills and contain an average of 5 to 8 tutorials.
- Comprehensive books are great for a full-semester class, and contain 9 to 12+ tutorials.
- Power Users or Advanced books are perfect for a highly accelerated introductory class or a second course in a given topic.

So if the book you're holding does not provide the right amount of coverage for you, there's probably another offering available. Go to our Web site or contact your Course Technology sales representative to find out what else we offer.

Instructor Resources

We offer more than just a book. We have all the tools you need to enhance your lectures, check students' work, and generate exams in a new, easier-to-use and completely revised package. This book's Instructor's Manual, ExamView testbank, PowerPoint presentations, data files, solution files, figure files, and a sample syllabus are all available on a single CD-ROM or for downloading at www.course.com.

How will your students master Microsoft Office?
SAM (Skills Assessment Manager) 2003 helps you energize your class exams and training assignments by allowing students to learn and test important computer skills in an active, hands-on environment. With SAM 2003, you create powerful interactive exams on critical Microsoft Office 2003 applications, including Word, Excel, Access, and PowerPoint. The exams simulate the application environment, allowing your students to demonstrate their knowledge and to think through the skills by performing real-world tasks. Designed to be used with the New Perspectives Series, SAM 2003 includes built-in page references so students can create study guides that match the New Perspectives textbooks you use in class. Powerful administrative options allow you to schedule exams and assignments, secure your tests, and run reports with almost limitless flexibility. Find out more about SAM 2003 by going to www.course.com or speaking with your Course Technology sales representative.

Distance Learning
Enhance your course with any of our online learning platforms. Go to www.course.com or speak with your Course Technology sales representative to find the platform or the content that's right for you.

www.course.com/NewPerspectives

About This Book

This book provides a short, hands-on introduction to word processing using the latest version of Microsoft Word, covering everything from creating business letters through simple desktop publishing.

- Updated for the new software! This book includes coverage of the new Research task pane and the new Reading Layout view.
- Tutorial 1 gives students the fundamental skills they need to create a document in Word. In this edition, the tutorial has been streamlined to move through basic topics more quickly, while still providing thorough coverage.
- For this edition, Tutorial 2 also has been restructured to move more quickly through editing and formatting tasks in Word, while still including thorough explanations.
- Tutorial 3 teaches students how to create a document containing multiple pages and how to create and modify tables.
- Tutorial 4 covers Word features and functions that students use to desktop publish a newsletter. In this edition, by popular demand, coverage of mail merge is also provided.

New to this edition!

- Screenshots are now 20% larger for improved readability.
- Sequential page numbering makes it easier to refer to specific pages in the book.
- The new Tutorial Summary and Key Terms sections at the end of each tutorial provide additional conceptual review for students.
- New labels and descriptions for the end-of-tutorial exercises make it easy for you to select the right exercises for your students.

Acknowledgments

Many thanks to the tireless reviewers, for all their detailed comments and suggestions: Kathleen Bent, Cape Cod Community College; Michael Feiler, Merritt College; Shui-lien Huang, Mt. San Antonio College; Glen Johansson, Spokane Community College; Mary Logan, Delgado Community College; and Kathy Winters, The University of Tennessee at Chattanooga. Thanks as well to Steven Freund, Dave Nuscher, and Rebekah Tidwell for their work on the Instructor Resources. Thank you also to the following members of the Quality Assurance team at Course Technology for verifying the technical accuracy of every step: John Bosco and John Freitas, Quality Assurance Managers; and Vitaly Davidovich, Sean Franey, and Susan Whalen, Quality Assurance Testers. Thanks to the smart, helpful people on the New Perspectives team, including Rachel Goldberg, Managing Editor; Brianna Germain, Product Manager; and Abbey Reider, Editorial Assistant. Special thanks to Kathy Finnegan, Senior Product Manager, who cheerfully steered our boat through a sea of details and complications. I'm grateful to Pam Conrad for her cheerful patience and careful editing, which introduced many improvements to this edition. Thanks, also, to Elena Montillo, Production Editor, for patiently managing the transformation of the manuscript into a published book. Finally, a thousand thanks to Beverly and Scott Zimmerman, writers and teachers extraordinaire, for giving me a chance to be a part of their team.

Ann Shaffer

We likewise want to thank all those who made this book possible. We especially want to thank Ann Shaffer, our co-author, for her expertise, hard work, and creative talents. Special thanks also go to Pam Conrad for her dedication and expertise as Developmental Editor in bringing this new edition to fruition.

Beverly and Scott Zimmerman

www.course.com/NewPerspectives

Table of Contents

Tutorial 3   WD 89

Creating a Multiple-Page Report .... WD 89
Writing a Recommendation ....WD 89

Tutorial 4   WD 135

Desktop Publishing and Mail Merge................. WD 135
Creating a Newsletter and Cover Letter ....WD 135

New Perspectives on

Using Common Features of Microsoft® Office 2003

Preparing Promotional Materials   OFF 3

Read This Before You Begin

To the Student

Data Files

To complete the Using Common Features of Microsoft Office 2003 tutorial, you need the starting student Data Files. Your instructor will either provide you with these Data Files or ask you to obtain them yourself.

The Using Common Features of Microsoft Office 2003 tutorial requires the folder named "OFF" to complete the Tutorial, Review Assignments, and Case Problems. You will need to copy this folder from a file server, a stand-alone computer, or the Web to the drive and folder where you will be storing your Data Files. Your instructor will tell you which computer, drive letter, and folder(s) contain the files you need. You can also download the files by going to www.course.com; see the inside back or front cover for

more information on downloading the files, or ask your instructor or technical support person for assistance.

If you are storing your Data Files on floppy disks, you will need one blank, formatted, high-density disk for this tutorial. Label your disk as shown, and place on it the folder indicated.

▼ **Common Features of Office: Data Disk**
   OFF folder

When you begin this tutorial, refer to the Student Data Files section at the bottom of the tutorial opener page, which indicates which folders and files you need for the tutorial. Each end-of-tutorial exercise also indicates the files you need to complete that exercise.

To the Instructor

The Data Files are available on the Instructor Resources CD for this title. Follow the instructions in the Help file on the CD to install the programs to your network or standalone computer. See the "To the Student" section above for information on how to set up the Data Files that accompany this text.

You are granted a license to copy the Data Files to any computer or computer network used by students who have purchased this book.

System Requirements

If you are going to work through this book using your own computer, you need:

- **Computer System** Microsoft Windows 2000 or Windows XP Professional or higher must be installed on your computer. This tutorial assumes a typical installation of Microsoft Office 2003. Additionally, to

complete the steps for accessing Microsoft's Online Help for Office, an Internet connection and a Web browser are required.

- **Data Files** You will not be able to complete the tutorals or exercises in this book using your own computer until you have the necessary starting Data Files.

www.course.com/NewPerspectives

Objectives

- Explore the programs that comprise Microsoft Office
- Start programs and switch between them
- Explore common window elements
- Minimize, maximize, and restore windows
- Use personalized menus and toolbars
- Work with task panes
- Create, save, close, and open a file
- Use the Help system
- Print a file
- Exit programs

Using Common Features of Microsoft Office 2003

Preparing Promotional Materials

Case

Delmar Office Supplies

Delmar Office Supplies, a company in Wisconsin founded by Jake Alexander in 1996, sells recycled office supplies to businesses and home-based offices around the world. The demand for quality recycled papers, reconditioned toner cartridges, and renovated office furniture has been growing each year. Jake and all his employees use Microsoft Office 2003, which provides everyone in the company the power and flexibility to store a variety of information, create consistent files, and share data. In this tutorial, you'll review how the company's employees use Microsoft Office 2003.

Student Data Files

▼OFF folder

▽ **Tutorial folder**

    (no starting Data Files)

▽ **Review folder**

    Finances.xls

    Letter.doc

Exploring Microsoft Office 2003

Microsoft Office 2003, or simply **Office**, is a collection of the most popular Microsoft programs: Word, Excel, PowerPoint, Access, and Outlook. Each Office program contains valuable tools to help you accomplish many tasks, such as composing reports, analyzing data, preparing presentations, compiling information, sending e-mail, and planning schedules.

Microsoft Word 2003, or simply **Word**, is a word-processing program you use to create text documents. The files you create in Word are called **documents**. Word offers many special features that help you compose and update all types of documents, ranging from letters and newsletters to reports, brochures, faxes, and even books—all in attractive and readable formats. You can also use Word to create, insert, and position figures, tables, and other graphics to enhance the look of your documents. The Delmar Office Supplies sales representatives create their business letters using Word.

Microsoft Excel 2003, or simply **Excel**, is a spreadsheet program you use to display, organize, and analyze numerical data. You can do some of this in Word with tables, but Excel provides many more tools for recording and formatting numbers as well as performing calculations. The graphics capabilities in Excel also enable you to display data visually. You might, for example, generate a pie chart or a bar chart to help readers quickly see the significance of and the connections between information. The files you create in Excel are called **workbooks**. The Delmar Office Supplies operations department uses a line chart in an Excel workbook to visually track the company's financial performance.

Microsoft Access 2003, or simply **Access**, is a database program you use to enter, organize, display, and retrieve related information. The files you create in Access are called **databases**. With Access you can create data entry forms to make data entry easier, and you can create professional reports to improve the readability of your data. The Delmar Office Supplies operations department tracks the company's inventory in a table in an Access database.

Microsoft PowerPoint 2003, or simply **PowerPoint**, is a presentation graphics program you use to create a collection of slides that can contain text, charts, pictures, and so on. The files you create in PowerPoint are called **presentations**. You can show these presentations on your computer monitor, project them onto a screen as a slide show, print them, share them over the Internet, or display them on the World Wide Web. You can also use PowerPoint to generate presentation-related documents such as audience handouts, outlines, and speakers' notes. The Delmar Office Supplies sales department has created an effective slide presentation with PowerPoint to promote the company's latest product line.

Microsoft Outlook 2003, or simply **Outlook**, is an information management program you use to send, receive, and organize e-mail; plan your schedule; arrange meetings; organize contacts; create a to-do list; and jot down notes. You can also use Outlook to print schedules, task lists, phone directories, and other documents. Jake Alexander uses Outlook to send and receive e-mail, plan his schedule, and create a to-do list.

Although each Office program individually is a strong tool, their potential is even greater when used together.

Integrating Office Programs

One of the main advantages of Office is **integration**, the ability to share information between programs. Integration ensures consistency and accuracy, and it saves time because you don't have to re-enter the same information in several Office programs. The staff at Delmar Office Supplies uses the integration features of Office daily, including the following examples:

- The accounting department created an Excel bar chart on the previous two years' fourth-quarter results, which they inserted into the quarterly financial report created in Word. They included a hyperlink in the Word report that employees can click to open the Excel workbook and view the original data.
- The operations department included an Excel pie chart of sales percentages by divisions of Delmar Office Supplies on a PowerPoint slide, which is part of a presentation to stockholders.
- The marketing department produced a mailing to promote the company's newest products by combining a form letter created in Word with an Access database that stores the names and addresses of customers.
- A sales representative wrote a letter in Word about a sales incentive program and merged the letter with an Outlook contact list containing the names and addresses of his customers.

These are just a few examples of how you can take information from one Office program and integrate it into another.

Starting Office Programs

You can start any Office program by clicking the Start button on the Windows taskbar, and then selecting the program you want from the All Programs menu. Once the program starts, you can immediately begin to create new files or work with existing ones. If you or another user has recently used one of the Office programs, then that program might appear on the most frequently used programs list on the left side of the Start menu. You can click the program name to start the program.

Starting Office Programs | Reference Window

- Click the Start button on the taskbar.
- Point to All Programs.
- Point to Microsoft Office.
- Click the name of the program you want to start.
or
- Click the name of the program you want to start on the most frequently used programs list on the left side of the Start menu.

You'll start Excel using the Start button.

To start Excel and open a new, blank workbook:

▶ **1.** Make sure your computer is on and the Windows desktop appears on your screen.

Trouble? If your screen varies slightly from those shown in the figures, then your computer might be set up differently. The figures in this book were created while running Windows XP in its default settings, but how your screen looks depends on a variety of things, including the version of Windows, background settings, and so forth.

▶ **2.** Click the **Start** button on the taskbar, and then point to **All Programs** to display the All Programs menu.

▶ **3.** Point to **Microsoft Office** on the All Programs menu, and then point to **Microsoft Office Excel 2003**. See Figure 1. Depending on how your computer is set up, your desktop and menu might contain different icons and commands.

Figure 1 ▶ **Start menu with All Programs submenu displayed**

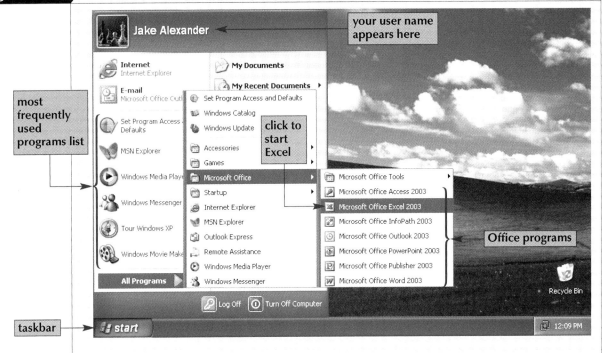

Trouble? If you don't see Microsoft Office on the All Programs menu, point to Microsoft Office Excel 2003. If you still don't see Microsoft Office Excel 2003, ask your instructor or technical support person for help.

▶ **4.** Click **Microsoft Office Excel 2003** to start Excel and open a new, blank workbook. See Figure 2.

New, blank Excel workbook ◀ **Figure 2**

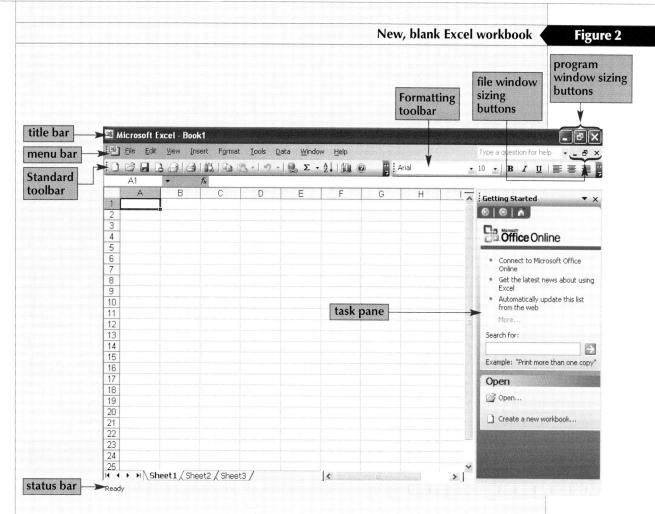

Trouble? If the Excel window doesn't fill your entire screen, the window is not maximized, or expanded to its full size. You'll maximize the window shortly.

You can have more than one Office program open at once. You'll use this same method to start Word and open a new, blank document.

To start Word and open a new, blank document:

▶ **1.** Click the **Start** button on the taskbar.

▶ **2.** Point to **All Programs** to display the All Programs menu.

▶ **3.** Point to **Microsoft Office** on the All Programs menu.

  Trouble? If you don't see Microsoft Office on the All Programs menu, point to Microsoft Office Word 2003. If you still don't see Microsoft Office Word 2003, ask your instructor or technical support person for help.

▶ **4.** Click **Microsoft Office Word 2003**. Word opens with a new, blank document. See Figure 3.

Figure 3	New, blank document in Word

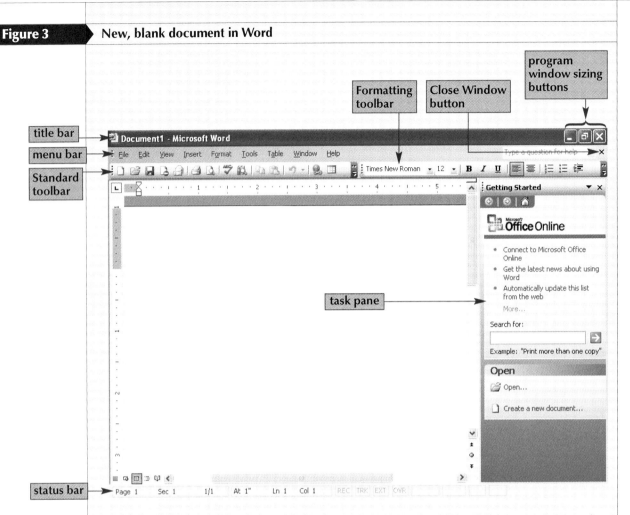

Trouble? If the Word window doesn't fill your entire screen, the window is not maximized. You'll maximize the window shortly.

When you have more than one program or file open at a time, you can switch between them.

Switching Between Open Programs and Files

Two programs are running at the same time—Excel and Word. The taskbar contains buttons for both programs. When you have two or more programs running, or two files within the same program open, you can use the taskbar buttons to switch from one program or file to another. The employees at Delmar Office Supplies often work in several programs at once.

To switch between Word and Excel:

1. Click the **Microsoft Excel – Book1** button on the taskbar to switch from Word to Excel. See Figure 4.

Excel and Word programs opened simultaneously ◀ **Figure 4**

button for active program appears in darker blue

click to switch back to Word

Ready

🔲 start | Microsoft Excel - Book1 | Document1 - Microsof... | 12:15 PM

2. Click the **Document1 – Microsoft Word** button on the taskbar to return to Word.

As you can see, you can start multiple programs and switch between them in seconds.

Exploring Common Window Elements

The Office programs consist of windows that have many similar features. As you can see in Figures 2 and 3, many of the elements you see in both the Excel program window and the Word program window are the same. In fact, all the Office programs have these same elements. Figure 5 describes some of the most common window elements.

Common window elements ◀ **Figure 5**

Element	Description
Title bar	A bar at the top of the window that contains the filename of the open file, the program name, and the program window sizing buttons
Menu bar	A collection of menus for commonly used commands
Toolbars	Collections of buttons that are shortcuts to commonly used menu commands
Sizing buttons	Buttons that resize and close the program window or the file window
Task pane	A window that provides access to commands for common tasks you'll perform in Office programs
Status bar	An area at the bottom of the program window that contains information about the open file or the current task on which you are working

Because these elements are the same in each program, once you've learned one program, it's easy to learn the others. The next sections explore the primary common features—the window sizing buttons, the menus and toolbars, and the task panes.

Using the Window Sizing Buttons

There are two sets of sizing buttons. The top set controls the program window and the bottom set controls the file window. There are three different sizing buttons. The Minimize button ▬, which is the left button, hides a window so that only its program button is visible on the taskbar. The middle button changes name and function depending on the status of the window—the Maximize button ☐ expands the window to the full screen size or to the program window size, and the Restore button ⧉ returns the window to a predefined size. The right button, the Close button ✕, exits the program or closes the file.

Most often you'll want to maximize the program and file windows as you work to take advantage of the full screen size you have available. If you have several files open, you might want to restore the files so that you can see more than one window at a time or you might want to minimize the programs with which you are not working at the moment. You'll try minimizing, maximizing, and restoring windows now.

To resize windows:

▶ **1.** Click the **Minimize** button 🔲 on the Word title bar to reduce the Word program window to a taskbar button. The Excel window is visible again.

▶ **2.** If necessary, click the **Maximize** button 🔲 on the Excel title bar. The Excel program window expands to fill the screen.

▶ **3.** Click the **Restore Window** button 🔲 on the Excel menu bar. The file window, referred to as the workbook window in Excel, resizes smaller than the full program window. See Figure 6.

| Figure 6 | Resized Excel windows |

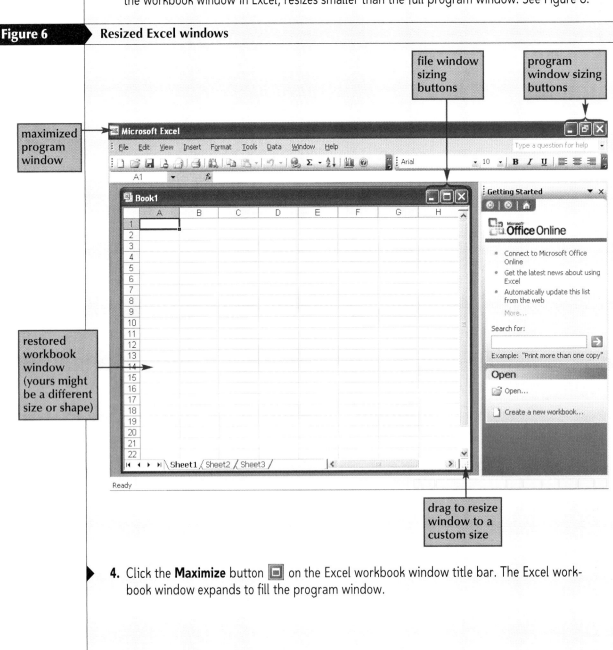

▶ **4.** Click the **Maximize** button 🔲 on the Excel workbook window title bar. The Excel workbook window expands to fill the program window.

   5. Click the **Document1 - Microsoft Word** button on the taskbar. The Word program window returns to its previous size.

   6. If necessary, click the **Maximize** button 🔲 on the Word title bar. The Word program window expands to fill the screen.

   The sizing buttons give you the flexibility to arrange the program and file windows on your screen to best fit your needs.

Using Menus and Toolbars

In each Office program, you can perform tasks using a menu command, a toolbar button, or a keyboard shortcut. A **menu command** is a word on a menu that you click to execute a task; a **menu** is a group of related commands. For example, the File menu contains commands for managing files, such as the Open command and the Save command. The File, Edit, View, Insert, Format, Tools, Window, and Help menus appear on the menu bar in all the Office programs, although some of the commands they include differ from program to program. Other menus are program specific, such as the Table menu in Word and the Data menu in Excel.

   A **toolbar** is a collection of buttons that correspond to commonly used menu commands. For example, the Standard toolbar contains an Open button and a Save button. The Standard and Formatting toolbars (as well as other toolbars) appear in all the Office programs, although some of the buttons they include differ from program to program. The Standard toolbar has buttons related to working with files. The Formatting toolbar has buttons related to changing the appearance of content. Each program also has program-specific toolbars, such as the Tables and Borders toolbar in Word for working with tables and the Chart toolbar in Excel for working with graphs and charts.

   A **keyboard shortcut** is a combination of keys you press to perform a command. For example, Ctrl+S is the keyboard shortcut for the Save command (you hold down the Ctrl key while you press the S key). Keyboard shortcuts appear to the right of many menu commands.

Viewing Personalized Menus and Toolbars

When you first use a newly installed Office program, the menus and toolbars display only the basic and most commonly used commands and buttons, streamlining the program window. The other commands and buttons are available, but you have to click an extra button to see them (the Expand button on a menu and the Toolbar Options button on a toolbar). As you select commands and click buttons, the ones you use often are put on the short, personalized menu and on the visible part of the toolbars. The ones you don't use remain available on the full menus and toolbars. This means that the Office menus and toolbars might display different commands and buttons on each person's computer.

To view a personalized and full menu:

   1. Click **Insert** on the Word menu bar to display the short, personalized menu. See Figure 7. The Bookmark command, for example, does not appear on the short menu.

Figure 7 ▶ **Short, personalized menu**

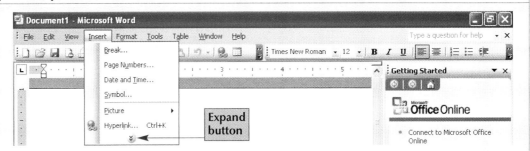

Trouble? If the Insert menu displays different commands than those shown in Figure 7, you need to reset the menus. Click Tools on the menu bar, click Customize (you might need to pause until the full menu appears to see the command), and then click the Options tab in the Customize dialog box. Click the Always show full menus check box to remove the check mark, if necessary, and then click the Show full menus after a short delay check box to insert a check mark, if necessary. Click the Reset menu and toolbar usage data button, and then click the Yes button to confirm that you want to reset the commands. Click the Close button. Repeat Step 1.

You can display the full menu in one of three ways: (1) pause until the full menu appears, which might happen as you read this; (2) click the Expand button at the bottom of the menu; or (3) double-click the menu name on the menu bar.

▶ **2.** Pause until the full Insert menu appears, as shown in Figure 8. The Bookmark command and other commands are now visible.

Figure 8 ▶ **Full, expanded menu**

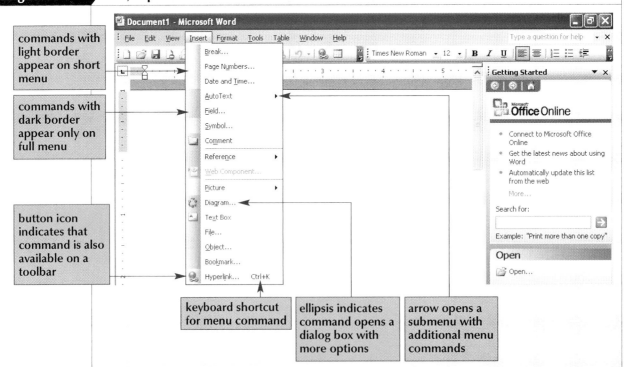

▶ **3.** Click the **Bookmark** command. A dialog box opens when you click a command whose name is followed by an ellipsis (...). In this case, the Bookmark dialog box opens.

4. Click the **Cancel** button to close the Bookmark dialog box.

5. Click **Insert** on the menu bar again to display the short, personalized menu. The Bookmark command appears on the short, personalized menu because you have recently used it.

6. Press the **Esc** key on the keyboard twice to close the menu.

As you can see, the menu changed based on your actions. Over time, only the commands you use frequently will appear on the personalized menu. The toolbars work similarly.

To use the personalized toolbars:

1. Observe that the Standard and Formatting toolbars appear side by side below the menu bar.

   Trouble? If the toolbars appear on two rows, you need to reset them to their default state. Click Tools on the menu bar, click Customize, and then click the Options tab in the Customize dialog box. Click the Show Standard and Formatting toolbars on two rows check box to remove the check mark. Click the Reset menu and toolbar usage data button, and then click the Yes button to confirm you want to reset the commands. Click the Close button. Repeat Step 1.

2. Click the **Toolbar Options** button ⧉ on the Standard toolbar. See Figure 9.

Toolbar Options palette ◀ **Figure 9**

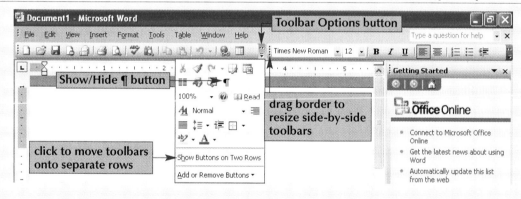

Trouble? If you see different buttons on the Toolbar Options palette, your side-by-side toolbars might be sized differently than the ones shown in Figure 9. Continue with Step 3.

3. Click the **Show/Hide ¶** button 🔲 on the Toolbar Options palette to display the nonprinting screen characters. The Show/Hide ¶ button moves to the visible part of the Standard toolbar, and another button may be moved onto the Toolbar Options palette to make room for the new button.

   Trouble? If the Show/Hide ¶ button already appears on the Standard toolbar, click another button on the Toolbar Options palette. Then click that same button again in Step 4 to turn off that formatting, if necessary.

   Some buttons, like the Show/Hide ¶ button, act as a toggle switch—one click turns on the feature and a second click turns it off.

4. Click the **Show/Hide ¶** button 🔲 on the Standard toolbar again to hide the nonprinting screen characters.

Some people like that the menus and toolbars change to meet their work habits. Others prefer to see all the menu commands or to display the default toolbars on two rows so that all the buttons are always visible. You'll change the toolbar setting now.

To turn off the personalized toolbars:

▶ **1.** Click the **Toolbar Options** button ▪ on the right side of the Standard toolbar.

▶ **2.** Click the **Show Buttons on Two Rows** command. The toolbars move to separate rows (the Standard toolbar on top) and you can see all the buttons on each toolbar.

You can easily access any button on the Standard and Formatting toolbars with one mouse click. The drawback is that when the toolbars are displayed on two rows, they take up more space in the program window, limiting the space you have to work.

Using Task Panes

A **task pane** is a window that provides access to commands for common tasks you'll perform in Office programs. For example, the Getting Started task pane, which opens when you first start any Office program, enables you to create new files and open existing ones. Task panes also help you navigate through more complex, multi-step procedures. All the Office programs include the task panes described in Figure 10. The other available task panes vary by program.

Figure 10 ▶ **Common task panes**

Task pane	Description
Getting Started	The home task pane; allows you to create new files, open existing files, search the online and offline Help system by keyword, and access Office online
Help	Allows you to search the online and offline Help system by keyword or table of contents, and access Microsoft Office Online
Search Results	Displays available Help topics related to entered keyword and enables you to initiate a new search
New	Allows you to create new files; name changes to New Document in Word, New Workbook in Excel, New File in Access, and New Presentation in PowerPoint
Clip Art	Allows you to search for all types of media clips (pictures, sound, video) and insert clips from the results
Clipboard	Allows you to paste some or all of the items that have been cut or copied from any Office program during the current work session
Research	Allows you to search a variety of reference material and other resources from within a file

No matter what their purpose, you use the same processes to open, close, and navigate between the task panes.

Opening and Closing Task Panes

When you first start any Office program, the Getting Started task pane opens by default along the right edge of the program window. You can resize or move the task pane to suit your work habits. You can also close the task pane to display the open file in the full available program window. For example, you might want to close the task pane when you are typing the body of a letter in Word or entering a lot of data in Excel.

You will open and close the task pane.

To open and close the task pane:

▶ 1. If necessary, click **View** on the menu bar, and then click **Task Pane**. The most recently viewed task pane opens on the right side of the screen. See Figure 11.

Getting Started task pane ◄ Figure 11

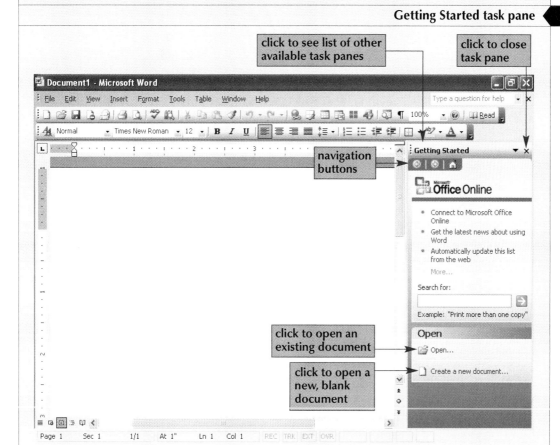

Trouble? If you do not see the task pane, you probably closed the open task pane in Step 1. Repeat Step 1 to reopen the task pane.

Trouble? If a different task pane than the Getting Started task pane opens, then another task pane was the most recently viewed task pane. You'll learn how to open different task panes in the next section; continue with Step 2.

▶ 2. Click the **Close** button ⊠ on the task pane title bar. The task pane closes, leaving more room on the screen for the open file.

▶ 3. Click **View** on the menu bar, and then click **Task Pane**. The task pane reopens.

There are several ways to display different task panes.

Navigating Among Task Panes

Once the task pane is open, you can display different task panes to suit the task you are trying to complete. For example, you can display the New task pane when you want to create a new file from a template. The name of the New task pane varies, depending on the program you are using: Word has the New Document task pane, Excel has the New Workbook task pane, PowerPoint has the New Presentation task pane, and Access has the New File task pane.

One of the quickest ways to display a task pane is to use the Other Task Panes button. When you point to the name of the open task pane in the task pane title bar, it becomes the Other Task Panes button. When you click the Other Task Panes button, all the available task panes for that Office program are listed. Just click the name of the task pane you want to display to switch to that task pane.

There are three navigation buttons at the top of the task pane. The Back and Forward buttons enable you to scroll backward and forward through the task panes you have opened during your current work session. The Back button becomes available when you display two or more task panes. The Forward button becomes available after you click the Back button to return to a previously viewed task pane. The Home button returns you to the Getting Started task pane no matter which task pane is currently displayed.

You'll use each of these methods to navigate among the task panes.

To navigate among task panes:

1. Point to **Getting Started** in the task pane title bar. The title bar becomes the Other Task Panes button.

2. Click the **Other Task Panes** button. A list of the available task panes for Word is displayed. The check mark before Getting Started indicates that this is the currently displayed task pane.

3. Click **New Document**. The New Document task pane appears and the Back button is available.

4. Click the **Back** button in the task pane. The Getting Started task pane reappears and the Forward button is available.

5. Click the **Forward** button in the task pane. The New Document task pane reappears and the Back button is available.

6. Click the **Home** button in the task pane. The Getting Started task pane reappears.

Using the Research Task Pane

The Research task pane allows you to search a variety of reference materials and other resources to find specific information while you are working on a file. You can insert the information you find directly into your open file. The thesaurus and language translation tools are installed with Office and therefore are stored locally on your computer. If you are connected to the Internet, you can also use the Research task pane to access a dictionary, an encyclopedia, research sites, as well as business and financial sources. Some of the sites that appear in the search results are fee-based, meaning that you'll need to pay to access information on that site.

To use the Research task pane, you type a keyword or phrase into the Search for text box and then select whether you want to search all the books, sites, and sources; one category; or a specific source. The search results appear in the Research task pane. Some of the results appear as links, which you can click to open your browser window and display that information. If you are using Internet Explorer 5.01 or later as your Web browser, the Research task pane is tiled (appears side by side) with your document. If you are using another Web browser, you'll need to return to the task pane in your open file to click another link.

The Research task pane functions independently in each file. So you can open multiple files and perform a different search in each. In addition, each Research task pane stores the results of up to 10 searches, so you can quickly return to the results from any of your most recent searches. To move among the saved searches, click the Back and Forward buttons in the task pane.

Using the Research Task Pane

- Type a keyword or phrase into the Search for text box.
- Select a search category, individual source, or all references.
- If necessary, click a link in the search results to display more information.
- Copy and paste selected content from the task pane into your file.

Jake plans to send a copy of the next quarter's sales report to the office in France. You'll use the bilingual dictionaries in the Research task pane to begin entering labels in French into an Excel workbook for the sales report.

To use the bilingual dictionaries in the Research task pane:

1. Click the **Microsoft Excel – Book1** button on the taskbar to switch to the Excel window.
2. Click the **Other Task Panes** button on the Getting Started task pane, and then click **Research**. The Research task pane opens.
3. Click in the **Search for** text box, and then type **paper**.
4. Click the **Search for** list arrow and then click **Translation**. The bilingual dictionary opens in the Research task pane. You can choose from among 12 languages to translate to and from, including Japanese, Russian, Spanish, Dutch, German, and French.

   Trouble? If a dialog box opens stating the translation feature is not installed, click the Yes button to install it.
5. If necessary, click the **To** list arrow, and then click **French (France)**. See Figure 12.

Research task pane ◄ **Figure 12**

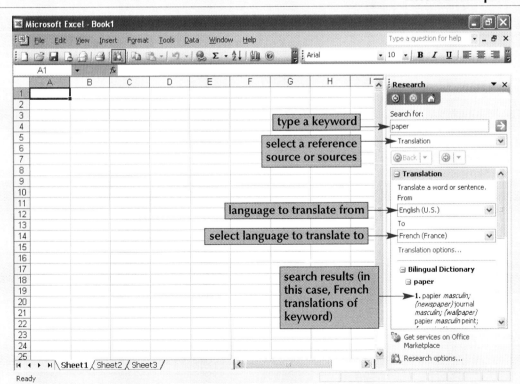

6. Scroll to read the different translations of "paper" in French.

After you locate specific information, you can quickly insert it into your open file. The information can be inserted by copying the selected content you want to insert, and then pasting it in the appropriate location in your file. In some instances, such as MSN Money Stock Quotes, a button appears enabling you to quickly insert the indicated information in your file at the location of the insertion point. Otherwise, you can use the standard Copy and Paste commands.

You'll copy the translation for "paper" into the Excel workbook.

To copy information from the Research task pane into a file:

1. Select **papier** in the Research task pane. This is the word you want to copy to the workbook.
2. Right-click the selected text, and then click **Copy** on the shortcut menu. The text is duplicated on the Office Clipboard.
3. Right-click cell **A1**, and then click **Paste**. The word "papier" is entered into the cell. See Figure 13.

Figure 13 ▶ **Translation copied into Excel**

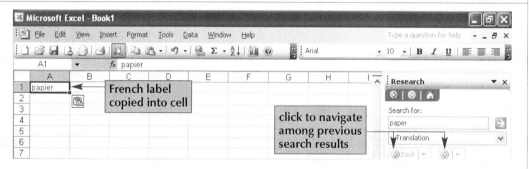

You'll repeat this process to look up the translation for "furniture" and copy it into cell A2.

To translate and copy another word into Excel:

1. Double-click **paper** in the Search for text box to select the text, type **furniture**, and then click the **Start searching** button ➡ in the Research task pane.
2. Verify that you're translating from English (U.S) to French (France).
3. Select **meubles** in the translation results, right-click the selected text, and then click **Copy**.
4. Right-click cell **A2**, and then click **Paste**. The second label appears in the cell.

The Research task pane works similarly in all the Office programs. You'll use other task panes later in this tutorial to perform specific tasks, including opening a file and getting assistance.

Working with Files

The most common tasks you'll perform in any Office program are to create, open, save, and close files. The processes for each of these tasks are the same in all the Office programs. In addition, there are several methods for performing most tasks in Office. This flexibility enables you to use Office in a way that fits how you like to work.

Creating a File

To begin working in a program, you need to create a new file or open an existing file. When you start Word, Excel, or PowerPoint, the program opens along with a blank file—ready for you to begin working on a new document, workbook, or presentation. When you start Access, the Getting Started task pane opens, displaying options for opening a new database or an existing one.

Jake has asked you to start working on the agenda for the stockholder meeting, which he suggests you create using Word. You enter text in a Word document by typing.

To enter text in a document:

1. Click the **Document1 – Microsoft Word** button on the taskbar to activate the Word program window.

2. Type **Delmar Office Supplies**, and then press the **Enter** key. The text you typed appears on one line in the Word document.

   Trouble? If you make a typing error, press the Backspace key to delete the incorrect letters, and then retype the text.

3. Type **Stockholder Meeting Agenda**, and then press the **Enter** key. The text you typed appears on the second line.

Next, you'll save the file.

Saving a File

As you create and modify Office files, your work is stored only in the computer's temporary memory, not on a hard disk. If you were to exit the programs, turn off your computer, or experience a power failure, your work would be lost. To prevent losing work, save your file to a disk frequently—at least every 10 minutes. You can save files to the hard disk located inside your computer or to portable storage disks, such as floppy disks, Zip disks, or read-write CD-ROMs.

The first time you save a file, you need to name it. This name is called a **filename**. When you choose a filename, select a descriptive one that accurately reflects the content of the document, workbook, presentation, or database, such as "Shipping Options Letter" or "Fourth Quarter Financial Analysis." Filenames can include a maximum of 255 letters, numbers, hyphens, and spaces in any combination. Office appends a **file extension** to the filename, which identifies the program in which that file was created. The file extensions are .doc for Word, .xls for Excel, .ppt for PowerPoint, and .mdb for Access. Whether you see file extensions depends on how Windows is set up on your computer.

You also need to decide where to save the file—on which disk and in what folder. A **folder** is a container for your files. Just as you organize paper documents within folders stored in a filing cabinet, you can organize your files within folders stored on your computer's hard disk or a removable disk. Store each file in a logical location that you will remember whenever you want to use the file again.

Reference Window | **Saving a File**

- Click the Save button on the Standard toolbar (*or* click File on the menu bar, and then click Save or Save As).
- In the Save As dialog box, click the Save in list arrow, and then navigate to the location where you want to save the file.
- Type a filename in the File name text box.
- Click the Save button.
- To resave the named file to the same location, click the Save button on the Standard toolbar (*or* click File on the menu bar, and then click Save).

The two lines of text you typed are not yet saved on disk. You'll do that now.

To save a file for the first time:

1. Click the **Save** button on the Standard toolbar. The Save As dialog box opens. The first few words of the first line appear in the File name text box, as a suggested filename. You'll replace this with a more descriptive filename.

2. Click the **Save in** list arrow, and then click the location that contains your Data Files.

   Trouble? If you don't have the Common Office Features Data Files, you need to get them before you can proceed. Your instructor will either give you the Data Files or ask you to obtain them from a specified location (such as a network drive). In either case, be sure that you make a backup copy of your Data Files before you start using them, so that the original files will be available on your copied disk in case you need to start over because of an error or problem. If you have any questions about the Data Files, see your instructor or technical support person for assistance.

3. Double-click the **OFF** folder in the list box, and then double-click the **Tutorial** folder. This is the location where you want to save the document. See Figure 14.

4. Type **Stockholder Meeting Agenda** in the File name text box.

Figure 14 | **Completed Save As dialog box**

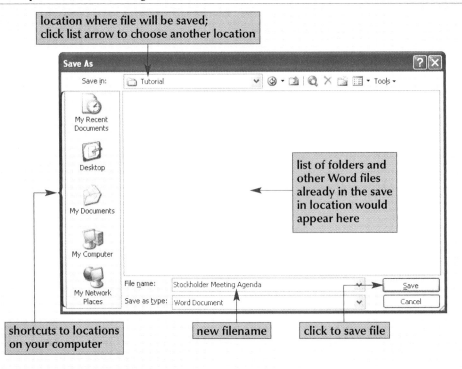

location where file will be saved; click list arrow to choose another location

list of folders and other Word files already in the save in location would appear here

shortcuts to locations on your computer

new filename

click to save file

Trouble? If the .doc file extension appears after the filename, then your computer is configured to show file extensions. Continue with Step 5.

▶ **5.** Click the **Save** button. The Save As dialog box closes, and the name of your file appears in the program window title bar.

The saved file includes everything in the document at the time you last saved it. Any edits or additions you then make to the document exist only in the computer's memory and are not saved in the file on the disk. As you work, remember to save frequently so that the file is updated to reflect the latest content of the document.

Because you already named the document and selected a storage location, the second and subsequent times you save, the Save As dialog box doesn't open. If you wanted to save a copy of the file with a different filename or to a different location, you would reopen the Save As dialog box by clicking File on the menu bar, and then clicking Save As. The previous version of the file remains on your disk as well.

You need to add your name to the agenda. Then you'll save your changes.

To modify and save a file:

▶ **1.** Type your name, and then press the **Enter** key. The text you typed appears on the next line.

▶ **2.** Click the **Save** button 🔲 on the Standard toolbar to save your changes.

When you're done with a file, you can close it.

Closing a File

Although you can keep multiple files open at one time, you should close any file you are no longer working on to conserve system resources as well as to ensure that you don't inadvertently make changes to the file. You can close a file by clicking the Close command on the File menu or by clicking the Close Window button in the upper-right corner of the menu bar.

As a standard practice, you should save your file before closing it. If you're unsure whether the file is saved, it cannot hurt to save it again. However, Office has an added safeguard: If you attempt to close a file or exit a program without saving your changes, a dialog box opens asking whether you want to save the file. Click the Yes button to save the changes to the file before closing the file and program. Click the No button to close the file and program without saving changes. Click the Cancel button to return to the program window without saving changes or closing the file and program. This feature helps to ensure that you always save the most current version of any file.

You'll add the date to the agenda. Then, you'll attempt to close the document without saving.

To modify and close a file:

▶ **1.** Type the date, and then press the **Enter** key. The text you typed appears under your name in the document.

▶ **2.** Click the **Close Window** button ⊠ on the Word menu bar to close the document. A dialog box opens, asking whether you want to save the changes you made to the document.

▶ **3.** Click the **Yes** button. The current version of the document is saved to the file, and then the document closes, and Word is still running.

Trouble? If Word is not running, then you closed the program in Step 2. Start Word, click the Close Window button on the menu bar to close the blank document.

Once you have a program open, you can create additional new files for the open program or you can open previously created and saved files.

Opening a File

When you want to open a blank document, workbook, presentation, or database, you create a new file. When you want to work on a previously created file, you must first open it. Opening a file transfers a copy of the file from the storage disk (either a hard disk or a portable disk) to the computer's memory and displays it on your screen. The file is then in your computer's memory and on the disk.

Reference Window	**Opening an Existing or a New File**

- Click the Open button on the Standard toolbar (*or* click File on the menu bar, and then click Open *or* click the More link in the Open section of the Getting Started task pane).
- In the Open dialog box, click the Look in list arrow, and then navigate to the storage location of the file you want to open.
- Click the filename of the file you want to open.
- Click the Open button.

or

- Click the New button on the Standard toolbar (*or* click File on the menu bar, click New, and then (depending on the program) click the Blank document, Blank workbook, Blank presentation, or Blank database link in the New task pane).

Jake asks you to print the agenda. To do that, you'll reopen the file. You'll use the Open button on the Standard toolbar.

To open an existing file:

▶ **1.** Click the **Open** button 📖 on the Standard toolbar. The Open dialog box, which works similarly to the Save As dialog box, opens.

▶ **2.** Click the **Look in** list arrow, and then navigate to the **OFF\Tutorial** folder included with your Data Files. This is the location where you saved the agenda document.

▶ **3.** Click **Stockholder Meeting Agenda** in the file list. See Figure 15.

Open dialog box ◀ **Figure 15**

4. Click the **Open** button. The file containing the agenda opens in the Word program window.

Next, you'll get information about printing files in Word.

Getting Help

If you don't know how to perform a task or want more information about a feature, you can turn to Office itself for information on how to use it. This information, referred to simply as **Help**, is like a huge encyclopedia available from your desktop. You can access Help in a variety of ways, including ScreenTips, the Type a question for help box, the Help task pane, and Microsoft Office Online.

Using ScreenTips

ScreenTips are a fast and simple method you can use to get help about objects you see on the screen. A **ScreenTip** is a yellow box with the button's name. Just position the mouse pointer over a toolbar button to view its ScreenTip.

Using the Type a Question for Help Box

For answers to specific questions, you can use the **Type a question for help box**, located on the menu bar of every Office program, to find information in the Help system. You simply type a question using everyday language about a task you want to perform or a topic you need help with, and then press the Enter key to search the Help system. The Search Results task pane opens with a list of Help topics related to your query. You click a topic to open a Help window with step-by-step instructions that guide you through a specific procedure and explanations of difficult concepts in clear, easy-to-understand language. For example, you might ask how to format a cell in an Excel worksheet; a list of Help topics related to the words you typed will appear.

Reference Window	**Getting Help from the Type a Question for Help Box**
	• Click the Type a question for help box on the menu bar.
	• Type your question, and then press the Enter key.
	• Click a Help topic in the Search Results task pane.
	• Read the information in the Help window. For more information, click other topics or links.
	• Click the Close button on the Help window title bar.

You'll use the Type a question for help box to obtain more information about printing a document in Word.

To use the Type a question for help box:

1. Click the **Type a question for help box** on the menu bar, and then type **How do I print a document?**

2. Press the **Enter** key to retrieve a list of topics. The Search Results task pane opens with a list of topics related to your query. See Figure 16.

Figure 16	**Search Results task pane displaying Help topics**

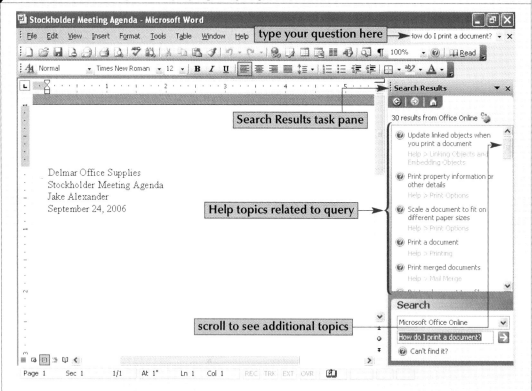

Trouble? If your search results list differs from the one shown in Figure 16, your computer is not connected to the Internet or Microsoft has updated the list of available Help topics since this book was published. Continue with Step 3.

3. Scroll through the list to review the Help topics.

4. Click **Print a document** to open the Help window and learn more about the various ways to print a document. See Figure 17.

click to arrange program and Help windows side by side

content of topic selected in task pane

click to close Help window

click to display all topic information

click any topic link to view more information

Trouble? If the Word program window and the Help window do not appear side by side, then you need to tile the windows. Click the Auto Tile button on the toolbar in the Help window.

▶ 5. Read the information, and then when you're done, click the **Close** button ☒ on the Help window title bar to close the Help window.

The Help task pane works similarly.

Using the Help Task Pane

For more in-depth help, you can use the **Help task pane**, a task pane that enables you to search the Help system using keywords or phrases. You type a specific word or phrase in the Search for text box, and then click the Start searching button. The Search Results task pane opens with a list of topics related to the keyword or phrase you entered. If your computer is connected to the Internet, you might see more search results because some Help topics are stored only online and not locally on your computer. The task pane also has a Table of Contents link that organizes the Help system by subjects and topics, like in a book. You click main subject links to display related topic links.

Getting Help from the Help Task Pane

- Click the Other Task Panes button on the task pane title bar, and then click Help (*or* click Help on the menu bar, and then click Microsoft Word/Excel/PowerPoint/Access/ Outlook Help).
- Type a keyword or phrase in the Search for text box, and then click the Start searching button.
- Click a Help topic in the Search Results task pane.
- Read the information in the Help window. For more information, click other topics or links.
- Click the Close button on the Help window title bar.

You'll use the Help task pane to obtain more information about getting help in Office.

To use the Help task pane:

▶ **1.** Click the **Other Task Panes** button on the task pane title bar, and then click **Help**.

▶ **2.** Type **get help** in the Search for text box. See Figure 18.

Figure 18 Microsoft Word Help task pane with keyword

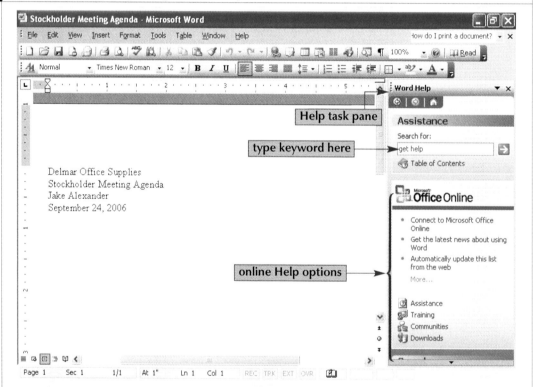

▶ **3.** Click the **Start searching** button ➡. The Search Results task pane opens with a list of topics related to your keywords.

▶ **4.** Scroll through the list to review the Help topics.

▶ **5.** Click **About getting help while you work** to open the Microsoft Word Help window and learn more about the various ways to obtain help in Word. See Figure 19.

About getting help while you work Help window ◄ **Figure 19**

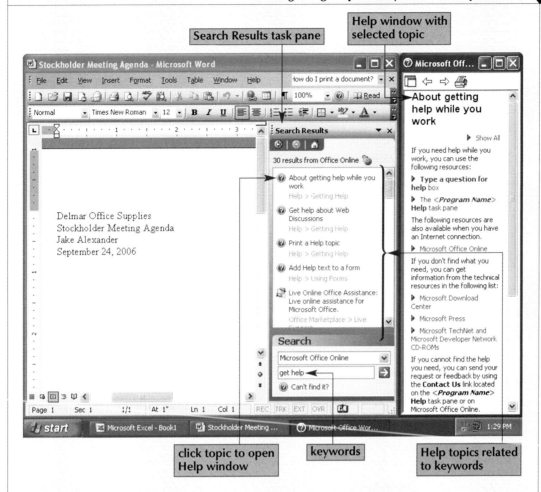

Trouble? If your search results list differs from the one shown in Figure 19, your computer is not connected to the Internet or Microsoft has updated the list of available Help topics since this book was published. Continue with Step 6.

Trouble? If the Word program window and the Help window do not appear side by side, then you need to tile the windows. Click the Auto Tile button on the toolbar in the Help window.

6. Click **Microsoft Office Online** in the right pane to display information about that topic. Read the information.

7. Click the other links about this feature and read the information.

8. When you're done, click the **Close** button ⊠ on the Help window title bar to close the Help window. The task pane remains open.

If your computer has a connection to the Internet, you can get more help information from Microsoft Office Online.

Using Microsoft Office Online

Microsoft Office Online is a Web site maintained by Microsoft that provides access to additional Help resources. For example, you can access current Help topics, read how-to articles, and find tips for using Office. You can search all or part of a site to find information about tasks you want to perform, features you want to use, or anything else you want more help with. You can connect to Microsoft Office Online from the Getting Started task pane, the Help task pane, or the Help menu.

To connect to Microsoft Office Online, you'll need Internet access and a Web browser such as Internet Explorer.

To connect to Microsoft Office Online:

▶ **1.** Click the **Back** button 🔘 in the Search Results task pane. The Word Help task pane reappears.

▶ **2.** Click the **Connect to Microsoft Office Online** link in the task pane. Internet Explorer starts and the Microsoft Office Online home page opens. See Figure 20. This Web page offers links to Web pages focusing on getting help and for accessing additional Office resources, such as additional galleries of clip art, software downloads, and training opportunities.

Figure 20 ▶ **Microsoft Office Online home page**

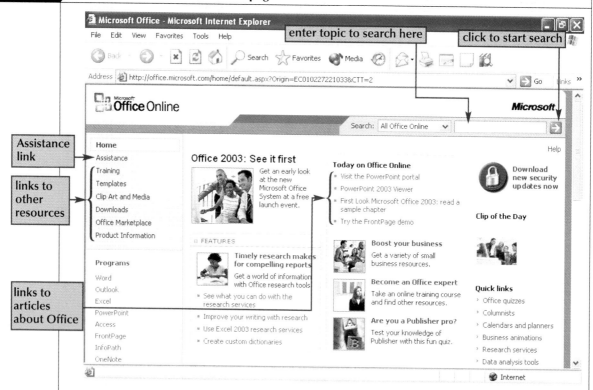

Trouble? If the content you see on the Microsoft Office Online home page differs from the figure, the site has been updated since this book was published. Continue with Step 3.

▶ **3.** Click the **Assistance** link. The Assistance page opens. From this page, you browse for help in each of the different Office programs. You can also enter a keyword or phrase pertaining to a particular topic you wish to search for information on using the Search box in the upper-right corner of the window.

▶ **4.** Click the **Close** button ⊠ on the Internet Explorer title bar to close the browser.

The Help features enable the staff at Delmar Office Supplies to get answers to questions they have about any task or procedure when they need it. The more you practice getting information from the Help system, the more effective you will be at using Office to its full potential.

Printing a File

At times, you'll want a paper copy of your Office file. The first time you print during each session at the computer, you should use the Print menu command to open the Print dialog box so you can verify or adjust the printing settings. You can select a printer, the number of copies to print, the portion of the file to print, and so forth; the printing settings vary slightly from program to program. For subsequent print jobs, you can use the Print button to print without opening the dialog box, if you want to use the same default settings.

Printing a File

Reference Window

- Click File on the menu bar, and then click Print.
- Verify the print settings in the Print dialog box.
- Click the OK button.

or

- Click the Print button on the Standard toolbar.

Now that you know how to print, you'll print the agenda for Jake.

To print a file:

▶ **1.** Make sure your printer is turned on and contains paper.

▶ **2.** Click **File** on the menu bar, and then click **Print**. The Print dialog box opens. See Figure 21.

Print dialog box ◀ **Figure 21**

▶ **3.** Verify that the correct printer appears in the Name list box in the Printer area. If the wrong printer appears, click the **Name** list arrow, and then click the correct printer from the list of available printers.

▶ **4.** Verify that **1** appears in the Number of copies text box.

▶ **5.** Click the **OK** button to print the document.

Trouble? If the document does not print, see your instructor or technical support person for help.

Now that you have printed the agenda, you can close Word and Excel.

Exiting Programs

Whenever you finish working with a program, you should exit it. As with many other aspects of Office, you can exit programs with a button or from a menu. You'll use both methods to close Word and Excel. You can use the Exit command to exit a program and close an open file in one step. If you haven't saved the final version of the open file, a dialog box opens, asking whether you want to save your changes. Clicking the Yes button saves the open file, closes the file, and then exits the program.

To exit a program:

▶ **1.** Click the **Close** button ☒ on the Word title bar to exit Word. The Word document closes and the Word program exits. The Excel window is visible again on your screen.

Trouble? If a dialog box opens, asking whether you want to save the document, you may have inadvertently made a change to the document. Click the No button.

▶ **2.** Click **File** on the Excel menu bar, and then click **Exit**. A dialog box opens asking whether you want to save the changes you made to the workbook.

▶ **3.** Click the **Yes** button. The Save As dialog box opens.

▶ **4.** Save the workbook in the **OFF\Tutorial** folder with the filename **French Sales Report**. The workbook closes, saving a copy to the location you specified, and the Excel program exits.

Exiting programs after you are done using them keeps your Windows desktop unclut-tered for the next person using the computer, frees up your system's resources, and prevents data from being lost accidentally.

Review

Quick Check

1. List the five programs included in Office.
2. How do you start an Office program?
3. Explain the difference between Save As and Save.
4. What is one method for opening an existing Office file?
5. What happens if you attempt to close a file or exit a program without saving the current version of the open file?
6. What are four ways to get help?

Review

Tutorial Summary

You have learned how to use features common to all the programs included in Microsoft Office 2003, including starting and exiting programs; resizing windows; using menus and toolbars; working with task panes; saving, opening, closing, and printing files; and getting help.

Key Terms

Access	menu	Outlook
database	menu bar	PowerPoint
document	menu command	presentation
Excel	Microsoft Access 2003	ScreenTip
file extension	Microsoft Excel 2003	task pane
filename	Microsoft Office 2003	toolbar
folder	Microsoft Office Online	Type a question for help box
Help	Microsoft Outlook 2003	Word
Help task pane	Microsoft PowerPoint 2003	workbook
integration	Microsoft Word 2003	
keyboard shortcut	Office	

Practice

Review Assignments

Practice the skills you learned in the tutorial using the same case scenario.

Data Files needed for the Review Assignments: Finances.xls, Letter.doc

Before the stockholders meeting at Delmar Office Supplies, you'll open and print documents for the upcoming presentation. Complete the following steps:

1. Start PowerPoint.
2. Use the Help task pane to learn how to change the toolbar buttons from small to large, and then do it. Use the same procedure to change the buttons back to regular size. Close the Help window when you're done.
3. Start Excel.
4. Switch to the PowerPoint window using the taskbar, and then close the presentation but leave open the PowerPoint program. (*Hint:* Click the Close Window button on the menu bar.)
5. Open a new, blank PowerPoint presentation from the Getting Started task pane. (*Hint:* Click Create a new presentation in the Open section of the Getting Started task pane.)
6. Close the PowerPoint presentation and program using the Close button on the PowerPoint title bar; do not save changes if asked.

7. Open the **Finances** workbook located in the **OFF\Review** folder included with your Data Files using the Open button on the Standard toolbar in Excel.
8. Use the Save As command to save the workbook as **Delmar Finances** in the **OFF\Review** folder.
9. Type your name, press the Enter key to insert your name at the top of the worksheet, and then save the workbook.
10. Print one copy of the worksheet using the Print command on the File menu.
11. Exit Excel using the File menu.
12. Start Word, and then use the Getting Started task pane to open the **Letter** document located in the **OFF\Review** folder included with your Data Files. (*Hint:* Click the More link in the Getting Started task pane to open the Open dialog box.)
13. Use the Save As command to save the document with the filename **Delmar Letter** in the **OFF\Review** folder.
14. Press and hold the Ctrl key, press the End key, and then release both keys to move the insertion point to the end of the letter, and then type your name.
15. Use the Save button on the Standard toolbar to save the change to the Delmar Letter document.
16. Print one copy of the document, and then close the document.
17. Exit the Word program using the Close button on the title bar.

Assess

SAM Assessment and Training

If you have a SAM user profile, you may have access to hands-on instruction, practice, and assessment of the skills covered in this tutorial. Log in to your SAM account and go to your assignments page to see what your instructor has assigned.

Review

Quick Check Answers

1. Word, Excel, PowerPoint, Access, Outlook
2. Click the Start button on the taskbar, point to All Programs, point to Microsoft Office, and then click the name of the program you want to open.
3. Save As enables you to change the filename and storage location of a file. Save updates a file to reflect its latest contents using its current filename and location.
4. Either click the Open button on the Standard toolbar or click the More link in the Getting Started task pane to open the Open dialog box.
5. A dialog box opens asking whether you want to save the changes to the file.
6. ScreenTips, Type a question for help box, Help task pane, Microsoft Office Online

New Perspectives on
Microsoft® Office Word 2003

Read This Before You Begin: Tutorials 1-4

To the Student

Data Files

To complete the Level I Word Tutorials (Tutorials 1 through 4), you need the starting student Data Files. Your instructor will either provide you with these Data Files or ask you to obtain them yourself.

The Level I Word tutorials require the folders shown in the next column to complete the Tutorials, Review Assignments, and Case Problems. You will need to copy these folders from a file server, a standalone computer, or the Web to the drive and folder where you will be storing your Data Files. Your instructor will tell you which computer, drive letter, and folder(s) contain the files you need. You can also download the files by going to www.course.com; see the inside back or front cover for more information on downloading the files, or ask your instructor or technical support person for assistance.

If you are storing your Data Files on floppy disks, you will need **one** blank, formatted, high-density disk for these tutorials. Label your disk as shown, and place on it the folders indicated.

▼ **Word 2003 Tutorials 1-4: Data Disk**
>   Tutorial.01 folder
>   Tutorial.02 folder
>   Tutorial.03 folder
>   Tutorial.04 folder

When you begin a tutorial, refer to the Student Data Files section at the bottom of the tutorial opener page, which indicates which folders and files you need for the tutorial. Each end-of-tutorial exercise also indicates the files you need to complete that exercise.

Course Labs

The Level I Word tutorials feature an interactive Course Lab to help you understand word processing concepts. There are Lab Assignments at the end of Tutorial 1 that relate to this lab. Contact your instructor or technical support person for assistance in accessing the lab.

To the Instructor

The Data Files and Course Labs are available on the Instructor Resources CD for this title. Follow the instructions in the Help file on the CD to install the programs to your network or standalone computer. See the "To the Student" section above for information on how to set up the Data Files that accompany this text.

You are granted a license to copy the Data Files and Course Labs to any computer or computer network used by students who have purchased this book.

System Requirements

If you are going to work through this book using your own computer, you need:

- **Computer System** Microsoft Windows 2000, Windows XP or higher must be installed on your computer. These tutorials assume a typical installation of Microsoft Word 2003.

- **Data Files** You will not be able to complete the tutorials or exercises in this book using your own computer until you have the necessary starting Data Files.

- **Course Labs** See your instructor or technical support person to obtain the Course Lab software for use on your own computer.

Objectives

Session 1.1
- Plan a document
- Identify the components of the Word window
- Choose commands using toolbars and menus
- Create a new document

Session 1.2
- Scroll a document and move the insertion point
- Correct errors and undo and redo changes
- Save, preview, and print a document
- Enter the date with AutoComplete
- Remove Smart Tags
- Create an envelope

Creating a Document

Writing a Business Letter

Case

Art4U, Inc.

Megan Grahs is the owner and manager of Art4U, Inc., a graphics design firm in Tucson, Arizona. When Megan founded Art4U in the early 1980s, the company drew most of its revenue from design projects for local magazines, newspapers, advertising circulars, and other print publications. The artists at Art4U laboriously created logos, diagrams, and other illustrations by hand, using watercolors, ink, pastels, and a variety of other media. Since the advent of the Internet, however, Art4U has become one of the Southwest's leading creators of electronic artwork. The firm's artists now work exclusively on computers, saving each piece of art as an electronic file that they can e-mail to a client in a matter of minutes.

Thanks to e-mail, Art4U is no longer limited to the local Tucson market. As a result, Art4U has nearly doubled in size over the past ten years. Most of the increase in business has come from Web page designers, who continually need fresh and innovative graphics to use in their Web pages. In fact, Megan has just signed a contract with Web Time Productions agreeing to create a series of logos for a high-profile Web site. She needs to return the signed contract to Web Time Productions' office in Chicago.

In this tutorial, you will create the cover letter that will accompany the contract. You will create the letter using **Microsoft Office Word 2003** (or simply **Word**), a popular word-processing program. Before you begin typing the letter, you will learn how to start the Word program, identify and use the elements of the Word screen, and adjust some Word settings. Next, you will create a new Word document, type the text of the cover letter, save the letter, and then print the letter for Megan. In the process of entering the text, you'll learn several ways to correct typing errors.

Lab

Student Data Files

There are no student Data Files needed for this tutorial.

Four Steps to a Professional Document

Word helps you produce quality work in minimal time. Not only can you type a document in Word, but you can also quickly make revisions and corrections, adjust margins and spacing, create columns and tables, and add graphics to your documents. The most efficient way to produce a document is to follow these four steps: (1) planning, (2) creating and editing, (3) formatting, and (4) printing.

In the long run, planning saves time and effort. First, you should determine what you want to say. State your purpose clearly and include enough information to achieve that purpose without overwhelming or boring your reader. Be sure to organize your ideas logically. Decide how you want your document to look as well. In this case, your letter to Web Time Productions will take the form of a standard business letter. It should be addressed to Web Time's president, Nicholas Brower. Megan has given you a handwritten note indicating what she would like you to say in the letter. This note is shown in Figure 1-1.

Figure 1-1	Megan's notes for the contract letter

Notes for Contract Letter

Please include the following questions in the Web Time Productions cover letter:

• When will we receive a complete schedule for the project?

• How many preliminary designs do you require?

• Will you be available to discuss the project with our artists via a conference call next week?

Send the letter to Web Time Productions' president, Nicholas Brower. The address is: 2015 Dubuque Avenue, Chicago, IL 60025.

After you plan your document, you can go ahead and create and edit it using Word. Creating the document generally means typing the text of your document. Editing consists of reading the document you've created, correcting your errors, and, finally, adding or deleting text to make the document easy to read.

Once your document is error-free, you can format it to make it visually appealing. Formatting features, such as adjusting margins to create white space (blank areas of a page), setting line spacing, and using bold and italic, can help make your document easier to read.

Printing is the final phase in creating an effective document. In this tutorial, you will preview your document before you spend time and resources to print it.

Exploring the Word Window

Before you can apply these four steps to produce a letter in Word, you need to start Word and learn about the general organization of the Word window. You'll do that now.

To start Microsoft Word:

▶ **1.** Click the **Start** button on the taskbar, point to **All Programs**, point to **Microsoft Office**, and then click **Microsoft Office Word 2003**. The Word window opens. See Figure 1-2.

Trouble? If you don't see the Microsoft Office Word 2003 option on the Microsoft Office submenu, look for it in a different submenu or as an option on the All Programs menu. If you still can't find the Microsoft Office Word 2003 option, ask your instructor or technical support person for help.

Maximized Word window ◀ **Figure 1-2**

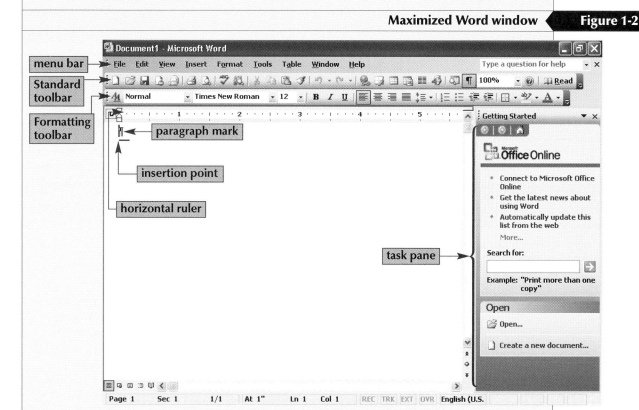

▶ **2.** If the Word window does not fill the entire screen, click the **Maximize** button 🔲 in the upper-right corner of the Word window. Your screen should now resemble Figure 1-2.

Trouble? If your screen looks slightly different from Figure 1-2, just continue with the steps. You will learn how to change the appearance of the Word window shortly.

Word is now running and ready to use. Don't be concerned if you don't see everything shown in Figure 1-2. You'll learn how to adjust the appearance of the Word window soon.

The Word window is made up of a number of elements, which are described in Figure 1-3. You are already familiar with some of these elements, such as the menu bar and toolbars, because they are common to all Windows programs.

Figure 1-3 **Parts of the Word window**

Screen Element	Description
Formatting toolbar	Contains buttons that affect how the document looks.
horizontal ruler	Shows page margins, tabs, and column widths.
insertion point	Shows where characters will appear when you start typing.
menu bar	Contains lists, or menus, of all the Word commands. When you first display a menu, you see a short list of the most frequently used commands. To see the full list of commands in the menu, you can click the menu and then wait a few seconds for the remaining commands to appear, double-click the menu, or click the menu and then click or point to the downward-facing double-arrow at the bottom of the menu.
paragraph mark	Marks the end of a paragraph.
Standard toolbar	Contains buttons for activating frequently used commands.
task pane	Provides links and buttons that you can use to perform common tasks.

If at any time you would like to check the name of a Word toolbar button, position the mouse pointer over the button without clicking. A ScreenTip, a small box with the name of the button, will appear. (If you don't see ScreenTips on your computer, click Tools on the Word menu bar, click Options, click the View tab, click the ScreenTips check box to insert a check, and then click OK.)

Keep in mind that the menus initially display the commands that are used most frequently on your particular computer. When you leave a menu open for a few seconds or point to the double-arrow, a complete list of commands appears. Throughout these tutorials, you should point to the double-arrow on a menu if you do not see the command you need.

Setting Up the Window Before You Begin Each Tutorial

Word provides a set of standard settings, called **default settings**, which control how the screen is set up and how a document looks when you first start typing. These settings are appropriate for most situations. However, these settings are easily changed, and most people begin a work session by adjusting Word to make sure it is set up the way they want it.

As you gain experience, you will learn how to customize Word to suit your needs. But to make it easier to follow the steps in these tutorials, you should take care to arrange your window to match the tutorial figures. The rest of this section explains what your window should look like and how to make it match those in the tutorials. Depending on how many people use your computer (and how much they adjust Word's appearance), you might have to set up the window to match the figures each time you start Word.

Setting the Document View to Normal

The View buttons in the lower-left corner of the Word window change the way your document is displayed. You will learn how to select the appropriate view for a document in a later tutorial. For now, you want the document displayed in Normal view.

To make sure the document is displayed in Normal view:

▶ **1.** Click the **Normal View** button ≡ to the left of the horizontal scroll bar. See Figure 1-4. If your Document window was not in Normal view, it changes to Normal view now. The Normal View button is now highlighted, indicating that it is selected.

Changing to Normal view ◀ **Figure 1-4**

Displaying the Toolbars, Task Pane, and Ruler

The Word toolbars allow you to perform common tasks quickly by clicking a button. To eliminate on-screen clutter while you work through these tutorials, you should check to make sure that only the Formatting and Standard toolbars appear on your screen. The Standard toolbar should be positioned on top of the Formatting toolbar, as shown previously in Figure 1-2.

Depending on the choices made by the last person to use your computer, you may not see both toolbars or you may see both toolbars on one row. You also may see additional toolbars. In the following steps, you will make sure that your Word window shows only the Standard and Formatting toolbars. At the same time, you will verify that the task pane is displayed as it is in Figure 1-2.

To verify that your Word window shows the correct toolbars and the task pane:

▶ **1.** Position the pointer over any toolbar and click the right mouse button. A shortcut menu appears. The menu lists all available toolbars with a check mark next to those currently displayed. If the Standard and Formatting toolbars are currently displayed on your computer, you should see check marks next to their names. You should also see a check mark next to "Task Pane," indicating that the task pane is displayed on the right side of the screen. (You saw the task pane earlier in Figure 1-2.)

▶ **2.** Verify that you see a check mark next to the word "Standard" in the shortcut menu. If you do not see a check mark, click **Standard** now. (Clicking any item on the shortcut menu closes the menu, so you will need to re-open it in the next step.)

▶ **3.** Redisplay the shortcut menu, and click **Formatting** if you don't see a check mark next to it.

▶ **4.** If you don't see the task pane, click View on the menu bar and then click **Task Pane**.

▶ **5.** Redisplay the shortcut menu. If any toolbar besides the Formatting and Standard toolbars is open, click the toolbar name to remove the check mark and hide the toolbar.

Trouble? If you see a task pane other than the Getting Started task pane, click the down pointing arrow at the top of the task pane, and then click Getting Started.

If the toolbars appear on one row, perform the next steps to arrange them in two rows.

To arrange the Standard and Formatting toolbars on two rows:

1. Click **Tools** on the menu bar, and then click **Customize**. The Customize dialog box opens.
2. Click the **Options** tab if it is not already selected, and then click the **Show Standard and Formatting toolbars on two rows** check box to select it (that is, to insert a check).
3. Click **Close**. The Customize dialog box closes. The toolbars and task pane on your screen should now match those shown earlier in Figure 1-2.

Setting Up Other Screen Elements

Next, you'll take care of a few other parts of the screen, including:

- The horizontal ruler, which appears below the Formatting toolbar and is used to adjust margins and align parts of a document
- The Zoom setting, which controls the document's on-screen magnification; a setting of 100% displays the text in the same size as it will appear when printed
- The default font setting, which controls the size and shape of the characters that appear when you start typing

You'll learn more about these topics later. For now, you simply need to make your screen match the figures in this book by displaying the horizontal ruler, setting the Zoom setting to 100%, and verifying that 12-point Times New Roman is the default font.

To display the ruler, check your Zoom setting, and select the correct default font:

1. Click **View** on the menu bar, and then point to the double-arrow at the bottom of the menu to display the hidden menu commands.
2. If "Ruler" does not have a check mark next to it, click **Ruler**. The horizontal ruler should now be displayed, as shown earlier in Figure 1-2.
3. Click the **Zoom** list arrow 100% on the Standard toolbar. A list of screen magnification settings appears. In Figure 1-5, the currently selected setting is 100%.

Figure 1-5 ▶ Zoom settings

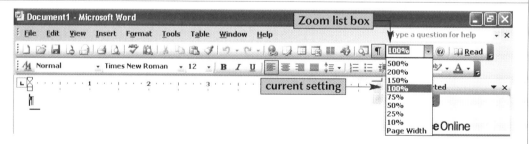

4. If 100% is not selected on your computer, click **100%** to select it. If you don't need to change your Zoom setting, press the **Esc** key to close the Zoom list. Next, you will check the default font setting.
5. Click **Format** on the menu bar, and then click **Font**. The Font dialog box opens. Click the **Font** tab if it is not already selected. See Figure 1-6.

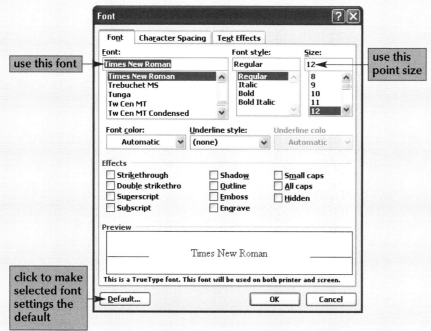

use this font

use this point size

click to make selected font settings the default

6. In the Font list box, click **Times New Roman**.

7. In the Size list box, click **12** if it is not already selected.

8. Click the **Default** button to make Times New Roman and 12 point the default settings. Word displays a message asking you to verify that you want to make 12-point Times New Roman the default font.

9. Click the **Yes** button.

Displaying Nonprinting Characters

Nonprinting characters are symbols that can appear on the screen but are not visible on the printed page. For example, one nonprinting character marks the end of a paragraph (¶) and another marks the space between words (•). It's helpful to display nonprinting characters so you can see whether you've typed an extra space, ended a paragraph, and so on.

Depending on how your computer is set up, nonprinting characters might have appeared automatically when you started Word. In Figure 1-7, you can see the paragraph symbol (¶) in the blank Document window. Also, the Show/Hide ¶ button is highlighted in the Standard toolbar. Both of these indicate that nonprinting characters are displayed. If they are not displayed on your screen, you need to perform the following step.

Figure 1-7 ▶ Nonprinting characters displayed

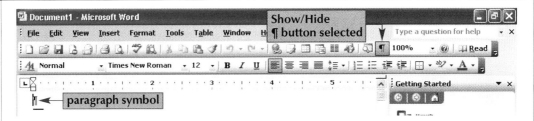

paragraph symbol

To display nonprinting characters:

1. Click the **Show/Hide ¶** button ¶ on the Standard toolbar. A paragraph mark (¶) appears at the top of the Document window. Your screen should now match Figure 1-7.

Trouble? If the Show/Hide ¶ button was already highlighted before you clicked it, you have now deactivated it. Click the Show/Hide ¶ button a second time to select it.

To make sure your window always matches the figures in these tutorials, remember to complete the checklist in Figure 1-8 each time you sit down at the computer.

Figure 1-8 ▶ Word window checklist

Screen Element	Setting
Default font	Times New Roman
Default font size	12 point
Document view	Normal view
Formatting toolbar	Displayed below Standard toolbar
Horizontal ruler	Displayed
Nonprinting characters	Displayed
Other toolbars	Hidden
Standard toolbar	Displayed below menu bar
Task pane	Displayed
Word window	Maximized
Zoom box	Setting identical to setting shown in figures

Now that you have planned your letter, opened Word, identified screen elements, and adjusted settings, you are ready to begin typing a letter.

Beginning a Letter

You're ready to begin typing Megan's letter to Nicholas Brower at Web Time Productions. Figure 1-9 shows the completed letter printed on company letterhead. You will create this letter by completing the steps in this tutorial.

Completed letter ◀ **Figure 1-9**

Art4U, Inc.
5725 Mesa Avenue
Tucson, AZ 85703
Art4U@Earth-World-Art.com

February 15, 2006

Nicholas Brower
Web Time Productions
2015 Dubuque Avenue
Chicago, IL 60025

Dear Nicholas:

Enclosed you will find the signed contract. As you can see, I am returning all three pages, with my signature on each.

Now that we have finalized the contract, I have a few questions: When will we receive a complete schedule for the project? Also, how many preliminary designs do you require? Finally, will you be available to discuss the project with our artists via a conference call some afternoon next week? Thursday or Friday afternoon would be ideal, if either of those options work for you.

Thanks again for choosing Art4U. We look forward to working with you.

Sincerely yours,

Megan L. Grahs

You'll begin by opening a new blank document (in case you accidentally typed something in the current page). Whenever you need to perform a common task such as opening a document, you can usually start with the task pane. In this case, you can use a special task pane that is devoted to creating new documents.

To open a new document:

▶ **1.** Click the **Create a new document** button 📄 in the Open section at the bottom of the Getting Started task pane. Instead of the Getting Started task pane, you now see the New Document task pane. See Figure 1-10.

Figure 1-10	New Document task pane

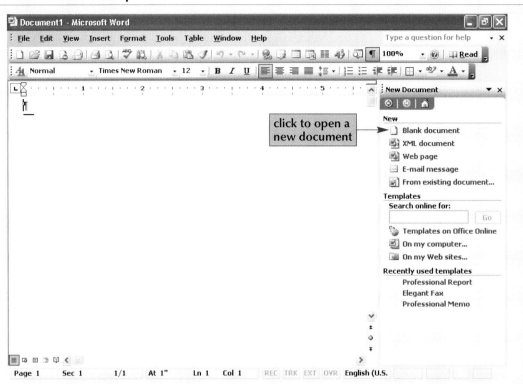

▶ **2.** Click the **Blank document** button ☐ in the New Document task pane. A new document named Document2 opens and the task pane closes.

Now that you have opened a new document, you need to insert some blank lines in the document to ensure that you leave enough room for the company letterhead.

To insert blank lines in the document:

▶ **1.** Press the **Enter** key eight times. Each time you press the Enter key, a nonprinting paragraph mark appears. In the status bar (at the bottom of the Document window), you should see the setting "At 2.5"," indicating that the insertion point is approximately 2.5 inches from the top of the page. Another setting in the status bar should read "Ln 9," indicating that the insertion point is in line 9 of the document. See Figure 1-11. (Your settings may be slightly different.)

Document window after inserting blank lines | **Figure 1-11**

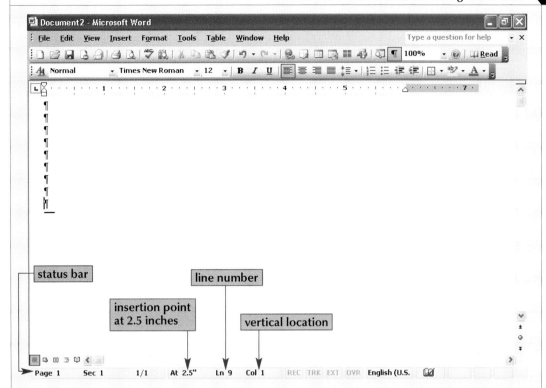

Trouble? If the paragraph mark doesn't appear each time you press the Enter key, the non-printing characters might be hidden. Click the Show/Hide ¶ button on the Standard toolbar.

Trouble? If you pressed the Enter key too many times, press the Backspace key to delete each extra line and paragraph mark. If you're on line 9 but the "At" number is not 2.5", don't worry. Different monitors produce slightly different measurements when you press the Enter key.

Pressing Enter is a simple, fast way to insert space in a document. When you are a more experienced Word user, you'll learn how to insert space without using the Enter key.

Entering Text

Normally, you begin typing a letter by entering the date. However, Megan tells you that she's not sure whether the contract will be ready to send today or tomorrow. So she asks you to skip the date for now and begin with the inside address. Making changes to documents is easy in Word, so you can easily add the date later.

In the following steps, you'll type the inside address (shown on Megan's note, in Figure 1-1). If you type a wrong character, press the Backspace key to delete the mistake and then retype the correct character.

To type the inside address:

▶ **1.** Type **Nicholas Brower**, and then press the **Enter** key. As you type, a nonprinting character (•) appears between words to indicate a space. See Figure 1-12.

Figure 1-12 First line of inside address

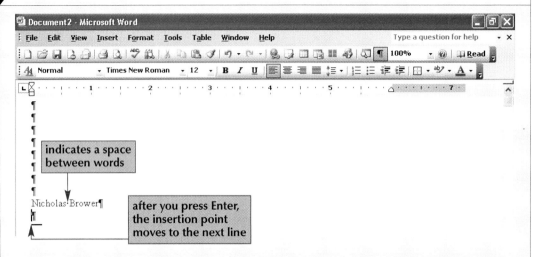

Trouble? If a wavy line appears beneath a word, check to make sure you typed the text correctly. If you did not, use the Backspace key to remove the error, and then retype the text correctly.

2. Type the following text, pressing the **Enter** key after each line to complete the inside address:

   Web Time Productions
   2015 Dubuque Avenue
   Chicago, IL 60025

   Be sure to press the Enter key after you type the ZIP code. Ignore the dotted underline below the street address. You'll learn the meaning of this underline later in this tutorial.

3. Press the **Enter** key again to add a blank line after the inside address. (You should see a total of two paragraph marks below the inside address.) Now you can type the salutation.

4. Type **Dear Nicholas:** and then press the **Enter** key twice to double space between the salutation and the body of the letter. See Figure 1-13.

Figure 1-13 Letter with inside address and salutation

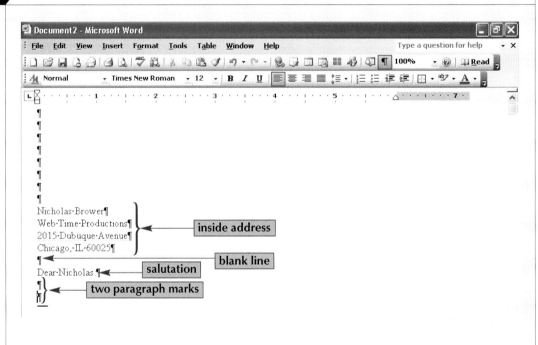

Before you continue with the rest of the letter, you should save what you have typed so far.

To save the document:

▶ 1. Click the **Save** button 🖫 on the Standard toolbar. The Save As dialog box opens. Note that Word suggests using the first few words of the letter ("Nicholas Brower") as the file-name. You will replace the suggested filename with something more descriptive.

▶ 2. Type **Web Time Contract Letter** in the File name text box. Next, you need to tell Word where you want to save the document. In this case, you want to use the Tutorial subfolder in the Tutorial.01 folder.

▶ 3. Click the **Save in** list arrow, click the drive containing your Data Files, double-click the **Tutorial.01** folder, and then double-click the **Tutorial** folder. The word "Tutorial" is now displayed in the Save in box, indicating that the Tutorial folder is open and ready for you to save the document. See Figure 1-14.

Trouble? The Tutorial.01 folder is included with the Data Files for this text. If you don't have the Word Data Files, you need to get them before you can proceed. Your instructor will either give you the Data Files or ask you to obtain them from a specified location (such as a network drive). In either case, be sure that you make a backup copy of your Data Files before you start using them, so that the original files will be available on your copied disk in case you need to start over because of an error or problem. If you have any questions about the Data Files, see your instructor or technical support person for assistance.

Save As dialog box | Figure 1-14

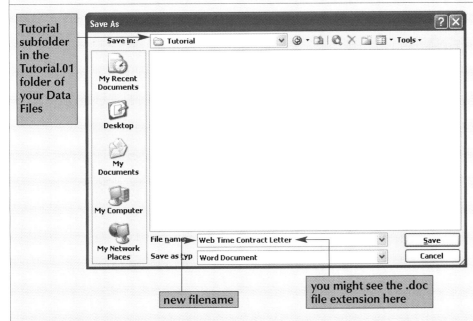

Trouble? If Windows XP is configured for Web style, you can single-click, rather than double-click, folders to open them in the Save As dialog box.

Trouble? If Word automatically adds the .doc extension to your filename, your computer is configured to show file extensions. Just continue with the tutorial.

▶ 4. Click the **Save** button in the Save As dialog box. The dialog box closes, and you return to the Document window. The new document name (Web Time Contract Letter) appears in the title bar.

Note that Word automatically appends the .doc extension to document filenames to identify them as Microsoft Word documents. However, unless your computer is set up to display file extensions, you won't see the .doc extension in any of the Word dialog boxes or in the title bar. These tutorials assume that file extensions are hidden.

You've made a good start on the letter, and you've saved your work so far. In the next session, you'll finish typing the letter and then you'll print it.

Review

Session 1.1 Quick Check

1. In your own words, list the steps in creating a document.
2. Define each of the following in your own words:
   a. nonprinting characters
   b. Zoom setting
   c. font settings
   d. default settings
3. Explain how to change the document view to Normal view.
4. Explain how to display or hide the Standard toolbar.
5. True or False: To display the Formatting toolbar, you need to use a button on the Standard toolbar.
6. True or False: Each time you press the Enter key, a nonprinting paragraph character (¶) appears in the status bar.
7. Word automatically appends the _____ extension to all document file names, even if you can't see the file extensions on the screen.

Session 1.2

Continuing Work on the Letter

Now that you have saved your document, you're ready to continue working on Megan's letter. As you type the body of the letter, you do not have to press the Enter key at the end of each line. Instead, when you type a word that extends into the right margin, both the insertion point and the word move automatically to the next line. This automatic line breaking is called **word wrap**. You'll see how word wrap works as you type the body of the letter.

To continue typing the letter:

▶ 1. If you took a break after the previous session, make sure that Word is running. Also, review the check list in Figure 1-8 and verify that your screen is set up to match the figures in this tutorial.

▶ 2. Make sure the insertion point is at Ln 16 (according to the setting in the status bar). If it's not, move it to line 16 by pressing the arrow keys.

▶ 3. Type the following sentence: **Enclosed you will find the signed contract.**

▶ 4. Press the **spacebar**.

▶ 5. Type the following sentence: **As you can see, I am returning all three pages, with my signature on each.** Notice how Word moves the last few words to a new line when the preceding line is full.

▶ 6. Press the **Enter** key to end the first paragraph, and then press the **Enter** key again to create a double space between the two paragraphs.

▶ **7.** Type the following text:

Now that we have finalized the contract, I have a few questions: When will we receive a complete schedule for the project? Also, how many preliminary designs do you require?

When you are finished, your screen should look similar to Figure 1-15, although the line breaks on your screen might be slightly different.

Beginning of second main paragraph ◀ **Figure 1-15**

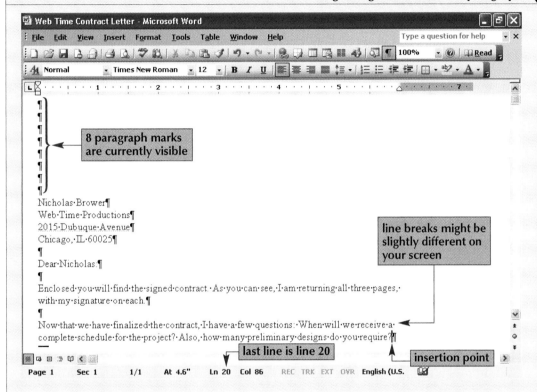

Trouble? If your screen does not match Figure 1-15 exactly, don't be concerned. The letter widths of the Times New Roman font can vary, which produces slightly different measurements on different monitors. As a result, the word or letter where the line wraps in your document might be different from the one shown in Figure 1-15.

Scrolling a Document

After you finish the last set of steps, the insertion point should be near the bottom of the Document window. Unless you are working on a large monitor, your screen probably looks like there's not enough room to type the rest of Megan's letter. However, as you continue to add text at the end of your document, the text that you typed earlier will **scroll** (or shift up) and disappear from the top of the Document window. You'll see how scrolling works as you enter the rest of the second paragraph.

To observe scrolling while you're entering text:

1. Make sure the insertion point is positioned to the right of the question mark after the word "require." The insertion point should be positioned at the end of line 20. See Figure 1-15.

2. Press the **spacebar**, and then type the following text:

   Finally, will you be available to discuss the project with our artists via a conference call some afternoon next week? Thursday or Friday afternoon would be ideal, if either of those options works for you.

3. Press the **Enter** key twice. The document scrolls up.

   At some point (either as you type the text in Step 2 or when you press the Enter key in Step 3), one or more paragraph marks at the top of the letter scroll off the top of the Document window. (Exactly when this happens depends on the size of your monitor.) When you are finished typing, your document should look like Figure 1-16. (Don't worry if you make a mistake in your typing. You'll learn a number of ways to correct errors in the next section.)

Figure 1-16   **Part of document scrolled off the screen**

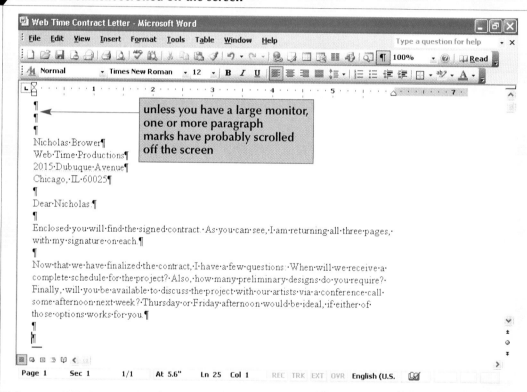

4. Type the following text:

   Thanks again for choosing Art4U. We look forward to working with you.

5. Press the **Enter** key twice.

6. Type **Sincerely yours,** (including the comma) to enter the complimentary closing.

7. Press the **Enter** key five times to allow space for a signature. Unless you have a very large monitor, part or even all of the inside address scrolls off the top of the Document window.

8. Type **Megan Grahs**, and then press the **Enter** key. A wavy red line appears below "Grahs." In Word, such lines indicate possible spelling errors. Because Megan's last name is not in the Word dictionary, Word suggests that it might be spelled incorrectly. You'll learn more about Word's error checking features in the next section. For now, you can ignore the wavy red line.

   You've completed the letter, so you should save your work.

9. Click the **Save** button 🔲 on the Standard toolbar. Word saves your letter with the same name and in the same location you specified earlier. Don't be concerned about any typing errors. You'll learn how to correct them in the next section.

In the last set of steps, you watched the text at the top of your document move off your screen. You can scroll this hidden text back into view so you can read the beginning of the letter. When you do, the text at the bottom of the screen will scroll out of view. To scroll the Document window, you can click the up or down arrows in the vertical scroll bar, click anywhere in the vertical scroll bar, or drag the scroll box. See Figure 1-17.

Note: If you are using a very large monitor, your insertion point may still be some distance from the bottom of the screen. In that case, you may not be able to perform the scrolling steps that follow. Read the steps to familiarize yourself with the process of scrolling. You'll have a chance to scroll longer documents later.

Parts of the scroll bar ◀ **Figure 1-17**

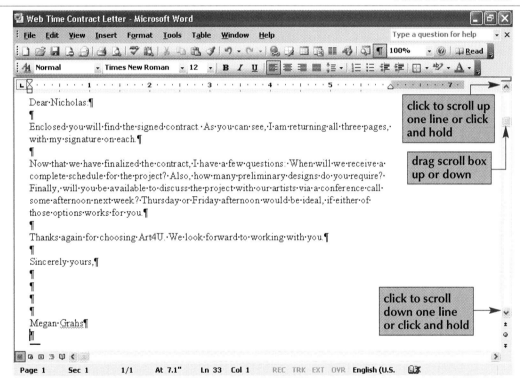

In the next set of steps, you will practice using the vertical scroll bar.

To scroll the document using the vertical scroll bar:

1. Position the mouse pointer on the up arrow at the top of the vertical scroll bar. Press and hold the mouse button to scroll the text. When the text stops scrolling, you have reached the top of the document and can see the beginning of the letter. Note that scrolling does not change the location of the insertion point in the document.

2. Click the down arrow on the vertical scroll bar several times. The document scrolls down one line at a time.

▶ 3. Click anywhere in the vertical scroll bar, below the scroll box. The document scrolls down one full screen.

▶ 4. Drag the scroll box up until the first line of the inside address ("Nicholas Brower") is positioned at the top of the Document window.

▶ 5. Scroll down to show the last line of the letter.

Correcting Errors

If you notice a typing error as soon as you make it, you can press the Backspace key, which deletes the characters and spaces to the left of the insertion point one at a time. Backspacing erases both printing and nonprinting characters. After you erase the error, you can type the correct character(s). You can also press the Delete key, which deletes characters to the right of the insertion point one at a time.

In many cases, however, Word's **AutoCorrect** feature will do the work for you. Among other things, AutoCorrect automatically corrects common typing errors, such as typing "adn" for "and." For example, you might have noticed AutoCorrect at work if you forgot to capitalize the first letter in a sentence as you typed the letter. AutoCorrect can automatically correct this error as you type the rest of the sentence. You'll learn more about using AutoCorrect as you become a more experienced Word user. For now, just keep in mind that AutoCorrect corrects certain spelling errors automatically. Depending on how your computer is set up, some or all AutoCorrect features might be turned off. You'll learn how to turn AutoCorrect on in the following steps.

Whether or not AutoCorrect is turned on, you can always rely on Word's **Spelling and Grammar checker**. This feature continually checks your document against Word's built-in dictionary and a set of grammar rules. If you type a word that doesn't match the correct spelling in Word's dictionary or if a word isn't in the dictionary at all (as is the case with Megan's last name, Grahs), a wavy red line appears beneath the word. A wavy red line also appears if you type duplicate words (such as "the the"). If you accidentally type an extra space between words or make a grammatical error (such as typing "He walk to the store." instead of "He walks to the store."), a wavy green line appears beneath the error.

The easiest way to see how these features work is to make some intentional typing errors.

To correct intentional typing errors:

▶ 1. Click to the left of the last paragraph mark to position the insertion point there (if it is not already there), and then press the **Enter** key to create a double space after Megan's last name, which is in the signature line. Before you start typing, you'll check to make sure AutoCorrect is turned on.

▶ 2. Click **Tools** on the menu bar, and then click **AutoCorrect Options**. The AutoCorrect: English (U.S.) dialog box opens.

▶ 3. Click the **Capitalize first letter of sentences** check box and the **Replace text as you type** check box to insert checks if these options are not already checked, and then click **OK**. (It is okay if other check boxes have checks.)

▶ 4. Carefully and slowly type the following sentence exactly as it is shown, including the spelling errors and the extra space between the last two words: **microsoft Word corects teh commen typing misTakes you make**. Press the **Enter** key when you are finished typing.

Notice that as you press the spacebar after the word "commen," a wavy red line appears beneath it, indicating that the word might be misspelled. Notice also that Word automatically capitalized the word "Microsoft" because it's the first word in the sentence. And, when you pressed the spacebar after the words "corects," "teh," and "misTakes," Word automatically corrected the spelling. After you pressed the Enter key, a wavy green line appeared under the last two words, alerting you to the extra space. See Figure 1-18.

Document with intentional typing errors ◀ **Figure 1-18**

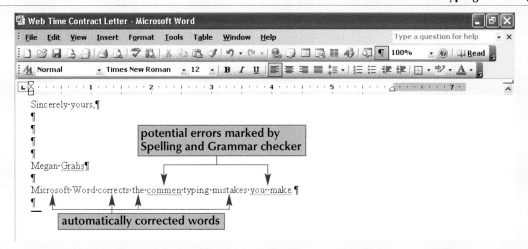

Trouble? If red and green wavy lines do not appear beneath mistakes, Word is probably not set to check spelling and grammar automatically as you type. Click Tools on the menu bar, and then click Options to open the Options dialog box. Click the Spelling & Grammar tab. If necessary, insert check marks in the "Check spelling as you type" and the "Check grammar as you type" check boxes, and then click OK.

Working with AutoCorrect

Whenever AutoCorrect makes a change, Word inserts an **AutoCorrect Options button** in the document. You can use this button to undo a change, or to prevent AutoCorrect from making the same change in the future. To see an AutoCorrect Options button, you position the mouse pointer over a word that has been changed by AutoCorrect.

To display an AutoCorrect Options button:

▶ **1.** Position the mouse pointer over the word "corrects." A small blue rectangle appears below the first few letters of the word, as shown in Figure 1-19.

Word changed by AutoCorrect ◀ **Figure 1-19**

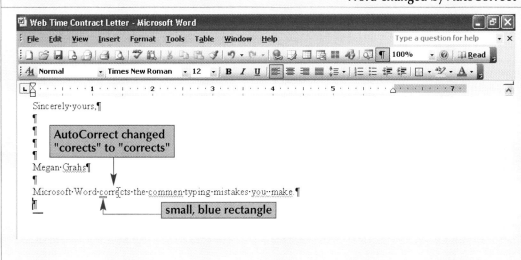

Trouble? If you see a blue button with a lightning bolt, move the pointer slightly to the right so that only the rectangle is visible, and then continue with the next step.

2. Point to the blue rectangle below "corrects." The blue rectangle is replaced by the AutoCorrect Options button and the entire word "corrects" is highlighted.

3. Click the **AutoCorrect Options** button. A menu with commands related to AutoCorrect appears. You could choose to change "corrects" back to "corects." You could also tell AutoCorrect to stop automatically correcting "corects." This second option might be useful if you found that AutoCorrect continually edited a word, such as a brand name or technical term, which was in fact spelled correctly. In the "corects" example, the change made by AutoCorrect is acceptable, so you can simply close the AutoCorrect menu.

4. Click anywhere in the document. The AutoCorrect menu closes.

Correcting Spelling and Grammar Errors

After you verify that AutoCorrect made changes you want, you should review your document for wavy underlines. Again, the red underlines indicate potential spelling errors, while the green underlines indicate potential grammar or punctuation problems. In the following steps, you will learn a quick way to correct such errors.

To correct spelling and grammar errors:

1. Position the I-Beam pointer over the word "commen," and then click the right mouse button. A shortcut menu appears with suggested spellings. See Figure 1-20.

Figure 1-20 ▶ Shortcut menu with suggested spellings

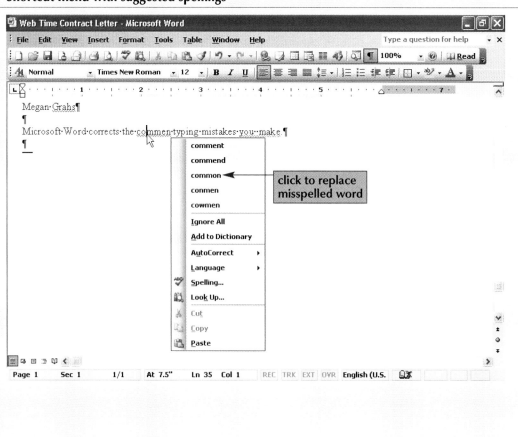

Trouble? If the shortcut menu doesn't appear, repeat Step 1, making sure you click the right mouse button, not the left one. If you see a different menu from the one shown in Figure 1-20, you didn't right-click exactly on the word "commen." Press the Esc key to close the menu, and then repeat Step 1.

2. Click **common** in the shortcut menu. The menu disappears, and the correct spelling appears in your document. Notice that the wavy red line disappears after you correct the error.

3. Click to the right of the letter "u" in the word "you." Press the **Delete** key to delete the extra space.

You can see how quick and easy it is to correct common typing errors with AutoCorrect and the Spelling and Grammar checker. Remember, however, to proofread each document you create thoroughly. AutoCorrect will not catch words that are spelled correctly, but used improperly (such as "your" for "you're").

Proofreading the Letter

Before you can proofread your letter, you need to delete the practice sentence.

To delete the practice sentence:

1. Confirm that the insertion point is to the right of "you" in the sentence you just typed, and then press the **Delete** key repeatedly to delete any spaces and characters to the right of the insertion point, including one paragraph mark.

2. Press the **Backspace** key repeatedly until the insertion point is to the left of the paragraph mark below Megan's name. There should only be one paragraph mark below her name. If you accidentally delete part of the letter, retype it, using Figure 1-17 as a guide.

Now you can proofread the letter for any typos. You can also get rid of the wavy red underline below Megan's last name.

To respond to possible spelling errors:

1. Be sure the signature line is visible. Because Word doesn't recognize "Grahs" as a word, it is marked as a potential error. You need to tell Word to ignore this name wherever it occurs in the letter.

2. Right-click **Grahs**. A shortcut menu opens.

3. Click **Ignore All**. The wavy red underline disappears from below "Grahs."

4. Scroll up to the beginning of the letter, and proofread it for typos. If a word has a wavy red or green underline, right-click it and choose an option in the shortcut menu. To correct other errors, click to the right or left of the error, use the Backspace or Delete key to remove it, and then type a correction.

5. Click the **Save** button 🖫 on the Standard toolbar. Word saves your letter with the same name and to the same location you specified earlier.

Inserting a Date with AutoComplete

The beauty of using a word-processing program such as Microsoft Word is that you can easily make changes to text you have already typed. In this case, you need to insert the current date at the beginning of the letter. Megan tells you that she wants to send the contract to Web Time Productions on February 15, so you need to insert that date into the letter now.

Before you can enter the date, you need to move the insertion point to the right location. In a standard business letter, the date belongs approximately 2.5 inches from the top. (As you recall, this is where you started the inside address earlier.) You also need to insert some blank lines to allow enough space between the date and the inside address.

To move the insertion point and add some blank lines:

1. Scroll up to display the top of the document.

2. Click to the left of the "N" in "Nicholas Brower" in the inside address. The status bar indicates that the insertion point is on line 9, 2.5 inches from the top. (Your status bar might show slightly different measurements.)

3. Press the **Enter** key four times, and then press the ↑ key four times. Now the insertion point is positioned at line 9, with three blank lines between the inside address and the line where you will insert the date. See Figure 1-21.

Figure 1-21 ▶ **Position of insertion point**

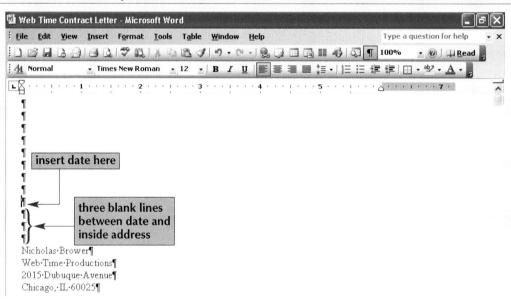

You're ready to insert the date. To do this you can take advantage of Word's **AutoComplete** feature, which automatically inserts dates and other regularly used items for you. In this case, you can type the first few characters of the month, and let Word insert the rest. (This only works for long month names like February.)

To insert the date:

▶ **1.** Type **Febr** (the first four letters of February). A rectangular box appears above the line, as shown in Figure 1-22. If you wanted to type something other than February, you could continue typing to complete the word. In this case, though, you want to accept the AutoComplete suggestion, which you will do in the next step.

AutoComplete suggestion | **Figure 1-22**

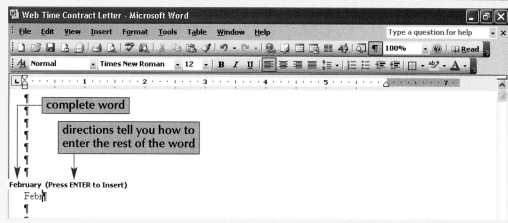

Trouble? If the AutoComplete suggestion doesn't appear, this feature may not be active. Click Tools on the menu bar, click AutoCorrect Options, click the AutoText tab, click the Show AutoComplete suggestions check box to insert a check, and then click OK. Delete the characters "Febr" and begin again with Step 1.

▶ **2.** Press the **Enter** key. The rest of the word "February" is inserted in the document.

▶ **3.** Press the **spacebar**, and then type **15, 2006**.

Trouble? If February happens to be the current month, you will see a second AutoComplete suggestion displaying the current date after you press the spacebar. To ignore that AutoComplete suggestion, continue typing the rest of the date as instructed in Step 3.

▶ **4.** Click one of the blank lines below the date. Depending on how your computer is set up, you may see a dotted underline below the date. (You will learn the meaning of this underline later in this tutorial.) You have finished entering the date. See Figure 1-23.

Date entered in the document | **Figure 1-23**

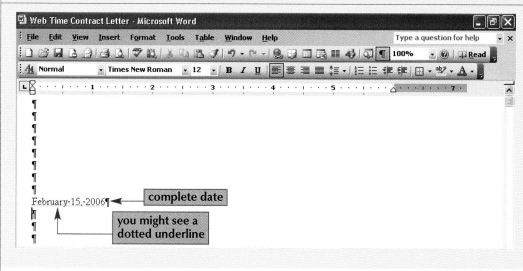

Moving the Insertion Point Around a Document

When you scroll a document, you change the part of the document that is displayed on the screen. But to change the location in the document where new text will appear when you type, you need to move the insertion point. In the last section, you moved the insertion point by scrolling up and then clicking where you wanted to insert new lines and text. You can also use the arrow keys on your keyboard, ←, →, ↑, and ↓, to move the insertion point one character at a time to the left or right, or one line at a time up or down. In addition, you can press a combination of keys to move the insertion point. As you become more experienced with Word, you'll decide which method you prefer.

Megan asks you to add her middle initial to the signature line. Before you can do that, you need to make sure you're comfortable moving the insertion point around the document. To see how quickly you can move through the document, you'll use keystrokes to move the insertion point to the beginning and end of the document.

To move the insertion point with keystrokes:

▶ 1. Press the **Ctrl** key and hold it down while you press the **Home** key. The insertion point moves to the beginning of the document.

▶ 2. Press the **Page Down** key to move the insertion point down to the top of the next screen.

▶ 3. Press the ↓ key several times to move the insertion point down one line at a time, and then press the → key several times to move the insertion point to the right one character at a time.

▶ 4. Press the **Ctrl+End** keys. The insertion point moves to the end of the document.

▶ 5. Use the arrow keys to position the insertion point to the right of the "n" in "Megan."

▶ 6. Press the **spacebar**, and then type the letter **L** followed by a period.

Figure 1-24 summarizes the keystrokes you can use to move the insertion point around the document. When you simply need to display a part of a document, you'll probably want to use the vertical scroll bar. But when you actually need to move the insertion point to a specific spot, it's helpful to use these special keystrokes.

Figure 1-24 ▶ **Keystrokes for moving the insertion point**

Press	To move the insertion point
← or →	Left or right one character at a time
↑ or ↓	Up or down one line at a time
Ctrl+ ← or Ctrl+ →	Left or right one word at a time
Ctrl+ ↑ or Ctrl+ ↓	Up or down one paragraph at a time
Home or End	To the beginning or to the end of the current line
Ctrl+Home or Ctrl+End	To the beginning or to the end of the document
Page Up or Page Down	To the previous screen or to the next screen
Alt+Ctrl+Page Up or Alt+Ctrl+Page Down	To the top or to the bottom of the document window

Using the Undo and Redo Commands

To undo (or reverse) the very last thing you did, click the **Undo button** on the Standard toolbar. If you want to restore your original change, the **Redo button** reverses the action of the Undo button (or redoes the undo). To undo more than your last action, you can click the Undo list arrow on the Standard toolbar. This list shows your most recent actions. Undo reverses the action only at its original location. You can't delete a word or phrase, move the surrounding text, and then undo the deletion at a different location.

Megan asks you to undo the addition of her middle initial, to see how the signature line looks without it.

To undo the addition of the letter "L":

1. Place the mouse pointer over the **Undo** button 🔄 on the Standard toolbar. The label "Undo Typing" appears in a ScreenTip, indicating that your most recent action involved typing. See Figure 1-25.

Using the Undo button ◄ **Figure 1-25**

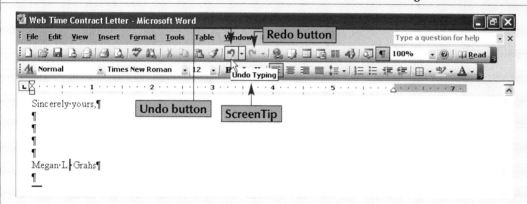

2. Click the **Undo** button 🔄. The letter "L," the period, and the space you typed earlier are deleted.

   Trouble? If something else changes, you probably made another edit or change to the document between the addition of Megan's middle initial and the undo. Click the Undo button on the Standard toolbar until the letter "L," the period, and the space following it are deleted. If a list of possible changes appears under the Undo button, you clicked the list arrow next to the Undo button rather than the Undo button itself. Press the Esc key to close the list.

   As she reviews the signature line, Megan decides that she does want to include her middle initial after all. Instead of retyping it, you'll redo the undo.

3. Place the mouse pointer over the **Redo** button 🔄 on the Standard toolbar and observe the "Redo Typing" ScreenTip.

4. Click the **Redo** button 🔄. Megan's middle initial (along with the period and an additional space) are reinserted into the signature line.

5. Click the **Save** button 💾 on the Standard toolbar to save your changes to the document.

Your letter is nearly finished. All that remains is to remove the straight dotted underlines and then print the letter.

Removing Smart Tags

A straight dotted underline below a date or address indicates that Word has inserted a Smart Tag in the document. A **Smart Tag** is a feature that allows you to perform actions (such as sending e-mail or scheduling a meeting) that would normally require a completely different program. When you point to Smart Tag text, a Smart Tag Actions button appears, which you can click to open a menu with commands related to that item. (For example, you might click a Smart Tag on an address to add that address to your e-mail address book.) You don't really need Smart Tags in this document, though, so you will delete them. (Your computer may not be set up to show Smart Tags at all, or it might show them on dates but not addresses. If you do not see any Smart Tags in your document, simply read the following steps.)

To remove the Smart Tags from the document:

▶ **1.** Scroll up so you can see the inside address. If you see a straight dotted underline below the street address (2015 Dubuque Avenue), position the mouse pointer over that line. A Smart Tag icon ⓘ appears over the street address.

▶ **2.** Move the mouse pointer over the **Smart Tag** icon ⓘ. The icon is transformed into the Smart Tag Actions button ⓘ ▾, as shown in Figure 1-26.

Figure 1-26 ▶ Displaying the Smart Tag Actions button

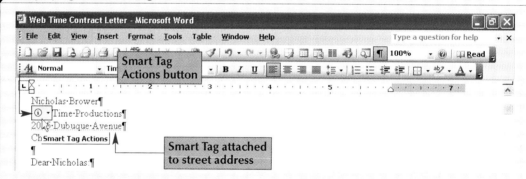

▶ **3.** Click the **Smart Tag Actions** button ⓘ ▾. A menu of commands related to addresses appears.

▶ **4.** Click **Remove this Smart Tag**. The Smart Tag menu closes. The address is no longer underlined, indicating that the Smart Tag has been removed. Depending on how your computer is set up, the Smart Tag on the street address may have been the only one in your document. But it's possible you see others.

▶ **5.** Remove any other Smart Tags in the document, including any on the date or elsewhere in the inside address.

▶ **6.** Click the **Save** button 🖫 on the Standard toolbar.

Previewing and Printing a Document

Do you think the letter is ready to print? You could find out by clicking the Print button on the Standard toolbar and then reviewing the printed page. With that approach, however, you risk wasting paper and printer time. For example, if you failed to insert enough space for the company letterhead, you would have to add more space, and then print the letter all over again. To avoid wasting paper and time, you should first display the document in the **Print Preview window**. By default, the Print Preview window shows you the full page; there's no need to scroll through the document.

To preview the document:

1. Proof the document one last time and correct any new errors. Always remember to proof your document immediately before printing it.

2. Replace "Megan L. Grahs" with your first and last name, at the end of the letter. This will ensure that you will be able to identify your copy of the letter.

3. Click the **Print Preview** button ☐ on the Standard toolbar. The Print Preview window opens and displays a full-page version of your letter, as shown in Figure 1-27. This shows how the letter will fit on the printed page. The Print Preview toolbar includes a number of buttons that are useful for making changes that affect the way the printed page will look.

Full page displayed in Print Preview window | **Figure 1-27**

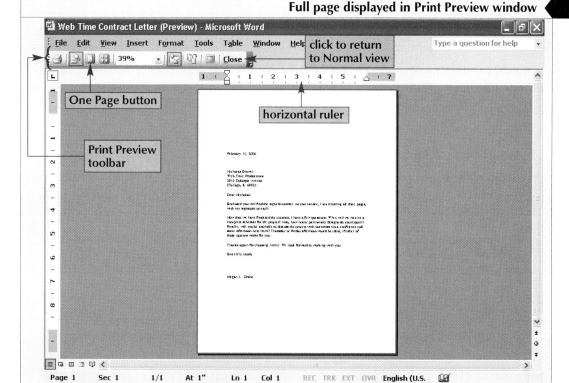

Trouble? If your letter in the Print Preview window is smaller and off to the left rather than centered in the window, click the One Page button on the Print Preview toolbar.

Trouble? If you don't see a ruler above the document, your ruler is not displayed. To show the ruler in the Print Preview window, click View on the menu bar and then click Ruler.

4. Click the **Close** button on the Print Preview toolbar to return to Normal view.

5. Click the **Save** button ☐ on the Standard toolbar.

Note that it is especially important to preview documents if your computer is connected to a network so that you don't keep a shared printer tied up with unnecessary printing. In this case, the text looks well spaced and the letterhead will fit at the top of the page. You're ready to print the letter.

When printing a document, you have two choices. You can use the Print command on the File menu, which opens the Print dialog box in which you can adjust some printer settings. Or, if you prefer, you can use the Print button on the Standard toolbar, which prints the document using default settings, without opening a dialog box. In these tutorials, the first time you print from a shared computer, you should check the settings in the Print dialog box and make sure the number of copies is set to 1. After that, you can use the Print button.

To print the letter document:

► 1. Make sure your printer is turned on and contains paper.

► 2. Click **File** on the menu bar, and then click **Print**. The Print dialog box opens.

► 3. Make sure the Printer section of the dialog box shows the correct printer. If you're not sure what the correct printer is, check with your instructor or technical support person. Also, make sure the number of copies is set to 1.

   Trouble? If the Print dialog box shows the wrong printer, click the Name list arrow, and then select the correct printer from the list of available printers.

► 4. Click the **OK** button. Assuming your computer is attached to a printer, the letter prints.

Your printed letter should look similar to Figure 1-9, but without the Art4U letterhead. The word wraps, or line breaks, might not appear in the same places on your letter because the size and spacing of characters vary slightly from one printer to the next.

Creating an Envelope

After you print the letter, Megan asks you to print an envelope in which to mail the contracts. Creating an envelope is a simple process because Word automatically uses the inside address from the letter as the address on the envelope.

Reference Window	**Printing an Envelope**

- Click Tools on the menu bar, point to Letters and Mailings, and then click Envelopes and Labels.
- In the Envelopes and Labels dialog box, verify that the Delivery address box contains the correct address. If necessary, you can type a new address or edit the existing one.
- If necessary, type a return address. If you are using preprinted stationery that already includes a return address, click the Omit check box to insert a check.
- To print the envelope immediately, insert an envelope in your printer, and then click Print.
- To store the envelope along with the rest of the document, click Add to Document.
- To print the envelope after you have added it to the document, open the Print dialog box and print the page containing the envelope.

Megan tells you that your printer is not currently stocked with envelopes. She asks you to create the envelope and add it to the document. Then she will print the envelope later, when she is ready to mail the contracts to Web Time Productions.

To create an envelope:

▶ **1.** Click **Tools** on the menu bar, point to **Letters and Mailings**, and then click **Envelopes and Labels**. The Envelopes and Labels dialog box opens, as shown in Figure 1-28. By default, Word uses the inside address from the letter as the delivery address. Depending on how your computer is set up, you might see an address in the Return address box. Because Megan will be using Art4U's printed envelopes, you don't need to include a return address on this envelope.

Envelopes and Labels dialog box ◀ **Figure 1-28**

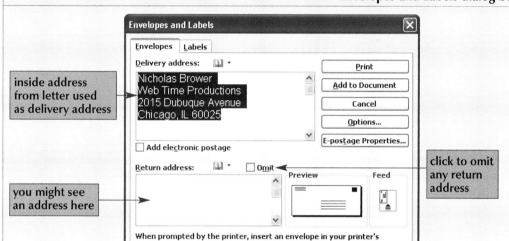

▶ **2.** Click the **Omit** check box to insert a check, if necessary.

▶ **3.** Click the **Add to Document** button. The dialog box closes, and you return to the Document window. The envelope is inserted at the top of the document, above a double line with the words "Section Break (Next Page)." The double line indicates that the envelope and the letter are two separate parts of the document. The envelope will print in the standard business envelope format. The letter will still print on standard 8.5 x 11-inch paper. (You'll have a chance to print an envelope in the exercises at the end of this tutorial.)

▶ **4.** Click the **Save** button 🖫 on the Standard toolbar.

You are finished with the letter and the envelope, so you can close the document.

To close the document:

▶ **1.** Click the **Close Window** button ⊠ on the menu bar. The Web Time Contract Letter document closes.

Trouble? If you see a dialog box with the message "Do you want to save the changes to 'Web Time Contract Letter?'," click the Yes button.

▶ **2.** Close any other open documents without saving them.

Congratulations on creating your first letter in Microsoft Word. You'll be able to use the skills you learned in this tutorial to create a variety of professional documents.

Session 1.2 Quick Check

1. True or False: The term "word wrap" refers to automatic line breaking.
2. Explain how to enter the name of a month using AutoComplete.
3. What button can you use to reverse your most recent edit immediately?
4. List the steps required to print an envelope.
5. In your own words, define each of the following:
   a. scrolling
   b. AutoComplete
   c. Redo button
   d. Smart Tag
   e. Print Preview

Tutorial Summary

In this tutorial you learned how to set up your Word window to match the figures in this book, create a new document from scratch, and type a professional-looking cover letter. You practiced correcting errors, and moving the insertion point. You learned how to undo and redo changes, how to insert a date with AutoComplete and how to remove Smart Tags from a document. Finally, you previewed and printed a document, and created an envelope.

Key Terms

AutoComplete
AutoCorrect
AutoCorrect Options button
default settings
nonprinting characters

Print Preview window
Redo button
scroll
Smart Tag

Spelling and Grammar
  checker
Undo button
word wrap

Practice

Practice the skills you learned in the tutorial using the same case scenario.

Review Assignments

There are no Data Files needed for the Review Assignments.

Megan received an e-mail from Nicholas Brower at Web Time Productions, confirming their plans for a conference call. Megan has e-mailed the graphic artists at Art4U, informing them about the call. To make sure everyone remembers, she would like you to post a memo on the bulletin board in the break room. She also asks you to create an envelope so the memo can be mailed to freelance artists who work outside the Art4U offices. Create the memo shown in Figure 1-29 by completing the following steps. The steps show quotation marks around text you type; do not include the quotation marks in your letter.

Figure 1-29

Art4U, Inc.
5725 Mesa Avenue
Tucson, AZ 85703
Art4U@Earth-World-Art.com

TO: Art4U Staff Artists

FROM: Megan L. Grahs

DATE: February 20, 2006

SUBJECT: Conference Call

Please plan to join us for a conference call at 3 p.m. on Friday, March 1. Nicholas Brower, president of Web Time Productions, will be taking part, as will five of his company's most experienced Web page designers. This will be your chance to ask the designers some important questions.

You will be able to join the call from your desk by dialing an 800 number and a special access code. You'll receive both of these numbers via e-mail the day of the call.

1. Make sure a new blank document is open.
2. Compare your screen to the checklist in Figure 1-8 and change any settings if necessary. In particular, make sure that nonprinting characters are displayed and the Getting Started task pane is open.
3. Press the Enter key eight times to insert enough space for the company letterhead.
4. Type "TO:" in capital letters, and then press the spacebar.
5. Turn off capitalization if you turned it on in Step 4, and then type "Art4U Staff Artists". Throughout the rest of this exercise, turn capitalization on and off as needed.
6. Press the Enter key twice, type "FROM:", press the spacebar, turn off capitalization, and then type your name.

7. Press the Enter key twice, type "DATE:", and then press the spacebar.
8. Enter the date February 20, 2006 using AutoComplete when possible to reduce the amount of typing required.
9. Press the Enter key twice, type "SUBJECT:", press the spacebar, type "Conference Call", and then press the Enter key three times.
10. Continue typing the rest of the memo as shown in Figure 1-29. (You will have a chance to correct any typing errors later.) Ignore any AutoCorrect suggestions that are not relevant to the text you are typing.
11. Save your work as **Call Memo** in the Tutorial.01\Review folder provided with your Data Files.
12. Practice using the keyboard to move the insertion point around the document. Use the arrow keys so the insertion point is positioned immediately to the left of the "A" in "Art4U" in the "TO" line.
13. Type "All" and a space, so the TO line reads "TO: All Art4U Staff Artists".
14. Undo the change and then redo it.
15. Scroll to the beginning of the document and proofread your work.
16. Correct any misspelled words marked by wavy red lines. If the correct spelling of a word does not appear in the shortcut menu, close the list, and then make the correction yourself. Remove any red wavy lines below words that are actually spelled correctly. Then correct any grammatical or other errors indicated by wavy green lines. Delete any extra words or spaces.
17. Remove any Smart Tags.
18. Save your most recent changes.
19. Preview and print the memo.
20. Add an envelope to the document. Use your own address as the delivery address. Do not include a return address.
21. Save your changes and close the Call Memo document. If any other documents are open, close them without saving any changes.

Case Problem 1

There are no Data Files needed for this Case Problem.

Luis Sotelo Elementary School You are a teacher at Luis Sotelo Elementary School. Your students have been raising money all year for a trip to Roaring Rapids Water Park. Before you can finalize plans for the outing, you need to write for some information. Create the letter by completing the following steps. The steps show quotation marks around text you type; do not include the quotation marks.

1. Open a new blank document if one is not already open, and then check your screen to make sure your settings match those in Figure 1-8.
2. Type your name, press Enter, and then type the following address:
   Luis Sotelo Elementary School
   1521 First Avenue
   Raleigh, North Carolina 21101

3. Press the Enter key four times, and then type the name of the current month. (If an AutoComplete suggestion appears, accept it to complete the name of the month.) Press the spacebar. After you press the spacebar, an AutoComplete suggestion appears with the current date. Accept the suggestion.

4. Press the Enter key three times, and, using the proper business letter format, type the inside address: "Scott Shimanski, Roaring Rapids Water Park, 2344 West Prairie Street, Durham, North Carolina 27704".
5. Double space after the inside address (that is, press the Enter key twice), type the salutation "Dear Mr. Shimanski:", and then insert a blank line.
6. Type the paragraph as follows: "I'd like some information about a class field trip to Roaring Rapids Water Park. Please answer the following questions:"
7. Save your work as **Field Trip Information Letter** in the Tutorial.01\Cases folder provided with your Data Files.
8. Insert one blank line, and then type these questions on separate lines with one blank line between each:
   "How much is a day pass for a 10-year-old child?"
   "How much is a day pass for an adult?"
   "Are lockers available for storing clothes and other belongings?"
9. Move the insertion point up to the beginning of the third question (which begins "Are lockers available..."). Insert a new line, and add the following as the new third question in the list: "Can you offer a discount for a group of 25 children and 5 adults?"
10. Correct any spelling or grammar errors indicated by red or green wavy lines. Because "Sotelo" is spelled correctly, use the shortcut menu to remove the wavy red line under the word "Sotelo" and prevent Word from marking the word as a misspelling. Repeat to ignore "Shimanski."
11. Insert another blank line at the end of the letter, and type the complimentary closing "Sincerely," (include the comma).
12. Use the Enter key to leave room for the signature, and type your full name. Then press the Enter key and type "Luis Sotelo Elementary School". Notice that "Sotelo" is not marked as a spelling error this time.
13. Scroll up to the beginning of the document, and then remove any Smart Tags in the letter.
14. Save your changes to the letter, and then preview it using the Print Preview button.
15. Print the letter, and then close the document.

Case Problem 2

Apply

Apply the skills you learned to create a letter confirming the catering needs for a client's annual convention.

There are no Data Files needed for this Case Problem.

Rocky Mountain Convention Center As catering director for the Rocky Mountain Convention Center, you are responsible for managing food service at the city's convention center. The American Rock Climbers Association has scheduled a daily breakfast buffet during its annual convention (which runs July 6–10, 2006). You need to write a letter confirming plans for the daily buffet.

Complete the following steps to create the letter using the skills you learned in the tutorial. The steps show quotation marks around text you type; do not include the quotation marks in your letter.

1. Open a new, blank document if one is not already open, and then check your screen to make sure your settings match those in Figure 1-8.
2. Press the Enter key until the insertion point is positioned about two inches from the top of the page. (Remember that you can see the exact position of the insertion point, in inches, in the status bar.)

3. Enter "June 6, 2006" as the date.
4. Press the Enter key four times after the date, and, using the proper business letter format, type the inside address: "Neil Skinner, American Rock Climbers Association, 222 Sydney Street, Whitewater, CO 77332".
5. Double space after the inside address (that is, press the Enter key twice), type the salutation "Dear Mr. Skinner:", and then double space again.
6. Write one paragraph confirming the daily breakfast buffets for July 6–10, 2006.
7. Insert a blank line and type the complimentary closing "Sincerely,".
8. Use the Enter key to leave room for the signature, and then type your name and title.
9. Save the letter as **Buffet Confirmation Letter** in the Tutorial.01\Cases folder provided with your Data Files.
10. Remove any Smart Tags. Reread your letter carefully, and correct any errors. Use the arrow keys to move the insertion point, as necessary.
11. Save any new changes, and then preview and print the letter.

Explore

12. Create an envelope for the letter, and add it to the document. Click the Omit check box if necessary to deselect it, and then, for the return address, type your own address. Add the envelope to the document. If you are asked if you want to save the return address as the new default return address, click No. If your computer is connected to a printer that is stocked with envelopes, click File on the menu bar, click Print, click the Pages option button, type 1 in the Pages text box, and then click OK.
13. Save your work, and then close the document.

Create

Use your skills to create the congratulatory letter shown in Figure 1-30.

Case Problem 3

There are no Data Files needed for this Case Problem.

Boundary Waters Technical College Liza Morgan, professor of e-commerce at Boundary Waters Technical College in northern Minnesota, was recently honored by the Northern Business Council for her series of free public seminars on developing Web sites for nonprofit agencies. She also was recently named Teacher of the Year by a national organization called Women in Technology. As one of her former students, you decide to write a letter congratulating her on these honors. To create the letter, complete the following steps:

1. Open a new blank document if one is not already open, and then check your screen to make sure your settings match those in Figure 1-8.
2. Create the letter shown in Figure 1-30. Replace "Your Name" with your first and last name.

Figure 1-30

August 13, 2006

Professor Liza Morgan
Department of Business Administration
Boundary Waters Technical College
1010 Sturgeon Drive
Blue Pines, Minnesota 50601

Dear Professor Morgan:

I was happy to hear about your recent honors. You certainly deserve to be recognized
for your Web site development seminars. As a grateful former student, I heartily endorse
your Teacher of the Year award. Congratulations!

Sincerely,

Your Name

3. Save the document as **Congratulations Letter** in the Tutorial.01\Cases folder provided
   with your Data Files.
4. Correct any typing errors, remove any Smart Tags, and then preview and print
   the letter.
5. Create an envelope, using your address as the return address, and then add the
   envelope to the document. (*Hint*: Click the Omit check box to deselect it if it is
   selected before attempting to type the return address.) Do not save the return address
   as the default.
6. Save the document and close it.

Challenge

Go beyond what you've learned to write a memo for a small e-business company.

Case Problem 4

There are no Data Files needed for this Case Problem.

Head for the Hills You are the office manager for Head for the Hills, a small company that sells hiking equipment over the Internet. The company has just moved to a new building, which requires a special security key card after hours. Some employees have had trouble getting the key cards to work properly. You decide to hold a meeting to explain the security policies for the new building and to demonstrate the key cards. But first you need to post a memo announcing the meeting. The recently ordered letterhead (with the company's new address) has not yet arrived, so you will use a Word template to create the memo. Word provides templates—that is, models with predefined formatting—to help you create complete documents (including a professional-looking letterhead) quickly. To create the memo, do the following steps. The steps show quotation marks around text you type; do not include the quotation marks in your letter.

1. Open a new blank document if one is not already open, and then check your screen to make sure your settings match those in Figure 1-8.
2. Open the New Document task pane. You see a number of options related to creating new documents.
3. **Explore** In the "Templates" section, click On my computer. The Templates dialog box opens.
4. **Explore** Click the Memos tab, click Professional Memo, and then click the OK button. A memo template opens containing generic, placeholder text that you can replace with your own information.
5. Display the template in Normal view, if it is not already. Click immediately to the right of the last "e" in the text "Company Name Here" (at the top of the document), press the Backspace key repeatedly to delete the text, and type "Head for the Hills".
6. Click the text "Click here and type name" in the To: line, and type "All Employees". Click the text after "From:", and replace it with your name.
7. Click the text after "CC:", press Delete to delete the placeholder text, and then delete the entire "CC:" line. Note that Word inserts the current date automatically after the heading "Date."
8. Click the text after "Re:", and then type "Using key cards".
9. Delete the placeholder text that begins "How to Use..." but do not delete the paragraph mark (¶) at the end of the line, and then type "Meeting Tomorrow".
10. **Explore** Delete the text in the body of the letter but do not delete the paragraph mark (¶) at the end of the paragraph, and then type a paragraph announcing the meeting, which is scheduled for tomorrow at 2 p.m. in the Central Conference Room.
11. Save the letter as **Key Card Meeting Memo** in the Tutorial.01\Cases folder provided with your Data Files.
12. **Explore** To make it easier to review your work, you can change the Zoom setting in Normal view. Click the Zoom box in the Standard toolbar, type 110%, and then press the Enter key. Continue to type values in the Zoom text box until the document fills the window.
13. Review the memo. Correct any typos and delete any Smart Tags. Save the memo again, preview it, and then print it.
14. Close the document.

Research

Go to the Web to find information you can use to create documents.

Internet Assignments

The purpose of the Internet Assignments is to challenge you to find information on the Internet that you can use to work effectively with this software. The actual assignments are updated and maintained on the Course Technology Web site. Log on to the Internet and use your Web browser to go to the Student Online Companion for New Perspectives Office 2003 at **www.course.com/np/office2003**. Click the Internet Assignments link, and then navigate to the assignments for this tutorial.

Assess

SAM Assessment and Training

If you have a SAM user profile, you may have access to hands-on instruction, practice, and assessment of the skills covered in this tutorial. Log in to your SAM account and go to your assignments page to see what your instructor has assigned.

Reinforce

Lab Assignments

The New Perspectives Labs are designed to help you master some of the key concepts and skills presented in this text. The steps for completing this Lab are located on the Course Technology Web site. Log on to the Internet and use your Web browser to go to the Student Online Companion for New Perspectives Office 2003 at **www.course.com/np/office2003**. Click the Lab Assignments link, and then navigate to the assignments for this tutorial.

Review

Quick Check Answers

Session 1.1

1. (1) Plan the content, purpose, organization, and look of your document. (2) Create and then edit the document. (3) Format the document to make it visually appealing. (4) Preview and then print the document.
2. a. symbols you can display on-screen but that don't print
   b. controls the document's on-screen magnification
   c. settings that control the size and shape of the characters that appear when you start typing
   d. standard settings
3. Click the Normal View button.
4. Right-click a toolbar or the menu bar, and then click Standard.
5. False
6. False
7. .doc

Session 1.2

1. True
2. Type the first few characters of the month. When an AutoComplete suggestion appears, press the Enter key.
3. Undo
4. Click Tools on the menu bar, point to Letters and Mailings, and then click Envelopes and Labels. In the Envelopes and Labels dialog box, verify that the Delivery address contains the correct address. If necessary, you can type a new address or edit the existing one. If necessary, type a return address. If you are using preprinted stationery that already includes a return address, click the Omit check box to insert a check. To print the envelope immediately, insert an envelope in your printer, and then click Print. To store the envelope along with the rest of the document, click Add to Document. To print the envelope after you have added it to the document, open the Print dialog box, and then print the page containing the envelope.
5. a. the means by which text at the bottom of the document shifts out of view when you display the top of the document, and text at the top shifts out of view when you display the bottom of a document
   b. a feature that automatically enters dates and other regularly used items
   c. a button that redoes changes
   d. a window in which you can see how the document will look when printed
   e. a feature that that allows you to perform actions (such as sending e-mail or scheduling a meeting) that would normally require a completely different program.

Objectives

Session 2.1
- Check spelling and grammar
- Select and delete text
- Move text within the document
- Find and replace text

Session 2.2
- Change margins, line spacing, alignment, and paragraph indents
- Copy formatting with the Format Painter
- Change fonts and adjust font sizes
- Emphasize points with bullets, numbering, bold, underlining, and italic
- Preview formatted text
- Add a comment to a document
- Use the Research task pane

Editing and Formatting a Document

Preparing an FAQ Document

Case

Long Meadow Gardens

Marilee Brigham is the owner of Long Meadow Gardens, a landscape and gardening supply company. The firm's large nursery provides shrubs and trees to professional landscape contractors throughout the Minneapolis/St. Paul area. At the same time, Long Meadow Gardens' retail store caters to home gardeners, who often call the store with questions about planting and caring for their purchases.

Marilee has noticed that retail customers tend to ask the same set of questions. To save time, she would like to create a series of handouts designed to answer these common questions. (Such a document is sometimes known as an FAQ—which is short for "frequently asked questions.") The company's chief horticulturist, Peter Chi, has just finished creating an FAQ containing information on planting trees. Now that Marilee has commented on and corrected the draft, Peter asks you to make the necessary changes and print the document.

In this tutorial, you will edit the FAQ document according to Marilee's comments. You will open a draft of the document, resave it, and edit it. You will check the document's grammar and spelling, and then move text using two different methods. You will also find and replace one version of the company name with another.

Next, you will change the overall look of the document by changing margins and line spacing, indenting and justifying paragraphs, and copying formatting from one paragraph to another. You'll create a bulleted list to emphasize the species of water-tolerant trees and a numbered list for the steps involved in removing the burlap from around the base of a tree. Then you'll make the title more prominent by centering it, changing its font, and enlarging it. You'll add bold to the questions to set them off from the rest of the text and underline an added note about how to get further

Student Data Files

▼ Tutorial.02

▽ **Tutorial folder**

FAQ.doc

▽ **Review folder**

Statmnt.doc

▽ **Cases folder**

Form.doc   Training.doc
Product.doc Tribune.doc

information. Finally, before you print the FAQ document, you will add a comment, and look up information using the Research task pane.

Session 2.1

Reviewing the Document

Marilee's editing marks and notes on the first draft are shown in Figure 2-1. You'll begin by opening the first draft of the document, which has the filename FAQ.

Figure 2-1 ▶ Draft of FAQ with Marilee's edits (page 1)

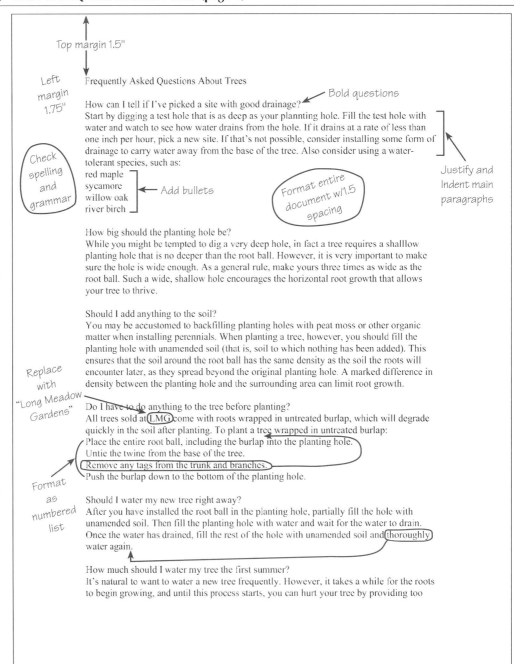

Draft of FAQ with Marilee's edits (page 2) **Figure 2-1 (cont.)**

much moisture. To avoid ~~any~~ root damage ~~or problems~~, water once a week. In times of heavy rainfall (more than 2 inches a week) don't water your tree at all.

Is mulch necessary?
You should definitely add some mulch, which helps prevent drying and discourages weeds. But take care not to add too much mulch. Too or three inches are all you need. You can choose from organic mulches (shredded bark, cocoa shells, composts) or ornamental gravel. To prevent damage from disease and pests, push the mulch back from the tree's base, forming a circle about 2 inches out from the trunk. Never use black plastic beneath mulch because it prevents the roots from getting the air and water they need. If you want an extra barrier to prevent weeds, use porous landscape cloth.

Any of our sales associates here at LMG would be happy to answer your questions about planting and caring for your tree. Call us at (501) 555-2325, from 10 A.M. to 8 P.M., seven days a week. For details on our upcoming series of horticulture classes, call 9 A.M. to 5 P.M, Monday through Friday.

insert
Marilee's
name

Note:

To open the document:

1. Start Word, and then verify that the Getting Started task pane is displayed.

2. In the Open section of the Getting Started task pane, click the **Open** button [icon]. You may have to point to the down arrow at the bottom of the task pane to scroll down in order to display the Open button. (Depending on how your computer is set up, the label next to this button might read "More" or "Open.") The Open dialog box opens, as shown in Figure 2-2. (Note that you could also use the Open button on the Standard toolbar to open this dialog box.)

Figure 2-2 Open dialog box

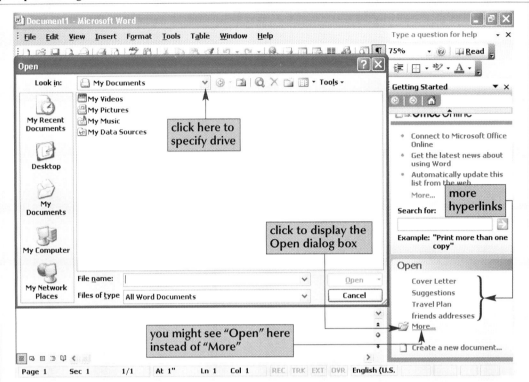

> **3.** Click the **Look in** list arrow, and then navigate to the Tutorial.02 folder included with your Data Files.

> **4.** Double-click the **Tutorial.02** folder, and then double-click the **Tutorial** folder.

> **5.** Click **FAQ** to select the file, if necessary.
>
> **Trouble?** If you see "FAQ.doc" in the folder, Windows is configured to display file extensions. Click FAQ.doc and continue with Step 6. If you can't find the file with or without the file extension, make sure you're looking in the Tutorial subfolder within the Tutorial.02 folder included with your Data Files, and check to make sure the Files of type text box displays All Word Documents or All Files. If you still can't locate the file, ask your instructor or technical support person for help.

> **6.** Click the **Open** button. The document opens with the insertion point at the beginning of the document. Notice that the document consists of a series of questions and answers.

> **7.** Verify that the document is displayed in Normal view, and then scroll down until you can see the question "Is mulch necessary?" Notice the dotted line in the middle of the preceding paragraph. This line shows where Word has inserted a page break, dividing the document into two pages. See Figure 2-3. Word automatically inserts a page break (called an **automatic page break**) whenever your text fills up all the available lines on a page. In Normal view, a page break is represented by the dotted line shown in Figure 2-3. In some views, page breaks are not visible at all.

Document with automatic page break

Figure 2-3

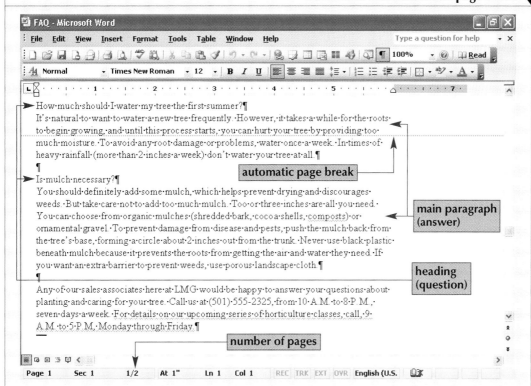

8. Check that your screen matches Figure 2-3. If necessary, click the **Show/Hide ¶** button ¶ to display nonprinting characters. This will make formatting elements (paragraph marks, spaces, and so forth) visible and easier to change.

Now that you've opened the document, you can save it with a new name. To avoid altering the original file, FAQ, you will save the document using the filename Tree FAQ. Saving the document with another filename creates a copy of the file and leaves the original file unchanged in case you want to work through the tutorial again.

To save the document with a new name:

1. Click **File** on the menu bar, and then click **Save As**. The Save As dialog box opens with the current filename highlighted in the File name text box. You could type an entirely new filename, or you could edit the current one.

2. Click to the left of "FAQ" in the File name text box, type **Tree**, and then press the **spacebar**.

3. Verify that the Tutorial.02\Tutorial folder is selected in the Save in box.

4. Click the **Save** button. The document is saved with the new filename "Tree FAQ".

Now you're ready to begin working with the document. First, you will check it for spelling and grammatical errors.

Using the Spelling and Grammar Checker

When typing a document, Word highlights possible spelling and grammatical errors. You can quickly recognize these possible errors by looking for words underlined in red (for possible spelling errors) or green (for possible grammatical errors). When you're working on a document that someone else typed, it's a good idea to start by using the Spelling and Grammar checker. This feature automatically checks a document word by word for a variety of errors. Among other things, the Spelling and Grammar checker can sometimes find words that, though spelled correctly, are not used properly.

Reference Window	**Checking a Document for Spelling and Grammatical Errors**

- Move the insertion point to the beginning of the document, and then click the Spelling and Grammar button on the Standard toolbar.
- In the Spelling and Grammar dialog box, review any errors highlighted in color. Possible grammatical errors appear in green; possible spelling errors appear in red. Review the suggested corrections in the Suggestions list box.
- To accept a suggested correction, click on it in the Suggestions list box, click Change to make the correction, and then continue searching the document for errors.
- Click Ignore Once to skip the current instance of the highlighted text and continue searching the document for errors.
- Click Ignore All to skip all instances of the highlighted text and continue searching the document for spelling errors. Click Ignore Rule to skip all instances of a highlighted grammatical error.
- To type your correction directly in the document, click outside the Spelling and Grammar dialog box, make the correction, and then click Resume in the Spelling and Grammar dialog box.
- To add an unrecognized word to the dictionary, click Add to dictionary.

The Spelling and Grammar Checker compares the words in your document to the default dictionary that is installed automatically with Word. If you regularly use terms that are not included in the main dictionary, you can create a custom dictionary and then select it as the new default dictionary. A custom dictionary includes all the terms in the main dictionary, plus any new terms that you add. To create a custom dictionary and select it as the new default dictionary, you would follow these steps:

1. Click **Tools** on the menu bar, click **Options**, click the **Spelling & Grammar** tab, and then click **Custom Dictionaries**. The Custom Dictionaries dialog box opens.
2. Click **New**. The Create Custom Dictionary dialog box opens.
3. Type a name for the custom dictionary in the File name text box, and click **Save**. You return to the Custom Dictionaries dialog box.
4. In the **Dictionary list** box, click the new custom dictionary to select it, click **Change Default**, and then click **OK**.

You'll see how the Spelling and Grammar checker works as you check the Tree FAQ document for mistakes.

To check the Tree FAQ document for spelling and grammatical errors:

▶ **1.** Press **Ctrl+Home** to verify that the insertion point is located at the beginning of the document, to the left of the "F" in "Frequently Asked Questions."

▶ **2.** Click the **Spelling and Grammar** button on the Standard toolbar. The Spelling and Grammar dialog box opens with the word "About" highlighted in green, indicating a possible grammatical error. The word "about" (with a lowercase "a") is suggested as a possible replacement. The line immediately under the dialog box title bar indicates the possible type of problem, in this case, Capitalization. See Figure 2-4. Prepositions of five or more letters are capitalized in titles so no change is required here.

Trouble? If you see the word "plannting" selected instead of "About," your computer is not set up to check grammar. Click the Check grammar check box to insert a check, and then click Cancel to close the Spelling and Grammar dialog box. Repeat Steps 1 and 2.

Spelling and Grammar dialog box ◀ **Figure 2-4**

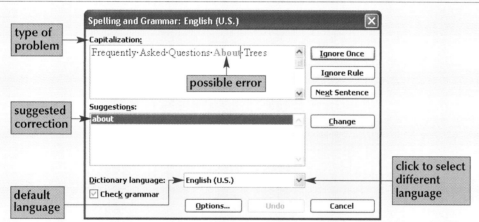

▶ **3.** Click the **Ignore Rule** button. The word "plannting" is highlighted in red, with "planting," "planning," and "plantings" listed as possible corrections.

▶ **4.** Verify that "planting" is highlighted in the Suggestions list box, and then click the **Change** button. "Planting" is inserted into the document, and the misspelled word "shalllow" is highlighted in the document.

▶ **5.** Verify that "shallow" is selected in the Suggestions list box, and then click the **Change** button. The word "composts" is highlighted in green, with "and composts" listed as a possible correction. The type of problem "Comma Use" has to do with using a comma without "and" before the last item in a list. Marilee likes the list as it stands, so you'll ignore this suggestion.

▶ **6.** Click the **Ignore Rule** button. You click Ignore Rule to ignore the rule throughout the entire document. (You can click Ignore Once to ignore a grammatical rule in the currently selected text.)

The last sentence of the document is selected. According to the type of problem listed at the top of the dialog box, the highlighted text is a sentence fragment. In this case, Word is correct. The word "call" lacks a direct object—that is, you need to indicate whom the reader should call. You can fix this problem by clicking outside the Spelling and Grammar dialog box and typing the change directly in the document.

7. Click outside the Spelling and Grammar dialog box just to the right of "call," press the **spacebar**, type **Marilee Brigham**, and then click the **Resume** button in the Spelling and Grammar dialog box. A message box opens indicating that the spelling and grammar check is complete. Notice that the last sentence is no longer a sentence fragment; that is because "Marilee Brigham" completes the sentence.

Trouble? If you don't see the word "call," the Spelling and Grammar checker dialog box is covering it. Click the title bar of the Spelling and Grammar dialog box, and drag the dialog box out of the way.

8. Click the **OK** button. The Spelling and Grammar dialog box closes. You return to the Tree FAQ document.

Although the Spelling and Grammar checker is a useful tool, remember that there is no substitute for careful proofreading. Always take the time to read through your document to check for errors the Spelling and Grammar checker might have missed. Keep in mind that the Spelling and Grammar checker probably won't catch *all* instances of words that are spelled correctly but used improperly. And, of course, the Spelling and Grammar checker cannot pinpoint phrases that are confusing or inaccurate. To produce a professional document, you must read it carefully several times, and, if necessary, ask a co-worker to read it, too.

To proofread the Tree FAQ document:

1. Scroll to the beginning of the document and begin proofreading. When you get near the bottom of the document, notice that the word "Too" is used instead of the word "Two" in the paragraph on mulch. See Figure 2-5. You will correct this error after you learn how to select parts of a document.

Figure 2-5 ▶ **Word "Too" used incorrectly**

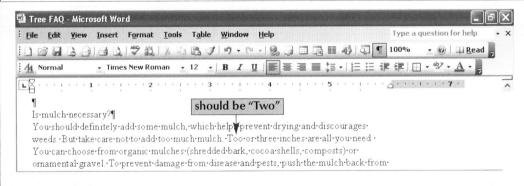

2. Finish proofreading the Tree FAQ document.

To make all of Marilee's changes, you need to learn how to select parts of a document.

Selecting Parts of a Document

Before you can do anything to text (such as deleting, moving, or formatting it), you often need to highlight, or **select** it. You can select text by using the mouse or the keyboard, although the mouse is usually easier and more efficient. With the mouse you can quickly select a line or paragraph by clicking the **selection bar** (the blank space in the left margin area of the Document window). You can also select text using various combinations of keys. Figure 2-6 summarizes methods for selecting text with the mouse and the keyboard. The notation "Ctrl+Shift" means you press and hold the two keys at the same time. Note that you will use the methods described in Figure 2-6 as you work on the Tree FAQ document.

Methods for selecting text ◀ **Figure 2-6**

To Select	Mouse	Keyboard	Mouse and Keyboard
A word	Double-click the word.	Move the insertion point to the beginning of the word, hold down Ctrl+Shift, and then press →.	
A line	Click in the selection bar next to the line.	Move the insertion point to the beginning of the line, hold down Shift, and then press →.	
A sentence	Click at the beginning of the sentence, then drag the pointer until the sentence is selected.		Press and hold down the Ctrl key, and click within the sentence.
Multiple lines	Click and drag in the selection bar next to the lines.	Move the insertion point to the beginning of the first line, hold down Shift, and then press → until all the lines are selected.	
A paragraph	Double-click in the selection bar next to the paragraph, or triple-click within the paragraph.	Move the insertion point to the beginning of the paragraph, hold down Ctrl+Shift, and then press ↓.	
Multiple paragraphs	Click in the selection bar next to the first paragraph in the group, and then drag in the selection bar to select the paragraphs.	Move the insertion point to the beginning of the first paragraph, hold down Ctrl+Shift, and then press ↓ until all the paragraphs are selected.	
An entire document	Triple-click in the selection bar.	Press Ctrl+A.	Press and hold down the Ctrl key and click in the selection bar.
A block of text	Click at the beginning of the block, then drag the pointer until the entire block is selected.		Click at the beginning of the block, press and hold down the Shift key, and then click at the end of the block.
Nonadjacent blocks of text	Press and hold the Ctrl key, then drag the mouse pointer to select multiple blocks of nonadjacent text.		

Deleting Text

When editing a document, you frequently need to delete text. You already have experience using the Backspace and Delete keys to delete a few characters. To delete an entire word or multiple words, you select the text. After you select the text, you can either replace it with something else by typing over it, or delete it by pressing the Delete key. You need to delete the word "Too" and replace it with "Two," so you'll use the first method now.

To replace "Too" with "Two":

1. Press **Ctrl+End**. The insertion point moves to the end of the document.

2. Press and hold the **Ctrl** key while you press the ↑ key three times. The insertion point is now positioned at the beginning of the paragraph that begins "You should definitely add some mulch." (The status bar indicates that this is line 5 of page 2.)

3. In the second line of the paragraph, double-click the word **Too** (in the phrase "Too or three inches"). The entire word is highlighted.

4. Type **Two**. The selected word is replaced with the correction. The sentence now correctly reads: "Two or three inches are all you need."

Next, Marilee wants you to delete the phrase "or problems" and the word "any" in the paragraph before the one you've just corrected. Peter explains that you can do this quickly by selecting multiple items and then pressing Delete. As you'll see in the following steps, selecting parts of a document by clicking and dragging takes a little practice, so don't be concerned if you don't get it right the first time. You can always try again.

To select and delete multiple items:

1. Press the ↑ key five times. As shown in Figure 2-7, the insertion point is now located in the sentence that begins "To avoid any root damage or problems." The status bar indicates that this is line 1 of page 2.

Figure 2-7 ▶ **Text to be deleted**

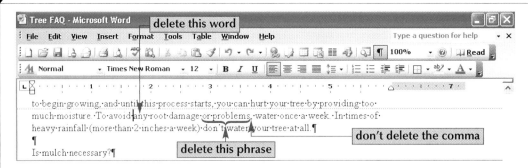

2. Double-click the word **any**. The word and the space following it are selected.

3. Press and hold the **Ctrl** key, click to the left of "or" and drag to select the phrase "or prob-lems," and then release the **Ctrl** key. Do not select the comma after the word "problems." At this point the word "any" and the phrase "or problems" should be selected.

   Trouble? If you don't get Step 3 right the first time (for instance, if you accidentally selected the word "damage"), click anywhere in the document and then repeat Steps 2 and 3.

4. Press the **Delete** key. The selected items are deleted and the words around them move in to fill the space. As you can see in Figure 2-8, you still need to delete the extra space before the comma.

Paragraph after deleting phrase | **Figure 2-8**

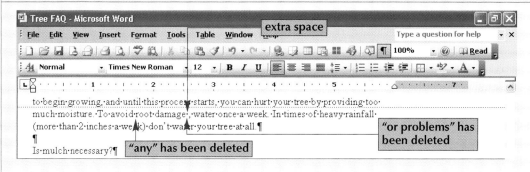

Trouble? If you deleted the wrong text, click the Undo button (not the Redo button) on the Standard toolbar to reverse your mistake, and then begin again with Step 2.

Trouble? If your screen looks slightly different from Figure 2-8, don't be concerned. The text may wrap differently on your monitor. Just make sure you deleted the correct text.

5. Click to the right of the word "damage," and then press the **Delete** key. The extra space is deleted.

6. Scroll down to display the last line of the document (if necessary), drag the mouse pointer to select "Marilee Brigham," press the **Delete** key, press the **spacebar**, and then type your first and last name. This change will make it easier for you to retrieve your document if you print it on a network printer used by other students.

You have edited the document by replacing "Too" with "Two" and by removing the text that Marilee marked for deletion. Now you are ready to make the rest of the edits she suggested.

Moving Text within a Document

One of the most useful features of a word-processing program is the ability to move text. For example, Marilee wants to reorder the four points Peter made in the section "Do I have to do anything to the tree before planting?" on page 1 of his draft. You could reorder the list by deleting an item and then retyping it at a new location, but it's easier to select and then move the text. Word provides several ways to move text: drag and drop, cut and paste, and copy and paste.

Dragging and Dropping Text

One way to move text within a document is called drag and drop. With **drag and drop**, you select the text you want to move, press and hold down the mouse button while you drag the selected text to a new location, and then release the mouse button.

Dragging and Dropping Text

- Select the text you want to move.
- Press and hold down the mouse button until the drag-and-drop pointer appears, and then drag the selected text to its new location.
- Use the dotted insertion point as a guide to determine exactly where the text will be inserted.
- Release the mouse button to drop the text at the insertion point.

Marilee wants you to change the order of the items in the list on page 1 of the document. You'll use the drag-and-drop method to reorder these items. At the same time, you'll practice using the selection bar to highlight a line of text.

To move text using drag and drop:

1. Scroll up until you see "Do I have to do anything to the tree before planting?" (line 29 of page 1). In the list of steps involved in planting a tree, Marilee wants you to move the third step ("Remove any tags from the trunk and branches.") to the top of the list.

2. Move the pointer to the selection bar to the left of the line "Remove any tags from the trunk and branches." The pointer changes from an I-beam I to a right-facing arrow $\overset{\curvearrowright}{\wedge}$.

3. Click to the left of the line "Remove any tags from the trunk and branches." The line is selected. Notice that the paragraph mark at the end of the line is also selected. See Figure 2-9.

Figure 2-9 Selected text to drag and drop

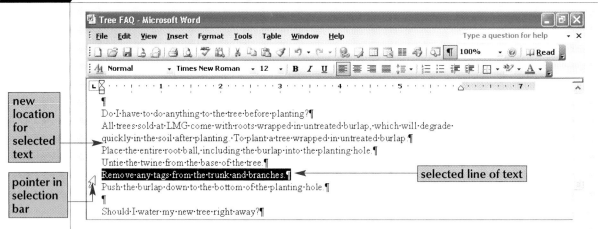

4. Position the pointer over the selected text. The pointer changes from a right-facing arrow $\overset{\curvearrowright}{\wedge}$ to a left-facing arrow $\overset{\curvearrowleft}{\wedge}$.

5. Press and hold down the mouse button until the drag-and-drop pointer $\overset{\downarrow}{\wedge}$ appears. Note that a dotted insertion point appears within the selected text. (You may have to move the mouse pointer slightly left or right to see the drag-and-drop pointer or the dotted insertion point.)

6. Drag the selected text up until the dotted insertion point appears to the left of the word "Place." Make sure you use the dotted insertion point, rather than the mouse pointer, to guide the text to its new location. The dotted insertion point indicates exactly where the text will appear when you release the mouse button. See Figure 2-10.

Moving text with drag-and-drop pointer | Figure 2-10

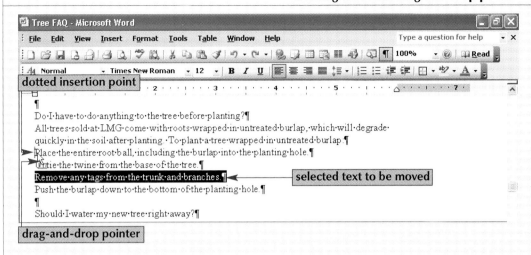

7. Release the mouse button. The selected text moves to its new location as the first step in the list. A Paste Options button appears near the newly moved text, as shown in Figure 2-11. When you move the mouse pointer over the Paste Options button, it changes to include a list arrow.

Paste Options button | Figure 2-11

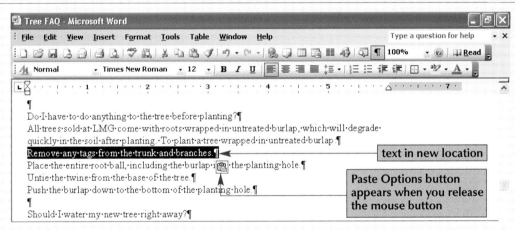

Trouble? If the selected text moves to the wrong location, click the Undo button 🔄 on the Standard toolbar, and then repeat Steps 2 through 7. Remember to hold down the mouse button until the dotted insertion point appears to the left of the word "Place."

Trouble? If you don't see the Paste Options button, your computer is not set up to display it. Read Step 8, and then continue with Step 9.

8. Click the **Paste Options** button 📋. A menu of text-moving commands appears. These commands are useful when you are inserting text that looks different from the surrounding text. For instance, suppose you selected text formatted in the Times New Roman font and then dragged it to a paragraph formatted in the Arial font. You could then use the Match Destination Formatting command to format the moved text in Arial.

9. Deselect the highlighted text by clicking anywhere in the document. The Paste Options menu closes, but the button remains visible. It will disappear as soon as you perform another task.

Dragging and dropping works well if you're moving text a short distance in a document. However, Word provides another method, called cut and paste, that works well for moving text both long and short distances.

Cutting or Copying and Pasting Text

To **cut** means to remove text from the document and place it on the **Clipboard**, a feature that temporarily stores text or graphics until you need them later. To **copy** means to copy text to the Clipboard, leaving the original material in its original location. To **paste** means to transfer a copy of the text from the Clipboard into the document at the insertion point. To **cut and paste**, you select the text you want to move, cut (or remove) it from the document, and then paste (or insert) it into the document in a new location. If you don't want to remove the text from its original location, you can copy it (rather than cutting it), and then paste the copy in a new location.

Reference Window	**Cutting or Copying and Pasting Text**

- Select the text you want to cut or copy.
- To remove the text, click the Cut button on the Standard toolbar.
- To make a copy of the text, click the Copy button on the Standard toolbar.
- Move the insertion point to the target location in the document.
- Click the Paste button on the Standard toolbar.

Depending on how your computer is set up, when you cut or copy more than one item, the **Clipboard task pane** may open automatically, making it easier for you to select which items you want to paste into the document. (To have the Clipboard task pane open automatically, click Options at the bottom of the Clipboard task pane, and then select Show Clipboard Automatically.) You can also choose to open the Clipboard task pane via the Office Clipboard command on the Edit menu. The Clipboard task pane contains a list of all the items currently stored on the Clipboard. The Clipboard can store a maximum of 24 items. The last item cut or copied to the Clipboard is the first item listed in the Clipboard task pane.

As indicated in Figure 2-1, Marilee suggested moving the word "thoroughly" (in the paragraph under the heading "Should I water my new tree right away?") to a new location. You'll use cut and paste to move this word.

To move text using cut and paste:

1. If necessary, scroll down until you can see the paragraph below the heading "Should I water my new tree right away?" near the bottom of page 1.

2. Double-click the word **thoroughly**. As you can see in Figure 2-12, you need to move this word to the end of the sentence.

Text to move using cut and paste Figure 2-12

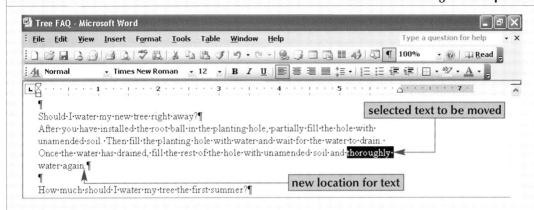

▶ **3.** Click the **Cut** button on the Standard toolbar to remove the selected text from the document.

▶ **4.** If the Clipboard task pane opens, click its **Close** button ✖ for now. You'll have a chance to use the Clipboard task pane shortly.

▶ **5.** Click between the "n" in "again" and the period that follows it. The insertion point marks the position where you want to move the text.

▶ **6.** Click the **Paste** button on the Standard toolbar. The word "thoroughly" appears in its new location, along with a Paste Options button. Note that Word also included a space before the word, so that the end of the sentence reads "and water again thoroughly." The Paste Options button that appeared in the previous set of steps (when you dragged text to a new location) disappears.

Trouble? If the Paste Options buttons on your computer do not behave exactly as described in these steps—for instance, if they do not disappear as described—this is not a problem, just continue with the tutorial.

Peter mentions that he'll be using the paragraph on mulch and the paragraph on watering for the FAQ he plans to write on flowering shrubs. He asks you to copy that information and paste it in a new document that he can use as the basis for the new FAQ. You can do this using copy and paste. In the process you'll have a chance to use the Clipboard task pane.

To copy and paste text:

▶ **1.** Click **Edit** on the menu bar, and then click **Office Clipboard**. The Clipboard task pane opens on the right side of the Document window. It contains the word "thoroughly," which you copied to the Clipboard in the last set of steps. See Figure 2-13.

Figure 2-13 ▶ Clipboard task pane

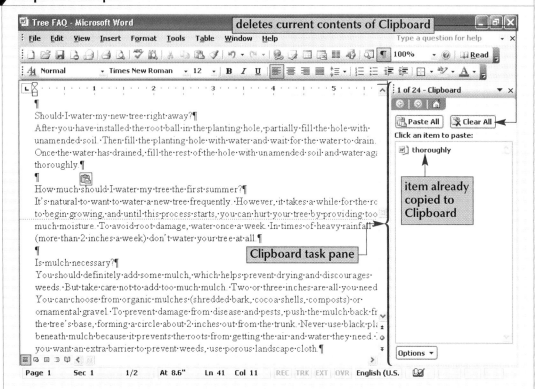

2. Click the **Clear All** button near the top of the task pane. The current contents of the Clipboard are deleted, and you see the following message on the Clipboard task pane: "Clipboard empty. Copy or cut to collect items."

3. Move the mouse pointer to the selection bar and double-click next to the paragraph that begins "After you have installed the root ball." The entire paragraph is selected.

4. Click the **Copy** button 🖹 on the Standard toolbar. The first part of the paragraph appears in the Clipboard task pane.

5. If necessary, scroll down until you can see the paragraph below the heading "Is mulch necessary?"

6. Select the paragraph below the heading (the paragraph that begins "You should definitely add . . . ").

7. Click the **Copy** button 🖹 on the Standard toolbar. The first part of the paragraph appears in the Clipboard task pane, as shown in Figure 2-14. Note the Clipboard icon 🖺 on the Windows taskbar indicating that the Clipboard task pane is currently active.

Trouble? If you do not see the Clipboard icon in the task pane, click the Options button at the bottom of the Clipboard task pane, and then click Show Office Clipboard Icon on Taskbar. When a check mark is next to this option, the Clipboard icon appears in the far right side of the Windows taskbar to the left of the time.

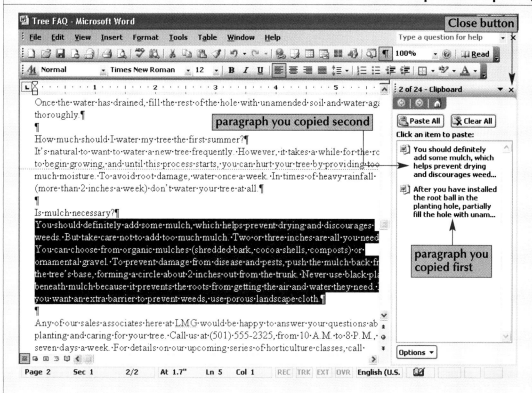

8. Click the **New Blank Document** button on the Standard toolbar. A new, blank document opens. The Clipboard icon on the Windows taskbar indicates that although the Clipboard task pane is no longer visible, it is still active.

9. Double-click the **Clipboard** icon on the right side of the Windows taskbar. The Clipboard task pane is now visible.

Now you can use the Clipboard task pane to insert the copied text into the new document.

To insert the copied text into the new document:

1. In the Clipboard task pane, click the item that begins "You should definitely add . . . " The text is inserted in the document.

2. Press the **Enter** key to insert a blank line, and then click the item that begins "After you have installed the root ball . . . " in the task pane. The text is inserted in the document.

3. Save the document as **Flowering Shrub FAQ** in the Tutorial.02\Tutorial folder, and then close the document. You return to the Tree FAQ document, where the Clipboard task pane is still open. You are finished using the Clipboard task pane, so you will delete its contents.

4. Click the **Clear All** button on the Clipboard task pane. The copied items are removed from the Clipboard task pane.

5. Click the **Close** button on the Clipboard task pane. The Clipboard task pane closes.

6. Click anywhere in the document to deselect the highlighted paragraph.

7. Save the document.

Finding and Replacing Text

When you're working with a longer document, the quickest and easiest way to locate a particular word or phrase is to use the **Find command**. To use the Find command, you type the text you want to find in the Find what text box, and then you click the Find Next button. The text in the Find what text box is the search text. After you click the Find Next button, Word finds and highlights the search text.

If you want to replace characters or a phrase with something else, you use the **Replace command**, which combines the Find command with a substitution feature. The Replace command searches through a document and substitutes the search text with the replacement text you specify. As you perform the search, Word stops and highlights each occurrence of the search text. You must determine whether or not to substitute the replacement text. If you want to substitute the highlighted occurrence, you click the Replace button. If you want to substitute every occurrence of the search text with the replacement text, you click the Replace All button.

When using the Replace All button with single words, keep in mind that the search text might be found within other words. To prevent Word from making incorrect substitutions in such cases, it's a good idea to select the Find whole words only check box along with the Replace All button. For example, suppose you want to replace the word "figure" with "illustration." Unless you select the Find whole words only check box, Word replaces "figure" in "configure" with "illustration" so the word becomes "conillustration."

As you search through a document, you can search from the current location of the insertion point down to the end of the document, from the insertion point up to the beginning of the document, or through the entire document.

| Reference Window | **Finding and Replacing Text** |

- Click Edit on the menu bar, and then click either Find or Replace.
- To find text, click the Find tab. To find and replace text, click the Replace tab.
- Click the More button to expand the dialog box to display additional options (including the Find whole words only option). If you see the Less button, the additional options are already displayed.
- In the Search list box, select Down if you want to search from the insertion point to the end of the document, select Up if you want to search from the insertion point to the beginning of the document, or select All to search the entire document.
- Type the characters you want to find in the Find what text box.
- If you are replacing text, type the replacement text in the Replace with text box.
- Click the Find whole words only check box to search for complete words. Click the Match case check box to insert the replacement text using the same case specified in the Replace with text box.
- Click the Find Next button.
- Click the Replace button to substitute the found text with the replacement text and find the next occurrence.
- Click the Replace All button to substitute all occurrences of the found text with the replacement text.

Marilee wants the company initials, LMG, to be spelled out as "Long Meadow Gardens" each time they appear in the text. You'll use the Replace command to make this change quickly and easily.

To replace "LMG" with "Long Meadow Gardens":

1. Press **Ctrl+Home** to move the insertion point to the beginning of the document.

2. Click **Edit** on the menu bar, and then click **Replace**. The Find and Replace dialog box opens.

3. If you see a **More** button, click it to display the additional search options. (If you see a Less button, the additional options are already displayed.) Also, click the **Search** list arrow, and then click **All** if it is not already selected in order to search the entire document.

4. Click the **Find what** text box, type **LMG**, press the **Tab** key, and then type **Long Meadow Gardens** in the Replace with text box.

   Trouble? If you already see the text "LMG" and "Long Meadow Gardens" in your Find and Replace dialog box, someone has recently performed these steps on your computer. Skip Step 4 and continue with Step 5.

5. Click the **Find whole words only** check box to insert a check.

6. Click the **Match case** check box to insert a check. This ensures that Word will insert the replacement text using initial capital letters, as you specified in the Replace with text box. Your Find and Replace dialog box should look like Figure 2-15.

Find and Replace dialog box ◀ **Figure 2-15**

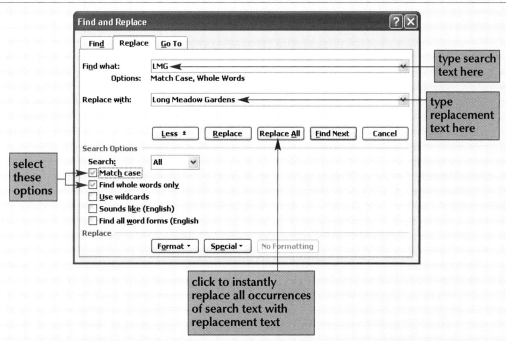

7. Click the **Replace All** button to replace all occurrences of the search text with the replacement text. When Word finishes making the replacements, you see a message box telling you that two replacements were made.

8. Click the **OK** button to close the message box, and then click the **Close** button in the Find and Replace dialog box to return to the document. The full company name has been inserted into the document, as shown in Figure 2-16. (You may have to scroll down to see this section.)

Figure 2-16 ▶ **Document with "Long Meadow Gardens" inserted**

9. Save the document.

Note that you can also search for and replace formatting, such as bold and special characters, in the Find and Replace dialog box. Click in the Find what text box, enter the search text, click the Format button, click Font to open the Font dialog box, and then select the formatting for the search text. Repeat this process for the replacement text, and then complete the search or replacement operation as usual.

You have completed the content changes Marilee requested. In the next session you will make some changes that will affect the document's appearance.

Review

Session 2.1 Quick Check

1. Explain how to use the Spelling and Grammar checker.
2. True or False: You should move the insertion point to the beginning of the document before starting the Spelling and Grammar checker.
3. Explain how to select the following items using the mouse:
   a. one word
   b. a block of text
   c. one paragraph
4. Define the following terms in your own words:
   a. selection bar
   b. drag and drop
   c. Replace
5. True or False: You can display the Clipboard via a command on the Format menu.
6. What is the difference between cut and paste, and copy and paste?
7. List the steps involved in finding and replacing text in a document.

Session 2.2

Changing Margins and Page Orientation

By default, text in a Word document is formatted in **portrait orientation**, which means the page is longer than it is wide (like a typical business letter). In Portrait orientation, the default margins are 1.25 inches for the left and right margins and 1 inch for the top and bottom margins. In **landscape orientation**, the page is wider than it is long, with slightly different margins, so that text spans the widest part of the page.

When working with margins, note that the numbers on the ruler indicate the distance in inches from the left margin, not from the left edge of the paper. You can change both page margins and page orientation from within the Page Setup dialog box.

Changing Margins and Page Orientation for the Entire Document   Reference Window

- With the insertion point anywhere in your document and no text selected, click File on the menu bar, and then click Page Setup.
- If necessary, click the Margins tab to display the margin settings.
- Click the Landscape icon if you want to switch to Landscape orientation.
- Use the arrows to change the settings in the Top, Bottom, Left, or Right text boxes, or type a new margin value in each text box.
- Make sure the Apply to list box displays Whole document.
- Click the OK button.

You need to change the top margin to 1.5 inches and the left margin to 1.75 inches, per Marilee's request. The left margin needs to be wider than usual to allow space for making holes so that the document can be inserted in a three-ring binder. In the next set of steps, you'll change the margins using the Page Setup command. You can also change margins in Print Layout view by dragging an icon on the horizontal ruler. You'll have a chance to practice this technique in the Case Problems at the end of this tutorial.

To change the margins in the Tree FAQ document:

1. If you took a break after the previous session, make sure Word is running, the Tree FAQ document is open in Normal view, and nonprinting characters are displayed.

2. Press **Ctrl+Home** to move the insertion point to the top of the document.

3. Click **File** on the menu bar, and then click **Page Setup** to open the Page Setup dialog box.

4. Click the **Margins** tab, if it is not already selected, to display the margin settings. Portrait orientation is selected by default. The Top margin setting is selected. See Figure 2-17. As you complete the following steps, keep an eye on the document preview, which changes to reflect changes you make to the margins.

Page Setup dialog box ◀ **Figure 2-17**

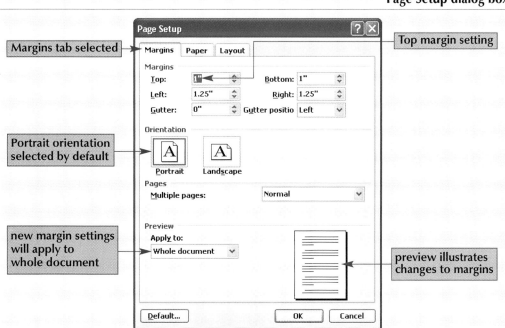

- Margins tab selected
- Top margin setting
- Portrait orientation selected by default
- new margin settings will apply to whole document
- preview illustrates changes to margins

5. Type **1.5** to change the Top margin setting. (You do not have to type the inches symbol.)

6. Press the **Tab** key twice to select the Left text box and highlight the current margin setting. The text area in the Preview box moves down to reflect the larger top margin.

7. Verify that the insertion point is in the Left text box, type **1.75**, and then press the **Tab** key. The left margin in the Preview box increases.

8. Make sure the **Whole document** option is selected in the Apply to list box, and then click the **OK** button to return to your document. Notice that the right margin on the ruler has changed to reflect the larger left margin setting and the resulting reduced page area. The document text is now 5.5 inches wide. See Figure 2-18.

| Figure 2-18 | **Ruler after setting left margin to 1.75 inches** |

Trouble? If a double dotted line and the words "Section Break" appear in your document, Whole document wasn't specified in the Apply to list box. If this occurs, click the Undo button on the Standard toolbar and repeat Steps 2 through 8, making sure you select the Whole document option in the Apply to list box.

Next, you will change the amount of space between lines of text.

Changing Line Spacing

The **line spacing** in a document determines the amount of vertical space between lines of text. In most situations, you will want to choose from three basic types of line spacing: **single spacing** (which allows for the largest character in a particular line as well as a small amount of extra space); **1.5 line spacing** (which allows for one and one-half times the space of single spacing); and **double spacing** (which allows for twice the space of single spacing). The Tree FAQ document is currently single-spaced because Word uses single spacing by default. The easiest way to change line spacing is to use the Line Spacing button on the Formatting toolbar. You can also use the keyboard to apply single, double, and 1.5 line spacing. Before changing the line-spacing setting, you need to click in the paragraph you want to change. To change line spacing for multiple paragraphs, select all of the paragraphs you want to change. Note that changes to line spacing affect entire paragraphs; you can't change the line spacing for individual lines within a paragraph.

Changing Line Spacing in a Document

- Click in the paragraph you want to change, or select multiple paragraphs.
- Click the list arrow next to the Line Spacing button on the Formatting toolbar, and then click the line spacing you want.

or

- Click in the paragraph you want to change, or select multiple paragraphs.
- Press Ctrl+1 for single spacing, Ctrl+5 for 1.5 line spacing, or Ctrl+2 for double spacing.

Marilee thinks the document will be easier to read with more spacing between the lines. She has asked you to change the line spacing for the entire Tree FAQ document to 1.5 line spacing. You will begin by selecting the entire document.

To change the document's line spacing:

1. Triple-click in the selection bar to select the entire document.

2. Move the mouse pointer over the **Line Spacing** button on the Formatting toolbar to display its ScreenTip. You see the text "Line Spacing (1)," indicating that single spacing is currently selected.

3. Click the **Line Spacing** list arrow on the Formatting toolbar. A list of line spacing options appears, as shown in Figure 2-19. To double space the document, you click 2.0, while to triple space it, you click 3.0. In this case, you need to apply 1.5 line spacing.

Line Spacing list box   **Figure 2-19**

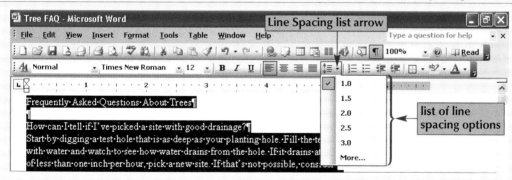

4. Click **1.5**. Notice the additional space between every line of text in the document.

5. Move the mouse pointer over the **Line Spacing** button on the Formatting toolbar to display a ScreenTip that reads "Line Spacing (1.5)." This tells you that 1.5 spacing is currently selected.

6. Click the title to deselect the text.

Now you are ready to make formatting changes that affect individual paragraphs.

Aligning Text

As you begin formatting individual paragraphs in the Tree FAQ document, keep in mind that in Word, a **paragraph** is defined as any text that ends with a paragraph mark symbol (¶). A paragraph can be a group of words that is many lines long, a single word, or even a blank line, in which case you see a paragraph mark alone on a single line. (The Tree FAQ document includes one blank paragraph before each question heading.)

The term **alignment** refers to how the text of a paragraph lines up horizontally between the margins. By default, text is aligned along the left margin but is **ragged**, or uneven, along the right margin. This is called **left alignment**. With **right alignment**, the text is aligned along the right margin and is ragged along the left margin. With **center alignment**, text is centered between the left and right margins and is ragged along both the left and right margins. With **justified alignment**, full lines of text are spaced between both the left and the right margins and the text is not ragged. Text in newspaper columns is often justified. The easiest way to apply alignment settings is by using the alignment buttons on the Formatting toolbar.

Marilee indicates that the title of the Tree FAQ should be centered and that the main paragraphs should be justified. First, you'll center the title.

To center-align the title:

1. Verify that the insertion point is located in the title "Frequently Asked Questions About Trees" at the beginning of the document.

2. Click the **Center** button ≣ on the Formatting toolbar. The text centers between the left and right margins. See Figure 2-20.

Figure 2-20 ▶ **Centered title**

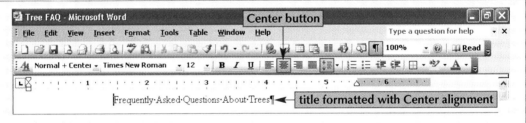

Next, you'll justify the text in the first two main paragraphs.

To justify the first two paragraphs using the Formatting toolbar:

1. Click anywhere in the paragraph that begins "Start by digging a test hole . . . "

2. Click the **Justify** button ≣ on the Formatting toolbar. The paragraph text spreads out so that it lines up evenly along the left and right margins.

3. Scroll down so you can move the insertion point to anywhere in the paragraph that begins "While you might be tempted . . . "

4. Click the **Justify** button ≣ on the Formatting toolbar again. The text is evenly spaced between the left and right margins. See Figure 2-21.

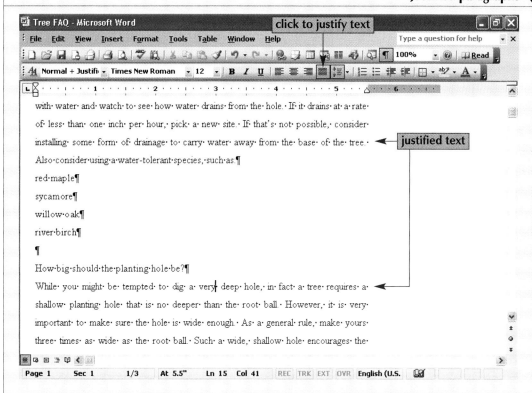

You'll justify the other paragraphs later. Now that you've learned how to change the paragraph alignment, you can turn your attention to indenting a paragraph.

Indenting a Paragraph

When you become a more experienced Word user, you might want to do some paragraph formatting, such as a **hanging indent** (where all lines except the first line of the paragraph are indented from the left margin) or a **right indent** (where all lines of the paragraph are indented from the right margin). You can select these types of indents on the Indents and Spacing tab of the Paragraph dialog box. To open this dialog box, you click Format on the menu bar and then click Paragraph.

In this document, though, you need to indent only the main paragraphs 0.5 inches from the left margin. This left indent is a simple paragraph indent. You can use the Indent buttons on the Formatting toolbar to increase or decrease paragraph indenting quickly. According to Marilee's notes, you need to indent all of the main paragraphs.

To indent a paragraph using the Increase Indent button:

▶ **1.** Press **Ctrl+Home**, and then click anywhere in the paragraph that begins "Start by digging a test hole . . . "

▶ **2.** Click the **Increase Indent** button 📑 on the Formatting toolbar twice. (Don't click the Decrease Indent button by mistake.) The entire paragraph moves right 0.5 inches each time you click the Increase Indent button. The paragraph is indented 1 inch, 0.5 inches more than Marilee wants.

> **3.** Click the **Decrease Indent** button ⬚ on the Formatting toolbar to move the paragraph left 0.5 inches. The paragraph is now indented 0.5 inches from the left margin. Don't be concerned about the list of tree species. You will indent the list later, when you format it as a bulleted list.

> **4.** Move the insertion point to anywhere in the paragraph that begins "While you might be tempted . . . " You may have to scroll down to see the paragraph.

> **5.** Click the **Increase Indent** button ⬚ on the Formatting toolbar. The paragraph is indented 0.5 inches. See Figure 2-22.

Figure 2-22 ▶ **Indented paragraphs**

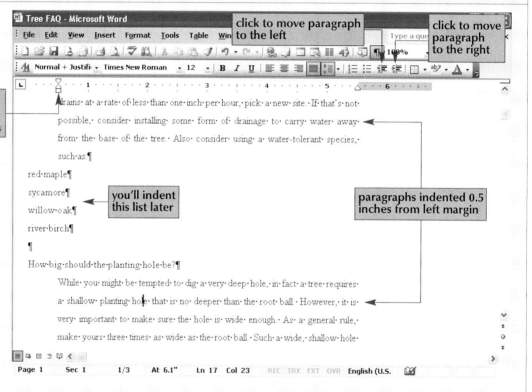

You can continue to indent and then justify each paragraph, or simply use the Format Painter command. The Format Painter allows you to copy both the indentation and alignment changes to all paragraphs in the document.

Using the Format Painter

The **Format Painter** makes it easy to copy all the formatting features of one paragraph to other paragraphs. You can use this button to copy formatting to one or multiple items.

Using the Format Painter

- Select the item whose formatting you want to copy.
- To copy formatting to one item, click the Format Painter button, and then use the mouse pointer to select the item you want to format.
- To copy formatting to multiple items, double-click the Format Painter button, and then use the mouse pointer to select each item you want to format. When you are finished, click the Format Painter button again to deselect it.

Use the Format Painter now to copy the formatting of the second paragraph to other main paragraphs. You'll begin by moving the insertion point to the paragraph whose format you want to copy.

To copy paragraph formatting with the Format Painter:

▶ **1.** Verify that the insertion point is located in the paragraph that begins "While you might be tempted . . . "

▶ **2.** Double-click the **Format Painter** button on the Standard toolbar. The Format Painter button will stay highlighted until you click the button again. When you move the pointer over text, the pointer changes to to indicate that the format of the selected paragraph can be painted (or copied) onto another paragraph.

▶ **3.** Scroll down, and then click anywhere in the paragraph that begins "You may be accustomed . . . " The format of the third paragraph shifts to match the format of the first two main paragraphs. See Figure 2-23. All three paragraphs are now indented and justified. The Format Painter pointer is still visible.

Formats copied with Format Painter | **Figure 2-23**

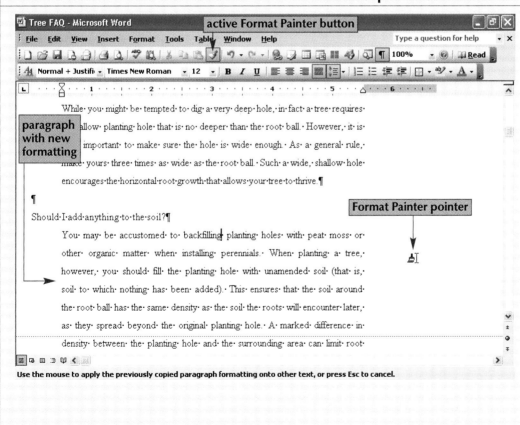

> **4.** Scroll down to click the remaining paragraphs that are preceded by a question heading. Take care to click only the paragraphs below the question headings. Do not click the document title, the one-line questions, the lists, or the last paragraph in the document.
>
> **Trouble?** If you click a paragraph and the formatting doesn't change to match the second paragraph, you single-clicked the Format Painter button rather than double-clicked it. Move the insertion point to a paragraph that has the desired format, double-click the Format Painter button, and then repeat Step 4.
>
> **Trouble?** If you accidentally click a title or one line of a list, click the Undo button 🔄 on the Standard toolbar to return the line to its original formatting. Then select a paragraph that has the desired format, double-click the Format Painter button 🖌, and finish copying the format to the desired paragraphs.
>
> **5.** After you are finished formatting paragraphs with the Format Painter pointer, click the **Format Painter** button 🖌 on the Standard toolbar to turn off the feature.
>
> **6.** Save the document.

All the main paragraphs in the document are formatted with the correct indentation and alignment. Your next job is to make the lists easier to read by adding bullets and numbers.

Adding Bullets and Numbers

You can emphasize a list of items by adding a heavy dot, or **bullet**, before each item in the list. For consecutive items, you can use numbers instead of bullets. Marilee requests that you add bullets to the list of tree species on page 1 to make them stand out.

To apply bullets to the list of items:

> **1.** Scroll to the top of the document until you see the list of tree species below the text "Also consider using a water-tolerant species such as:".
>
> **2.** Select the four items in the list (from "red maple" to "river birch"). It doesn't matter whether or not you select the paragraph mark after "river birch."
>
> **3.** Click the **Bullets** button 🔳 on the Formatting toolbar. A bullet, a dark circle, appears in front of each item. Each line indents to make room for the bullet.
>
> **4.** In order to make the bullets align with the first paragraph, make sure the list is still selected, and then click the **Increase Indent** button 🔳 on the Formatting toolbar. The bulleted list moves to the right.
>
> **5.** Click anywhere within the document window to deselect the text. Figure 2-24 shows the indented bulleted list.

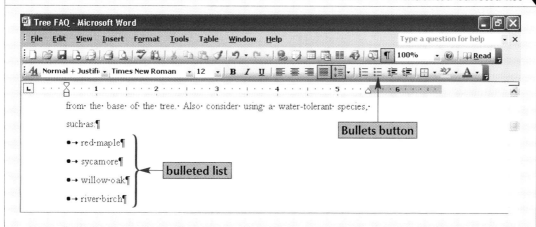

The bulleted list you just created includes the default bullet style. To select a different style of bullets (such as check marks or arrows) you can use the Bullets and Numbering command on the Format menu. You'll have a chance to try that command in the Case Problems at the end of this tutorial.

Next, you need to format the list of steps involved in planting a tree. Marilee asks you to format this information as a numbered list because this list shows sequential steps. This is an easy task thanks to the Numbering button, which automatically numbers selected paragraphs with consecutive numbers. If you insert a new paragraph, delete a paragraph, or reorder the paragraphs, Word automatically adjusts the numbers to make sure they remain consecutive.

To apply numbers to the list of steps:

1. Scroll down until you see the list that begins "Remove any tags . . . " and ends with "of the planting hole."

2. Select the entire list. It doesn't matter whether or not you select the paragraph mark at the end of the last item.

3. Click the **Numbering** button on the Formatting toolbar. Consecutive numbers appear in front of each item in the list. The list is indented, similar to the bulleted list. The list would look better if it was indented to align with the paragraph.

4. Click the **Increase Indent** button on the Formatting toolbar. The list moves to the right, so that the numbers align with the preceding paragraph.

5. Click anywhere in the document to deselect the text. Figure 2-25 shows the indented and numbered list.

Figure 2-25 ▶ **Indented numbered list**

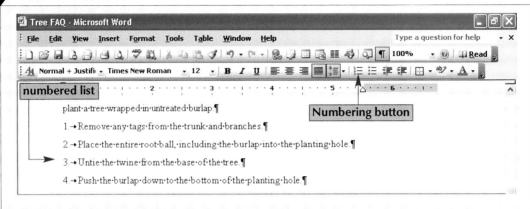

The text of the document is now properly aligned and indented. The bullets and numbers make the lists easy to read and give readers visual clues about the type of information they contain. Next, you need to adjust the formatting of individual words.

Changing the Font and Font Size

All of Marilee's remaining changes concern changing fonts, adjusting font sizes, and emphasizing text with font styles. The first step is to change the font of the title from 12-point Times New Roman to 14-point Arial. This will make the title stand out from the rest of the text.

Reference Window | **Changing the Font and Font Size**

- Select the text you want to change.
- Click the Font list arrow on the Formatting toolbar to display the list of fonts.
- Click the font you want to use.
- Click the Font Size list arrow, and then click the font size you want to use.

or

- Select the text that you want to change.
- Click Format on the menu bar, and then click Font.
- In the Font tab of the Font dialog box, select the font and font size you want to use.
- Click the OK button.

Marilee wants you to change the font of the title as well as its size and style. To do this, you'll use the Formatting toolbar. Marilee wants you to use a **sans serif font**, which is a font that does not have the small additional lines (called serifs) at the tops and bottoms of the letters. Sans serif fonts are often used in titles so they contrast with the body text. A **serif font** is a font that does include these small lines. Times New Roman is a serif font, and Arial is a sans serif font.

To change the font of the title:

1. Press **Ctrl+Home** to move the insertion point to the beginning of the document, and then click to the left of the title **Frequently Asked Questions About Trees** to select it.

2. Click the **Font** list arrow on the Formatting toolbar. A list of available fonts appears in alphabetical order, with the name of the current font in the Font text box. See Figure 2-26. Fonts that have been used recently might appear above a double line. Note that each name in the list is formatted with the relevant font. For example, "Arial" appears in the Arial font, and "Times New Roman" appears in the Times New Roman font.

Font list | **Figure 2-26**

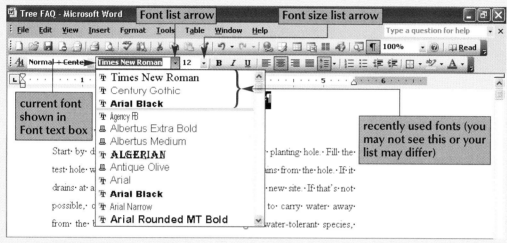

Trouble? If you don't see the fonts beginning with "A" at the top of your Font list, scroll up until you do.

3. Click **Arial** to select it as the new font. As you click, watch the font in the title change to reflect the new font.

Trouble? If Arial doesn't appear in the font list, use another sans serif font.

4. Click the **Font Size** list arrow on the Formatting toolbar, and then click **14** in the size list. As you click, watch the title's font increase from 12 to 14 points.

5. Save your work, and then click within the title to deselect it. See Figure 2-27. Note that the font settings in the Formatting toolbar reflect the font settings of the text that is currently selected, or, if no text is selected, of the text currently containing the insertion point.

Title font and font size changed | **Figure 2-27**

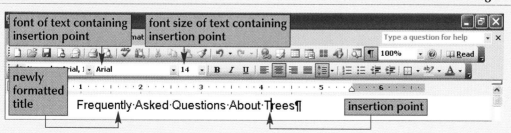

Trouble? If your font and font size settings don't match those in Figure 2-27, you might not have clicked the title. Click the title, view the font and font size settings displayed on the Formatting toolbar, and then make the necessary changes. Because of differences in fonts and monitors, the characters in your document might look different from the figure.

Emphasizing Text Using Bold, Underline, and Italic Styles

You can emphasize words in your document by formatting them with bold, underline, or italic styles. These styles help make specific thoughts, ideas, words, or phrases stand out. (You can also add special effects such as shadows to characters.) Marilee marked a few words on the document draft (shown in Figure 2-1) that need special emphasis. You add bold, underline, or italic styles by using the corresponding buttons on the Formatting toolbar. These buttons are **toggle buttons**, which means you can click them once to format the selected text, and then click again to remove the formatting from the selected text.

Bolding Text

Marilee wants to draw attention to the title and all of the question headings. You will do this by formatting them with the bold style.

To format the title and the questions in bold:

1. Select the title **Frequently Asked Questions About Trees**. It doesn't matter whether or not you select the paragraph mark following the title.
2. Press and hold the **Ctrl** key, and then select the first question in the document ("How can I tell if I've picked a site with good drainage?"). Again, whether or not you select the paragraph mark following the question is of no concern. Both the title and the first question are now selected. You can continue to select nonadjacent information by using the Ctrl key and scroll arrows.
3. Continue to hold down the **Ctrl** key, and then scroll down and select each of the remaining questions. Use the down arrow on the vertical scroll bar to view the questions. Again, whether or not you select the paragraph mark following each question is of no concern.
   Trouble? If you accidentally select something other than a question, keep the Ctrl key pressed while you click the incorrect item. This should deselect the incorrect item.
4. Release the **Ctrl** key, click the **Bold** button ⓑ on the Formatting toolbar, click anywhere in the document to deselect the text, and then scroll up to return to the beginning of the document. The title and the questions appear in bold, as shown in Figure 2-28.

Figure 2-28 ▶ Text in bold

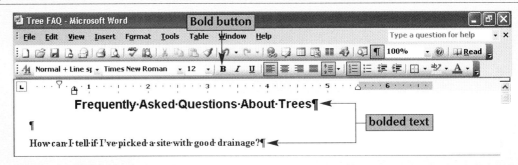

After reviewing this change, Marilee wonders if the title would look better without bold. You can easily remove bold by selecting the text and clicking the Bold button again to turn off, or toggle, bold.

5. To remove the bold, select the title, and then click the **Bold** button ⓑ on the Formatting toolbar. The title now appears without bold. Marilee decides she prefers to emphasize the title with bold after all.
6. Verify that the title is still selected, and then click the **Bold** button ⓑ on the Formatting toolbar. The title appears in bold again.

Underlining Text

The Underline button works in the same way as the Bold button. Marilee's edits indicate that the word "Note" should be inserted and underlined at the beginning of the final paragraph. Using the Underline button, you'll make both of these changes at the same time.

To underline text:

1. Press **Ctrl+End** to move the insertion point to the end of the document, then press **Ctrl+ ↑** to move the insertion point to the left of the word "Any" in the first line of the final paragraph.

2. Click the **Underline** button U on the Formatting toolbar to turn on underlining. The Underline button is highlighted. Whatever text you type now will be underlined on your screen and in your printed document.

3. Type **Note:** and then click the **Underline** button U on the Formatting toolbar to turn off underlining. The Underline button is no longer highlighted, and "Note:" is now underlined.

4. Press the **spacebar**. See Figure 2-29.

Word typed with underline | **Figure 2-29**

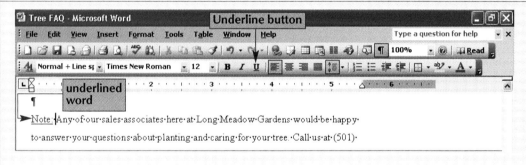

Italicizing Text

Next, you'll format each instance of "Long Meadow Gardens" in italic. This helps draw attention to the company name.

To italicize the company name:

1. Scroll up to the first question on the second page ("Do I have to do anything to the tree before planting?").

2. In the first line below the question, select **Long Meadow Gardens**.

3. Click the **Italic** button I on the Formatting toolbar. The company name changes from regular to italic text. In the next step, you'll learn a useful method for repeating the task you just performed.

4. Scroll down to the last paragraph of the document, select the company name, and then press the **F4** key. The F4 key enables you to repeat your most recent action. It is especially helpful when formatting parts of a document.

5. Save the document.

Previewing Formatted Text

You have made all the editing and formatting changes that Marilee requested for the Tree FAQ document. It's helpful to preview a document after formatting it, because the Print Preview window makes it easy to spot text that is not aligned correctly.

To preview and print the document:

1. Press **Ctrl+Home**, click the **Print Preview** button 🔍 on the Standard toolbar, click the **One Page** button 🔲 on the Print Preview toolbar if you see more than one page, and examine the first page of the document. Use the vertical scroll bar to display the second page. (If you notice any alignment or indentation errors, click the Close button on the Print Preview toolbar, correct the errors in Normal view, save your changes, and then return to the Print Preview window.)

2. Click the **Print** button 🖨 on the Print Preview toolbar. After a pause, the document prints.

3. Click the **Close** button on the Print Preview toolbar. You return to Normal view.

4. If you made any changes to the document after previewing it, save your work.

You now have a printed copy of the final Tree FAQ document, as shown in Figure 2-30.

Figure 2-30	Final version of Tree FAQ document

Adding Comments

Peter reviews the Tree FAQ document and is happy with its appearance. He wonders if he should add some information about fertilizing new trees. He asks you to insert a note to Marilee about this using Word's Comment feature. A **comment** is an electronic version of a self-sticking note that you might attach to a piece of paper. To insert a comment in a Word document, select a block of text, click Comment on the Insert menu, and then type your comment in the comment box. To display a comment, place the mouse pointer over text where the comment has been inserted. Comments are very useful when you are exchanging Word documents with co-workers electronically, whether via e-mail, disks, or on CDs, because they allow you to make notes or queries without affecting the document itself.

You'll insert Peter's comment at the document title so that Marilee will be sure to see it as soon as she opens the document. It's easiest to work with comments in Print Layout view.

To add the comment to the document:

1. Click the **Print Layout View** button ▣ in the lower-left corner of the Word window, then click the **Zoom** list arrow and click **100%** in the list if it is not already selected. The document view changes, allowing you to see the document margins.

2. Scroll up and down through the document and notice that, in Print Layout view, a page break is represented by something more noticeable than a dotted line. You can actually see the end of one page and the beginning of another.

3. Scroll up to the beginning of the document, and then select the title **Frequently Asked Questions About Trees**. (Do not select the paragraph mark after the title.)

4. Click **Insert** on the menu bar, and then click **Comment**. A comment balloon appears in the right margin, with the insertion point ready for you to type your comment. The Reviewing toolbar opens, displaying buttons that are useful for working with comments. See Figure 2-31.

Inserting a comment ◄ **Figure 2-31**

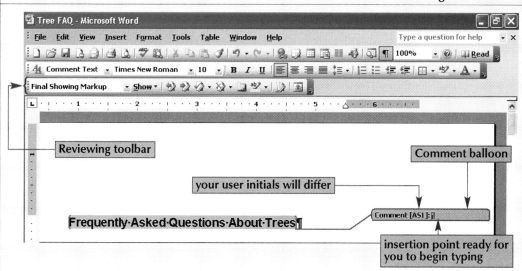

Trouble? If you can't see the entire comment balloon, scroll right to display it fully.

The comment is preceded by the user's initials and a number. Initials depend on the information entered on the Information tab in the Options dialog box. The numbers are sequential, with the first comment labeled #1, the second #2, and so on.

▶ 5. Type **Should we add a section on fertilizing new trees?** The newly typed comment is displayed in the comment balloon. Depending on the size of your monitor, you may need to scroll right to read the entire comment.

▶ 6. Click the **Normal View** button ≡ in the lower-left corner of the Word window. The title is highlighted in color with brackets around it, indicating that a comment has been inserted at this point in the document.

▶ 7. Place the mouse pointer over the title. The comment is displayed in a ScreenTip over the pointer. When you move the mouse pointer away from the title, the ScreenTip closes.

▶ 8. Save the document.

Note that to delete a comment, you can right-click the comment box in Print Layout view and click Delete Comment. To edit a comment, click in the comment box and make any deletions or additions you desire. After you insert comments in a document, you can choose to print the document with or without comments in the margin. To print the comments, select Document showing markup in the Print what list box of the Print dialog box. To print a document without comments, select Document in the Print what list box. You'll find comments useful when you need to collaborate on a document with your fellow students or co-workers.

Using the Research Task Pane

Before you finish your work for the day, Peter suggests that you use the Research task pane to look up information on plants sold at Long Meadow Gardens. The **Research task pane** provides a number of research tools, including a thesaurus, an Internet search engine, and access to the Encarta Encyclopedia and Dictionary. To take full advantage of these options, your computer must be connected to the Internet. To get started, Peter asks you to use the Research task pane to find the Latin name for "red maple."

To look up "red maple" in the Research task pane:

▶ 1. Verify that your computer is connected to the Internet. If your computer is not connected to the Internet, read, but do not attempt to perform, the following steps.

▶ 2. Use the Find command to locate and select the text "red maple". Close the Find and Replace dialog box.

▶ 3. Click the **Research** button 🔍 on the Standard toolbar. The Research task pane opens. See Figure 2-32. The term you selected in the document appears in the Search for text box, ready for you to look up the definition. Next, you need to specify the reference source you want to search.

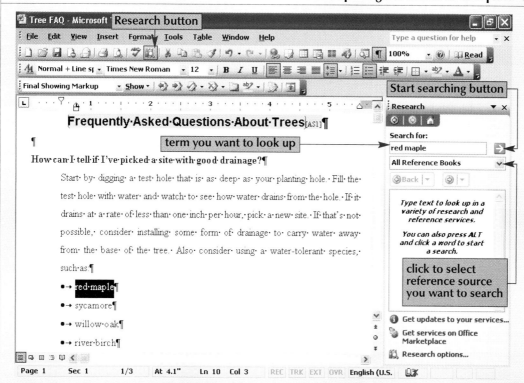

4. Verify that **All Reference Books** is selected in the list box below the Search for text box, and then click the **Start searching** button. A list of research results appears, as shown in Figure 2-33. At the top of the list is the Encarta Dictionary definition for "red maple," with the Latin name, *Acer rubrum*, at the end. If the initial search results don't provide the information you need, scroll down and click the "Can't find it?" link at the bottom of the Research task pane to display more research options. In some cases, when you click a link in the Research task pane, Internet Explorer might open a Web page with further information.

Trouble? If All Reference Books is not selected in the list box below the Search for text box, click the list arrow and select All Reference Books. At that point the search will begin; you do not have to click the Start searching button.

Figure 2-33 Research results

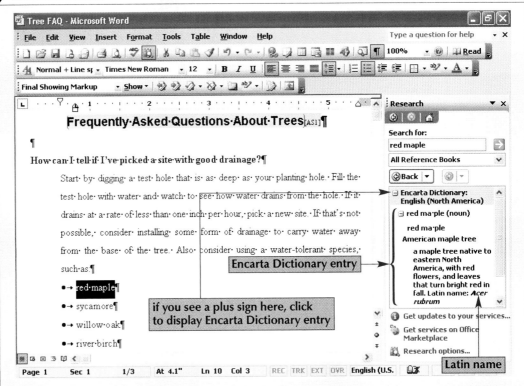

Trouble? If you see "Encarta Dictionary: English (North America)" but not the dictionary entry for "red maple," click the plus sign as indicated in Figure 2-33.

5. Click the **Close** button ⊠ at the top of the Research task pane. The Research task pane closes.

6. Close the Reviewing toolbar, save, and then close the document.

In this tutorial, you have helped Peter edit and format the Tree FAQ document that will be handed out to all customers purchasing a tree at Long Meadow Gardens. Peter will e-mail the file to Marilee later so that she can review your work and read the comment you inserted.

Review

Session 2.2 Quick Check

1. What are Word's default values for the left and right margins? For the top and bottom margins?
2. Describe the steps involved in changing the line spacing in a document.
3. Describe the four types of text alignment.
4. Explain how to indent a paragraph 1 inch or more from the left margin.
5. Describe a situation in which you would use the Format Painter.
6. Explain how to transform a series of short paragraphs into a numbered list.
7. Explain how to add underlining to a word as you type it.
8. True or False: Before you can take full advantage of the Research task pane, your computer must be connected to the Internet.

Review

Tutorial Summary

In this tutorial you learned how to use the Spelling and Grammar checker, select parts of a document, delete text, and move text within a document. You also learned how to find and replace text. Next, you focused on formatting a document, including changing margins and line spacing, aligning text, indenting paragraphs, using the Format Painter, changing the font and font size, and emphasizing text with bold, underlining, and italic styles. Finally, you learned how to add a comment to a document, preview formatted text, and look up information using the Research task pane.

Key Terms

¶	cut and paste	portrait orientation
1.5 line spacing	double spacing	ragged
alignment	drag and drop	Replace command
automatic page break	Find command	Research task pane
bullet	Format Painter	right alignment
center alignment	hanging indent	right indent
Clipboard	justified alignment	sans serif font
Clipboard task pane	landscape orientation	select
comment	left alignment	selection bar
copy	paragraph	serif font
copy and paste	paragraph symbol (¶)	single spacing
cut	paste	toggle button

Practice

Apply the skills you learned in the tutorial using the same case scenario.

Review Assignments

Data File needed for the Review Assignments: Statmnt.doc

Now that you have completed the Tree FAQ document, Marilee asks you to help her create a statement summarizing customer accounts for Long Meadow Gardens' wholesale nursery. She would also like you to create a document that contains contact information for Long Meadow Gardens. Remember to use the Undo and Redo buttons as you work to correct any errors.

1. Open the file **Statmnt** located in the Tutorial.02\Review folder included with your Data Files, and then check your screen to make sure your settings match those in the tutorial.
2. Save the document as **Monthly Statement** in the same folder.
3. Change the left and right margins to 1.5 inches using the Page Setup dialog box.
4. Make all edits and formatting changes shown in Figure 2-34, and then save your work.

Figure 2-34

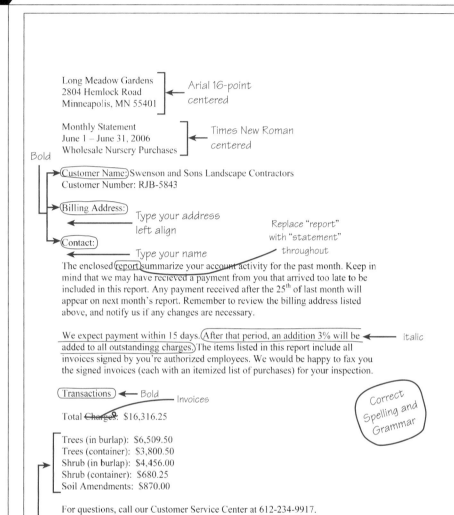

Long Meadow Gardens
2804 Hemlock Road
Minneapolis, MN 55401 ← Arial 16-point centered

Monthly Statement
June 1 – June 31, 2006
Wholesale Nursery Purchases ← Times New Roman centered

Bold

Customer Name: Swenson and Sons Landscape Contractors
Customer Number: RJB-5843

Billing Address: ← Type your address left align

Replace "report" with "statement" throughout

Contact: ← Type your name

The enclosed report summarize your account activity for the past month. Keep in mind that we may have recieved a payment from you that arrived too late to be included in this report. Any payment received after the 25th of last month will appear on next month's report. Remember to review the billing address listed above, and notify us if any changes are necessary.

We expect payment within 15 days. After that period, an addition 3% will be ← italic
added to all outstandingg charges. The items listed in this report include all invoices signed by you're authorized employees. We would be happy to fax you the signed invoices (each with an itemized list of purchases) for your inspection.

Transactions ← Bold — Invoices

Correct Spelling and Grammar

Total Charges: $16,316.25

Trees (in burlap): $6,509.50
Trees (container): $3,800.50
Shrub (in burlap): $4,456.00
Shrub (container): $680.25
Soil Amendments: $870.00

For questions, call our Customer Service Center at 612-234-9917.

Add bullets

5. Proofread the document carefully to check for any additional errors. Look for and correct two errors that were not reported when you used the Spelling and Grammar checker.

6. Remove any Smart Tags in the document.

7. Move the last sentence of the document (which begins "For questions, call . . . ") to create a new paragraph, just above the heading "Transactions."

8. Select the Transactions portion of the document, from the heading "Transactions" down to the end of the document. Increase the indentation by 0.5 inch.

9. Open the Clipboard task pane. Select the company name and address at the top of the document and copy it to the Clipboard. Then copy the Customer Service Center phone number (above Transactions) to the Clipboard.

10. Open a new, blank document. Type your name on the first line, and then "Customer Service Center" on the next line. Move the insertion point to the third line. Open the Clipboard task pane, and then click the company address to insert this information at the insertion point. Be sure the insertion point is below the address, and then click the phone number to insert it in the document. Notice that text inserted from the Clipboard retains its original formatting, though the alignment may not carry over perfectly.

11. Left-align any centered text, clear the contents of the Clipboard task pane, close the task pane, and print the document.

12. Switch to Print Layout view. Then select the company name and insert the following comment: "Marilee, please let me know how you want this document formatted."

13. Save the document as **Customer Service Contact** in the Tutorial.02\Review folder. Close the document.

14. Save the Monthly Statement document, and then preview and print it.

15. Select the term "Amendments," which appears in the bulleted list at the end of the document. Open the Research task pane and look up the definition of "amendment." *Note:* you must have an active Internet connection to complete this step.

16. Type an asterisk (*) after "Amendments," and then on a blank line at the end of the document type an asterisk (*) followed by the definition of "amendment." After the definition include a sentence indicating that the definition is taken from the Encarta Dictionary.

17. Close the Research task pane and the Reviewing toolbar, save the Monthly Statement document, and then close it.

Apply

Apply the skills you learned to create a one-page advertising brochure.

Case Problem 1

Data File needed for this Case Problem: Tribune.doc

Blue Ridge Tribune The *Blue Ridge Tribune* is a student-run newspaper published through the Blue Ridge College Student Services Association. The newspaper is distributed around campus each Friday. The online version of the newspaper is posted on the Blue Ridge College Web site. Local businesses have a long-established tradition of advertising in the print version of the newspaper, and the paper's advertising manager, Noah McCormick, would like to ensure that this same tradition carries over to the online newspaper. When he sends out the monthly statements to his print advertisers, he would like to include a one-page brochure encouraging them to purchase an online ad. He typed the text about online advertising that is currently found on the Blue Ridge Tribune Web site and saved it as unformatted text in a Word document.

1. Open the file **Tribune** located in the Tutorial.02\Cases folder included with your Data Files, and save the file as **Tribune Brochure** in the same folder.

2. Correct any spelling or grammar errors. Make sure the right correction is selected in the Suggestions list box before you click Change.

3. Proofread for other errors, such as words that are spelled correctly but used incorrectly.
4. In the second to last sentence, replace "the BRT Advertising Office" with your name.
5. Change the right margin to 1.5 inches and the left margin to 2 inches.
6. Format the entire document in 12-point Times New Roman font.
7. Format the four paragraphs below "Did you know?" as a bulleted list.
8. Drag the third bullet (which begins "You can include . . . ") up to make it the first bullet in the bulleted list.
9. Format the first line of the document using a font, font size, and alignment of your choice. Use bold or italic for emphasis.
10. Format the entire document using 1.5 line spacing.
11. Save your work, preview the document, and then switch back to Normal view to make any changes you think necessary.
12. Print the document and then return to the Print Preview window. Open the Page Setup dialog box and switch to Landscape orientation. (Don't change any margin settings.) Observe the change in the Print Preview window.
13. Save the document as **Tribune Brochure Landscape** in the Tutorial.02\Cases folder and print it.
14. Switch to Print Layout view, and add a comment to the first line (*Blue Ridge Tribune*) asking Noah if he would like you to leave a printed copy of the brochure in his mailbox.
15. As Noah reviews the brochure, he wonders if the word "Web" should actually be capitalized. Use the Research task pane to look up "Web" in the Encarta Dictionary. In the first definition, you can see that "Web" is short for "World Wide Web." You will use this information to explain to Noah that indeed Web should be capitalized. Close the Research task pane.
16. Close the Reviewing toolbar, save, and then close the document.

Apply

Use your skills to format the summary document shown in Figure 2-35.

Case Problem 2

Data File needed for this Case Problem: Training.doc

UpTime Productivity Training   UpTime, Inc. provides productivity training for large companies across the country. Matt Patterson is UpTime's marketing director for the Northeast region. He wants to provide interested clients with a one-page summary of UpTime's productivity training sessions.

1. Open the file **Training** located in the Tutorial.02\Cases folder included with your Data Files, and then check your screen to make sure your settings match those in the tutorials.
2. Save the file as **Training Summary** in the same folder.
3. Format the document as shown in Figure 2-35.

Figure 2-35

← change top margin to 1.5 inches

bold and centered — UpTime Productivity Training ← 16-point sans serif font
www.UpTimeTraining.com

UpTime productivity training focuses on improving productivity throughout your company. The productivity training we provide consists of four ~~general~~ components:

Improving employee morale through improved interpersonal communication.
Improving field services productivity through new technology
Improving personal productivity through improved time-management skills.
Improving company productivity through establishing management priorities.

Personal Productivity Training Seminar ← bold, italic

UpTime provides a half-day personal productivity-training seminar for all of your company's employees. This seminar has received national recognition for its effectiveness in helping employees set and attain goals. ~~This seminar improves employees' individual performances by maximizing their personal effectiveness in setting immediate and long-range goals and in prioritizing personal tasks.~~

As part of this personal productivity-training seminar, each employee in attendance ~~at the seminar~~ receives a customized personal log with planning sheets for recording events and managing daily activities. This personal log standardizes the method by which all of your employees organize and control events, improving their productivity and, at the same time, increasing your company's ability to bid contracts and bill clients.

Management Productivity Training ← bold, italic

(UpTime provides management training at our Leadership Retreat facilities at Garrison Lake, New York.) UpTime's management training program is designed to help managers create more effective relationships with the employees they supervise. This two-day training, focuses on helping company officials work together to identify your company's unique mission statement, guiding principles for each division, and personal role-based tasks. ←

Field Services Technology and Training ← bold, italic

reverse order ⎰ UpTime provides 30 hours of free on-site training and 6 months of free on-line consultation services. After 6 months, training and consultation are provided on a contractual basis.

UpTime's advanced technology system improves your communication field services. Our phone-fax-computer system connects your managers through e-mail, fax, and telephone to establish better communication throughout your company and to simplify procedures, streamline red tape, and eliminate bureaucracy.

For more information, contact your name.

replace with your first and last name, format in bold with underline

Explore

4. Change the left margin using the ruler, as follows:
   a. Make sure the horizontal ruler is displayed and the document is shown in Normal view.
   b. Select the entire document.
   c. Position the pointer on the small gray square on the ruler at the left margin. A ScreenTip with the words "Left Indent" appears.
   d. Press and hold down the mouse button. A vertical dotted line appears in the document window, indicating the current left margin. Drag the margin right to the 0.5-inch mark on the ruler, and then release the mouse button. Click anywhere to deselect the document.

Explore

5. Select the list of the four training components near the top of the document, click Format on the menu bar, then use the Bullets and Numbering dialog box to create a bulleted list using check marks as the bullet symbol.
6. Italicize both occurrences of the word "free" in the second text paragraph under the "Field Services Technology and Training" heading.
7. Use the Spelling and Grammar checker to make corrections as needed, proofread for additional errors, save, and preview the document.
8. Print the document, and then close the file.

Challenge

Expand your formatting skills to create a description of new products.

Case Problem 3

Data File needed for this Case Problem: Product.doc

Ridge Top Thomas McGee is vice president of sales and marketing at Ridge Top, an outdoor and sporting-gear store in Duluth, Minnesota. Each year Thomas and his staff mail a description of new products to Ridge Top's regular customers. Thomas has asked you to edit and format the first few pages of the description of new products he plans to use for this year's mailing.

1. Open the file **Product** located in the Tutorial.02\Cases folder included with your Data Files, and then check your screen to make sure your settings match those in the tutorials.
2. Save the file as **Ridge Top Products** in the same folder.

Explore

3. Switch to Print Layout view if necessary, and then read the comment inserted at the first line of the document. Right-click the comment (point to the comment in the right margin, and press the right mouse button), and then click Delete Comment in the Shortcut menu.
4. Switch to Normal view, search for the text "your name," and replace with your first and last name.
5. Replace all occurrences of "RidgeTop" with "Ridge Top".
6. Use the Spelling and Grammar checker to correct any errors in the document. Because of the nature of this document, it contains some words that the Word dictionary on your computer may not recognize. It also contains headings that the Spelling and Grammar checker may consider sentence fragments. Use the buttons in the Spelling and Grammar dialog box to respond to each Spelling and Grammar checker query. For example, use the Ignore All button to skip over brand names.
7. Delete the phrase "a great deal" from the first sentence of the paragraph below the heading "Snuggle Up to These Prices."
8. Reverse the order of the first two paragraphs under the heading "You'll Eat Up the Prices of This Camp Cooking Gear!"

9. Find the paragraph that begins "Finding camping gear . . . " Use a toolbar button to cut the last sentence ("Prices are good through . . . ") of the paragraph from the document. Then move the insertion point to the end of the document, press the Enter key twice, and insert the cut sentence as a new paragraph. Format it in 12-point Arial font, and then italicize it.

10. Format the five Ridge Top tip items as a numbered list.

Explore ▶ 11. Reorder the items under the "Ridge Top Tips" heading by moving the fourth product idea and the following blank paragraph to the top of the list.

Explore ▶ 12. Experiment with two special paragraph alignment options: first line and hanging. First, select everything from the heading "Ridge Top Guarantees Warmth at Cool Prices" through the paragraph just before the heading "Ridge Top Tips." Next, click Format on the menu bar, click Paragraph, and then click the Indents and Spacing tab if it is not already selected. Click the Special list arrow in the Paragraph dialog box, and notice the special alignment options. Experiment with both the First line and the Hanging options. When you are finished, return the document to its original format by choosing the (none) option.

13. Justify all the paragraphs in the document.

14. Apply a 12-point, bold, sans serif font to the first heading ("Ridge Top Guarantees . . . "). Be sure to pick a font that looks professional and is easy to read. Use the Format Painter to copy the formatting and apply it to the rest of the headings.

15. Change the title's and subtitle's font to the same font you used for the headings, except set the size to 16 point.

16. Bold the title and subtitle.

17. Underline the names and prices for all of the brand name products.

18. Save and preview the document.

19. Print the document and close it.

Explore ▶ 20. The Research task pane provides access to a variety of resources. Some (such as the Encarta Dictionary) are free, while others (such as the Encarta Encyclopedia) require you to pay a subscription fee. After you find the information you need in the Research task pane, you can copy and paste it into your document. Keep in mind that you must always cite your source when you use copyrighted material, such as the definitions from the Encarta Dictionary. To practice using the Research task pane, you will look up information on the word "mountain" for use later in a Ridge Top motivational brochure on mountain climbing. Open a new, blank document, connect your computer to the Internet (if necessary), and open the Research task pane. Change the document's Zoom setting to 75% so you can see the entire document next to the Research task pane. Replace the contents of the Search for text box with the word "mountain," click the list arrow below the Search for text box, and select an option that interests you. Experiment by clicking topics in the Research task pane. To display a topic more fully, click the box that contains a hyphen (to the left of the topic). In some cases, when you click a topic, Internet Explorer will open (with the Research task pane on the left)

Explore ▶ to display more information.

21. When you are finished experimenting, close Internet Explorer, if necessary, and return to the Word window. Click the list arrow below the Search for text box and select Encarta Dictionary: English (North America). Drag the mouse pointer to select the definition that begins "a high and often rocky area...," press Ctrl+C to copy the information to the Clipboard, click in the document, and then use the Paste button to paste the definition into the document. Add some text explaining that you copied the definition from the Encarta Dictionary to demonstrate how to copy and paste information from the Research task pane.

22. Save the document as **Definition** in the Tutorial.02\Cases folder, print it, close the Research task pane, and close the document.

Case Problem 4

Data File needed for this Case Problem: Form.doc

Gygs and Bytes Melissa Martinez is the purchasing manager for Gygs and Bytes, a wholesale distributor of computer parts based in Portland, Oregon. Most of the company's business is conducted via catalog or through the company's Web site, but local customers sometimes drop by to pick up small orders. In the past Melissa has had problems determining which of her customers' employees were authorized to sign credit invoices. To avoid confusion, she has asked all local customers to complete a form listing employees who are authorized to sign invoices. She plans to place the completed forms in a binder at the main desk, so the receptionist at Gygs and Bytes can find the information quickly.

1. Open the file **Form** located in Tutorial.02\Cases folder included with your Data Files, and save the file as **Invoice Authorization Form** in the same folder.
2. Correct any spelling or grammar errors. Ignore the name of the company "Gygs and Bytes."

3. When you type Web addresses or e-mail addresses in a document, Word automatically formats them as links. When you click a Web address formatted as a link, Windows automatically opens a Web browser (such as Microsoft Internet Explorer) and, if your computer is connected to the Internet, displays that Web page. If you click an e-mail address formatted as a link, Windows opens a program in which you can type an e-mail message. The address you clicked is automatically included as the recipient of the e-mail. You'll see how this works as you add a Web address and e-mail address to the statement. In the address at the top of the document, click at the end of the ZIP code, add a new line, and then type the address for the company's Web site: **www.G&B.com**. When you are finished, press Enter. Notice that as soon as you press Enter, Word formats the address in blue with an underline, marking it as a link. Move the mouse pointer over the link and read the ScreenTip. The company is fictitious and does not have a Web site.

4. In the line below the Web address, type G&B@worldlink.com and then press Enter. Word formats the e-mail address as a link. Press and hold the Ctrl key and then click the e-mail link. Your default e-mail program opens, displaying a window where you could type an e-mail message to Gygs and Bytes. (If your computer is not set up for e-mail, close any error messages that open.) Close the e-mail window without saving any changes. The link is now formatted in a color other than blue, indicating that the link has been clicked.
5. Change the top and left margins to 1.5 inches.
6. Center the first six lines of the document (containing the form title and the company addresses).
7. Format the first line of the document (the form title) in 16-point Arial, with italic.
8. Format lines 2 through 6 (the addresses, including the Web and e-mail addresses) in 12-point Arial.

9. Replace all instances of G&B, except the first two (in the Web and e-mail addresses), with the complete company name, Gygs and Bytes. In the Find and Replace dialog box, select the Match case check box to ensure that the replacement text is inserted exactly as you typed it in the Replace with text box. (Be sure to use the Find Next button to skip an instance of the search text.)

10. Format the blank ruled lines as a numbered list. Customers will use these blank lines to write in the names of authorized employees.

11. Format the entire document using 1.5 spacing. Then triple-space the numbered list (with the blank lines) and the Signature and Title lines as follows:
    a. Select the numbered list with the blank lines.
    b. Triple-space the selected text using the Line Spacing button on the Formatting toolbar.
    c. Select the "Signed:" and the "Title:" lines, and then press F4.

12. Save the document.

13. Drag "Customer Name:" up to position it before "Customer Number:".

14. Select "Customer Name:", "Customer Number:", and "Address:". Press Ctrl+B to format the selected text in bold. Note that it is sometimes easier to use this keyboard shortcut instead of the Bold button on the Formatting toolbar.

15. Delete the phrase "all employees" and replace it with "all authorized personnel".

16. Select the phrase "all authorized personnel will be required to show a photo I.D." Press Ctrl+I to format the selected text in italic. It is sometimes easier to use this keyboard shortcut instead of the Italic button on the Formatting toolbar.

17. Insert your name in the form to the right of "Customer Name:". Format your name without bold, if necessary.

18. Insert your address, left aligned, without bold, below the heading "Address:".

19. Click the Print Preview button on the Standard toolbar to check your work.

20. Click the Shrink to Fit button on the Print Preview toolbar to reduce the entire document to one page. Word reduces the font sizes slightly in order to fit the entire form on one page. Close the Print Preview window and save your work.

21. Use the Print command on the File menu to open the Print dialog box. Print two copies of the document by changing the Number of copies setting in the Print dialog box.

22. You can find out useful statistics about your documents by using the Word Count command on the Tools menu. Use this command to determine the number of words, characters (not including spaces), and paragraphs in the document, and then write these statistics in the upper-right corner of the printout.

23. Save and close the document.

Internet Assignments

The purpose of the Internet Assignments is to challenge you to find information on the Internet that you can use to work effectively with this software. The actual assignments are updated and maintained on the Course Technology Web site. Log on to the Internet and use your Web browser to go to the Student Online Companion for New Perspectives Office 2003 at **www.course.com/np/office2003**. Click the Internet Assignments link, and then navigate to the assignments for this tutorial.

SAM Assessment and Training

If you have a SAM user profile, you may have access to hands-on instruction, practice, and assessment of the skills covered in this tutorial. Log in to your SAM account and go to your assignments page to see what your instructor has assigned.

Quick Check Answers

Session 2.1

1. Click at the beginning of the document, and then click the Spelling and Grammar button on the Standard toolbar. In the Spelling and Grammar dialog box, review each error, which is displayed in color. Grammatical errors appear in green; spelling errors appear in red. Review the possible corrections in the Suggestions list box. To accept a suggested correction, click it in the Suggestions list box, and then click Change to make the correction and continue searching the document for errors.
2. True
3. a. double-click the word
   b. click at the beginning of the block, and then drag until the entire block is selected
   c. double-click in the selection bar next to the paragraph, or triple-click in the paragraph
4. a. the blank space in the left margin area of the Document window that allows you to select entire lines or large blocks of text easily
   b. the process of moving text by first selecting the text, then pressing and holding the mouse button while moving the text to its new location in the document, and finally releasing the mouse button
   c. a command on the Edit menu that is used to search for a set of characters and replace them with a different set of characters
5. False
6. Cut and paste removes the selected material from its original location and inserts it in a new location. Copy and paste makes a copy of the selected material and inserts the copy in a new location; the original material remains in its original location.
7. Click Edit on the menu bar, click Replace, type the search text in the Find what text box, type the replacement text in the Replace with text box, click Find Next, Replace, or click Replace all.

Session 2.2

1. The default top and bottom margins are 1 inch. The default left and right margins are 1.25 inches.
2. Select the text you want to change, click the Line Spacing list arrow on the Formatting toolbar, and then click the line spacing option you want. Or select the text, and then press Ctrl+1 for single spacing, Ctrl+5 for 1.5 line spacing, or Ctrl+2 for double spacing.
3. Left alignment: each line flush left, ragged right; Right alignment: each line flush right, ragged left; Center: each line centered, ragged right and left.; Justify: each line flush left and flush right.
4. To indent a paragraph, place the insertion point in the paragraph and then click the Increase Indent button on the Formatting toolbar. Each click indents the text .5 inches, so to indent 1 inch, click the button two times. Use the horizontal ruler to confirm that the text is indented to the correct position.
5. You might use the Format Painter to copy the formatting of a heading to the other headings in a document.
6. Select the paragraphs, and then click the Numbering button on the Formatting toolbar.
7. Click the Underline button on the Formatting toolbar, type the word, and then click the Underline button again to turn off underlining.
8. True

Objectives

Session 3.1
- Set tab stops
- Divide a document into sections
- Center a page between the top and bottom margins
- Create a header with page numbers
- Create a table

Session 3.2
- Sort the rows in a table
- Modify a table's structure
- Format a table
- Explore Reading Layout view

Creating a Multiple-Page Report

Writing a Recommendation

Case

Tyger Networks

Tyger Networks is a consulting company in Madison, Wisconsin, that specializes in setting up computer networks for small businesses and organizations. Susan Launspach, the program director at New Hope Social Services, recently contacted Tyger Networks about linking the computer networks at New Hope's three main offices. The offices are scattered throughout southern Wisconsin in Madison, Janesville, and Milwaukee. Each office has its own self-contained computer network. To make it easier for a social worker in one office to access data stored on a computer in another office, Susan would like to establish some kind of connection between the three networks.

Caitlyn Waller, an account manager at Tyger Networks, is responsible for the New Hope account. In a phone call, she explained to Susan that connecting the three offices will create a new type of a network known as a wide area network (WAN). Because Susan is unfamiliar with networking terminology, Caitlyn offered to write a report that summarizes the options for creating this type of a network. Working with a task force of sales and technical personnel, Caitlyn compiled the necessary information in a multi-page document. Now Caitlyn would like you to help her finish formatting the report. She also needs some help adding a table to the end of the report. Once the report is completed, Susan will present it to the board of directors at New Hope Social Services.

In this tutorial, you will format the report's title page so that it has a different layout from the rest of the report. The title page will contain only the title and subtitle and will not have page numbers like the rest of the report. You also will add a table to the report that summarizes the costs involved in creating a WAN.

Student Data Files

▼ **Tutorial.03**

▽ **Tutorial folder**

WAN.doc

▽ **Review folder**

Trouble.doc

▽ **Cases folder**

Budget.doc
Contacts.doc
SunRep.doc
Tour.doc

Planning the Document

Caitlyn divided the responsibility for the report among the members of the group. Each person gathered information about one topic and wrote the appropriate section of the report. Then Caitlyn compiled all the information into a coherent and unified report. In addition, she took care to follow the company's guidelines for content, organization, style, and format.

Because Caitlyn knows that some members of the New Hope board of directors will not have time to read the entire report, she began the report with an executive summary. The body of the report provides an in-depth explanation of the options for establishing a WAN. At the end of the report, she summarizes the costs of these options. The report's style follows established standards of business writing, and emphasizes clarity, simplicity, and directness.

In accordance with the company style guide, Caitlyn's report will begin with a title page, with the text centered between the top and bottom margins. Every page except the title page will include a line of text at the top, giving a descriptive name for the report, as well as the page number. The text and headings will be formatted to match all reports created at Tyger Networks, and will follow company guidelines for layout and text style.

Opening the Report

Caitlyn already has combined the individual sections into one document. She also has begun formatting the report by changing the font size of headings, adding formatting such as bold and italic, and by indenting paragraphs. You'll open the document and follow the steps in this section to perform the remaining formatting tasks, as indicated in Figure 3-1.

Options for Establishing a Wide Area Network

make this a vertically centered title page

Prepared for
Susan Launspach, Program Director
New Hope Social Services

set tab stop

Written by Tyger Networks:

type list of task force members and their titles

start new page

Executive Summary
This report presents options for connecting the three computer networks run by New Hope Social Services. First we describe the networks in the Madison, Janesville, and Milwaukee offices, and then we explain the options for integrating these networks into a larger structure, known as a Wide Area Network (WAN). Finally, in a table at the end of this report, we summarize the costs for implementing the various WAN connections.

New Hope's Existing LANs
The term Local Area Network (LAN) refers to a network of computers and other devices (such as printers) that are geographically close to each other (for example, on the same floor of a building). A LAN is managed via a special computer known as a server. The majority of the computers on the three New Hope LANs are used to run Microsoft Office applications. The network operating system on the Janesville and Madison servers has been upgraded to Windows 2000 Server, while the Milwaukee server continues to run Windows NT 4. Because the three LANs are separate, a social worker in one office cannot directly access data stored on a computer in one of the other two offices.

insert header in this section

WAN Technology
To allow inter-office data access, we propose connecting the three LANs, thereby creating a Wide Area Network (WAN). A WAN is a network that spans a geographical distance (between buildings, cities, or even countries). Strictly speaking, a WAN consists of one link between two points. It does not usually connect one site to several other sites in the way that a LAN connects multiple computers. Thus, to connect the three New Hope LANs, we would need to establish multiple WAN links. The following sections describe various options for creating these links. The

To open the document:

▶ **1.** Start Word, and then open the file **WAN** located in the Tutorial.03\Tutorial folder included with your Data Files.

▶ **2.** To avoid altering the original file, save the document as **New Hope WAN Report** in the same folder.

▶ **3.** Check your settings to make sure your screen matches figures in this tutorial. In particular, be sure to display the nonprinting characters and switch to Normal view if necessary. Note that throughout this tutorial, your Zoom settings may not automatically match the Zoom settings shown in the figures. As you work through the tutorial steps, adjust your Zoom settings as necessary if you want to make your screen match the figures exactly.

Setting Tab Stops

Tabs are useful for indenting paragraphs and for vertically aligning text or numerical data in columns. A **tab** adds space between the margin and text in a column or between text in one column and text in another column. A **tab stop** is the location where text moves when you press the Tab key. When Show/Hide ¶ is selected, the nonprinting tab character → appears wherever you press the Tab key. A tab character is just like any other character you type; you can delete it by pressing the Backspace key or the Delete key.

Word provides several **tab-stop alignment styles**. The five major styles are left, center, right, decimal, and bar, as shown in Figure 3-2. The first three tab-stop styles position text in a similar way to the Align Left, Center, and Align Right buttons on the Formatting toolbar. The difference is that with a tab, you determine line by line precisely where the left, center, or right alignment should occur.

Figure 3-2 ▶ Tab stop alignment styles

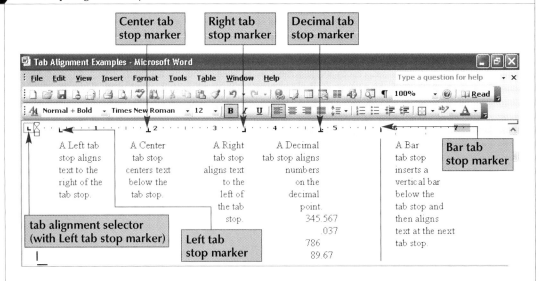

Left tabs position the left edge of text at the tab stop and extend the text to the right. **Center tabs** position text so that it's centered evenly on both sides of the tab stop. **Right tabs** position the right edge of text at the tab stop and extend the text to the left. **Decimal tabs** position numbers so that their decimal points are aligned at the tab stop.

Bar tabs insert a vertical bar at the tab stop and then align text to the right of the next tab stop. In addition, you can use a **First Line Indent tab**, which indents the first line of a paragraph, and a **Hanging Indent tab**, which indents every line of a paragraph *except* the first line.

The Word default tab-stop settings are every one-half inch, as indicated by the small gray tick marks at the bottom of the ruler shown in Figure 3-3. You set a new tab stop by selecting a tab-stop alignment style (from the tab alignment selector at the left end of the horizontal ruler) and then clicking the horizontal ruler to insert the tab stop. You can remove a tab stop from the ruler by clicking it and dragging the tab stop off the ruler.

Ruler with tab stops   **Figure 3-3**

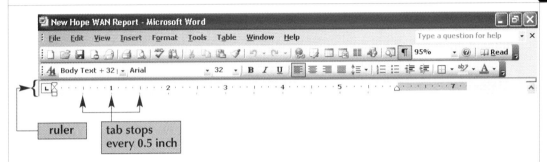

You should never try to align columns of text by adding extra spaces with the spacebar. Although the text might seem precisely aligned in the document window, it might not be aligned when you print the document. Furthermore, if you edit the text, the extra spaces might disturb the alignment. One of the main advantages of tab stops is that, if you edit text aligned with tabs, the alignment remains intact. If you want to align a lot of text in many columns, you'll find it easier to use a table, as described later in this tutorial.

To align columns using tabs, set tab stops on the horizontal ruler, type text in the first column, and then press the Tab key. The insertion point then moves to the next tab stop to the right, where you can type more text. You can continue in this way until you type the first row of each column. Then you can press the Enter key, and begin typing the next row of each column. However, sometimes you'll find that text in a column stretches beyond the next default tab stop, and as a result the columns fail to line up evenly.

Setting Tab Stops

Reference Window

- To set a tab stop, click the tab alignment selector on the far left of the horizontal ruler until the appropriate tab-stop alignment style appears, and then click the horizontal ruler where you want to position the tab stop. Press the Tab key to move the insertion point from one tab stop to another.
- To change the tab alignment or location for text that already contains tab stops, select the text and then move an existing tab stop to a new location, or click the tab alignment selector on the far left of the horizontal ruler until the appropriate tab-stop alignment style appears and then click the horizontal ruler where you want to set the tab stop.
- To remove a tab stop, click it and drag it off the horizontal ruler.

In the Tyger Networks report, you need to type the list of task force members and their titles. As you type, you'll discover whether Word's default tab stops are appropriate for this document, or whether you need to add a new tab stop.

To enter the task force list using tabs:

▸ **1.** Verify that nonprinting characters are displayed, and then move the insertion point to the line below the text "Written by Tyger Networks:."

▸ **2.** Type **Caitlyn Waller**, and then press the **Tab** key. A tab character appears, and the insertion point moves to the first tab stop after the "r" in "Waller." This tab stop is located at the 1.5-inch mark on the horizontal ruler. See Figure 3-4.

Figure 3-4 ▸ Tab character

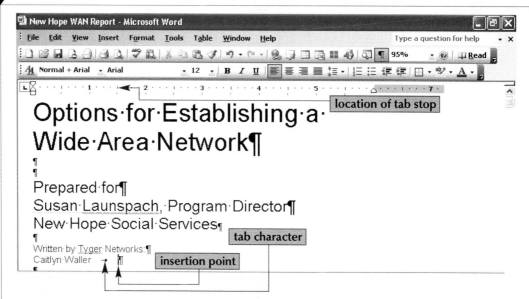

▸ **3.** Type **Account Manager**, and then press the **Enter** key. The insertion point moves to a new line, ready for you to enter the next name in the list.

▸ **4.** Type **Melissa J. Curlington**, and then press the **Tab** key. The insertion point moves to the first available tab stop, at the 2-inch mark on the horizontal ruler.

▸ **5.** Type **Product Manager**, and then press the **Enter** key.

As you can see, Melissa J. Curlington's title does not align with Caitlyn Waller's title on the line above. You'll fix this in a moment by inserting a new tab stop that overrides the default tab stops. But first continue typing the list of names.

▸ **6.** Type **Angelo Zurlo-Cuva**, press the **Tab** key, type **Sales Engineer**, press the **Enter** key, type your first and last name, press the **Tab** key, and then type **Network Engineer**. When you are finished, your document should look like Figure 3-5.

List of task force members | **Figure 3-5**

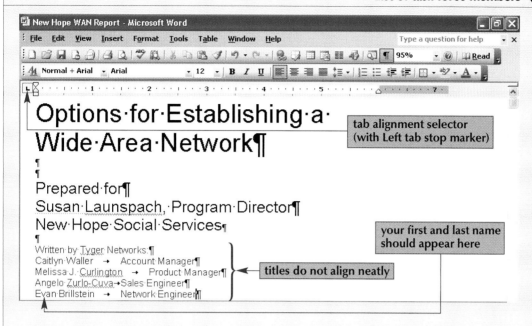

The list of names and titles is not aligned properly. You'll fix this by inserting a new tab stop.

To add a new tab stop to the horizontal ruler:

1. Click and drag the mouse pointer to select the list of task force members and titles.

2. Make sure the current tab-stop alignment style is Left tab ⌊L⌋, as shown in Figure 3-5. If ⌊L⌋ is not selected, click the **tab alignment selector** one or more times until ⌊L⌋ appears.

3. Click the **tick mark** on the ruler that occurs at 2.5 inches. Word automatically inserts a Left tab stop at that location and removes the tick marks to its left. The column of titles shifts to the new tab stop.

4. Deselect the highlighted text and then move the insertion point anywhere in the list of names and titles. See Figure 3-6.

Figure 3-6 **Left tab stop on ruler**

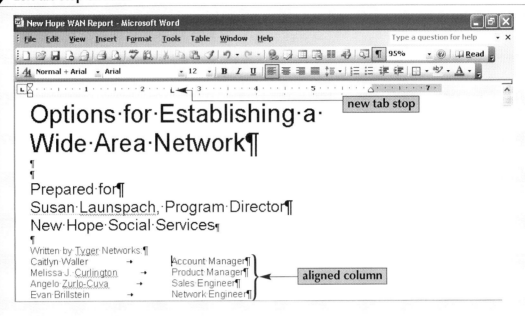

▶ **5.** Click the **Save** button on the Standard toolbar to save your work.

The two columns of information are now aligned, as Caitlyn requested. Notice that Word changed the tab stops only for the selected paragraphs, not for all the paragraphs in the document. In the Case Problems at the end of this tutorial you'll have a chance to work with tab stops using the Tabs dialog box (which you can open via the Tabs command on the Format menu). Among other things, the Tabs dialog box allows you to insert a leader, which is a row of dots (or other characters) between tabbed text. A dot leader makes it easier to read a long list of tabbed material because the eye can follow the dots from one item to the next. You can also use the Tabs dialog box to clear (or remove) tab stops from a document. Next, you need to change the layout of the title page.

Formatting the Document in Sections

According to the company guidelines, the title page of the report should be centered between the top and bottom margins of the page. To format the title page differently from the rest of the report, you need to divide the document into sections. A **section** is a unit or part of a document that can have its own page orientation, margins, headers, footers, and vertical alignment. Each section, in other words, is like a mini-document within a document.

To divide a document into sections, you insert a **section break**, which appears in a document as a dotted line with the words "Section Break." A section break marks the point at which one section ends and another begins. A section can start on a new page, or a section can continue on the same page as text not included in the new section. You insert a section break with the Break command on the Insert menu. To delete a section break (or a page break), click the line representing the break and press the Delete key.

To insert a section break after the title:

1. Position the insertion point immediately to the left of the "E" in the heading "Executive Summary." You want the text above this heading to be on a separate title page and the executive summary to begin on the second page of the report.

2. Click **Insert** on the menu bar, and then click **Break** to open the Break dialog box. See Figure 3-7.

Break dialog box | **Figure 3-7**

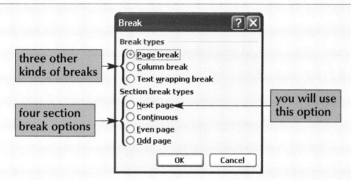

The Break dialog box can be a bit confusing, so you should study it carefully before continuing with these steps. The option buttons under "Break types" allow you to insert three different types of breaks, including a **page break**, which moves the text after it onto a new page. (You don't need to be concerned with the other options right now.) The four option buttons under "Section break types" allow you to insert four types of section breaks. Of these, the two most important types of section breaks are a Next page section break, which starts a new section on a new page, and a Continuous section break, which inserts a section break without starting a new page. If you simply want to start a new page, you can click the Page break option button in the Break dialog box. If you want to start a new page *and* insert a section break, you should click the Next page option button in the Break dialog box. Because you want the document to have a title page, and because you want to format the title page differently than the rest of the document, you will insert a section break that starts a new page. In other words, you need to click the Next page option button.

3. Under "Section break types," click the **Next page** option button, and then click the **OK** button. A double-dotted line and the words "Section Break (Next Page)" appear before the heading "Executive Summary," indicating that you have inserted a break that starts a new section on the next page. The status bar indicates that the insertion point is on page 2, section 2. See Figure 3-8.

Figure 3-8 | **Section break**

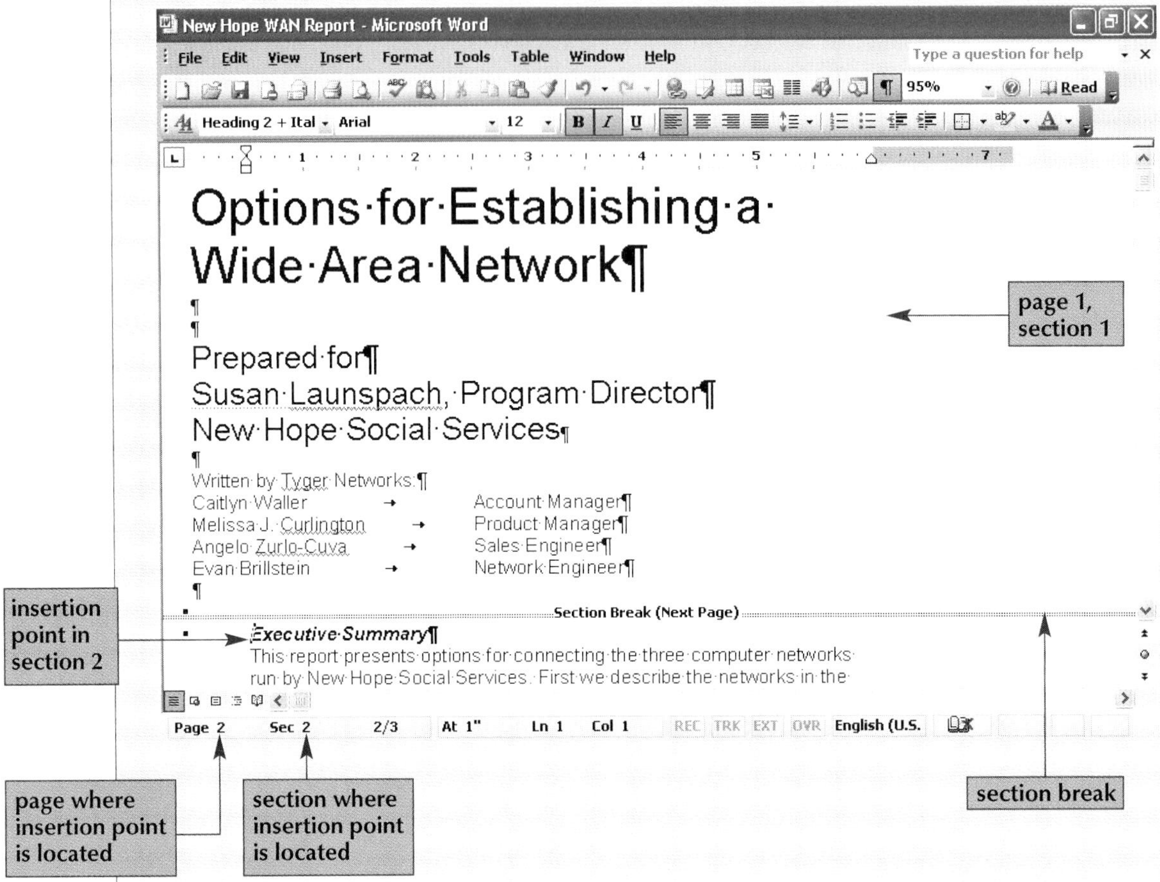

Trouble? If you see a single dotted line and the words "Page Break," you inserted a page break rather than a section break. Click the Undo button 🔄 on the Standard toolbar, and then repeat Steps 1 through 3.

▶ **4.** To practice deleting a section break, click the Section break line, and then press the **Delete** key. The section break line disappears and the status bar indicates that the insertion point is located in section 1, which is now the only section.

▶ **5.** Click the **Undo** button 🔄 on the Standard toolbar. The section break reappears.

▶ **6.** Save your work.

Now that the title page is a separate section and page from the rest of the report, you can make changes affecting only that section, leaving the rest of the document unchanged.

Changing the Vertical Alignment of a Section

You're ready to center the text of page 1 vertically on the page. But first you will switch to the Print Preview window, so you can more easily observe your changes to page 1.

To see the document in Print Preview:

1. Click the **Print Preview** button 🔍 on the Standard toolbar to open the Print Preview window.

2. If you don't see all three pages (as shown in Figure 3-9) click the **Multiple Pages** button 🔡 on the Print Preview toolbar, and then click and drag across the top three pages in the list box to select "1 × 3 Pages." The three pages of the report are reduced in size and appear side by side. See Figure 3-9. Although you cannot read the text on the pages, you can see the general layout.

Report in Print Preview window ◀ **Figure 3-9**

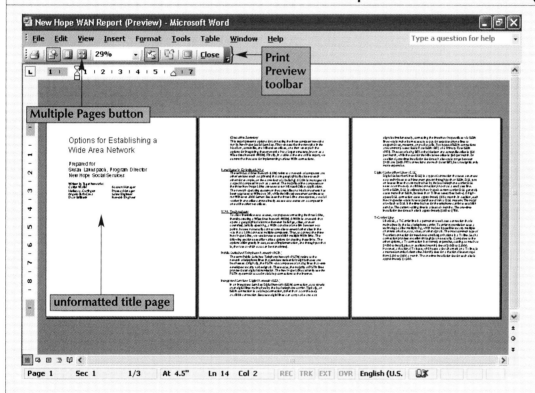

Now you can change the vertical alignment to center the lines of text between the top and bottom margins. The **vertical alignment** specifies how a page of text is positioned on the page between the top and bottom margins—flush at the top, flush at the bottom, or centered between the top and bottom margins.

You'll center the title page text from within the Print Preview window.

To change the vertical alignment of the title page:

▶ **1.** Click the **Magnifier** button 🔍 on the Print Preview toolbar once to deselect it. When the magnifier button is deselected, you can edit the document.

▶ **2.** Click the **leftmost page** in the Print Preview window to move the insertion point to page 1 (the title page). The status bar indicates that page 1 is the current page.

Trouble? If the size of page 1 increases when you click it, you selected the Magnifier button 🔍 in Step 1 instead of deselecting it. Click the Multiple Pages button 📑 on the Print Preview toolbar, drag to select "1 × 3 Pages," and then repeat Steps 1 and 2.

▶ **3.** Click **File** on the menu bar, and then click **Page Setup**. The Page Setup dialog box opens.

▶ **4.** Click the **Layout** tab. In the Apply to list box, select **This section** (if it is not already selected) so that the layout change affects only the section containing the insertion point (that is, the first section) and not both sections of your document.

▶ **5.** Click the **Vertical alignment** list arrow, and then click **Center** to center the pages of the current section—in this case, just page 1—vertically between the top and bottom margins.

▶ **6.** Click the **OK** button to return to the Print Preview window. The text of the title page is centered vertically, as shown in Figure 3-10.

Figure 3-10 ▶ **Title page vertically centered**

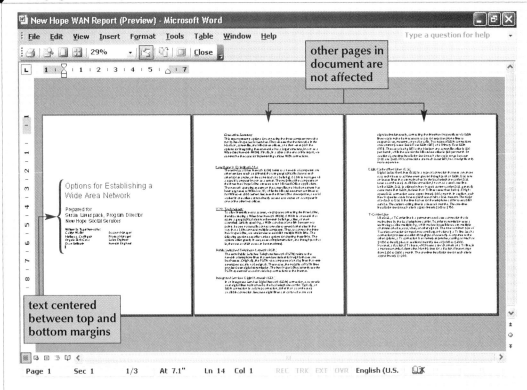

▶ **7.** Click the **Close** button on the Print Preview toolbar to return to Normal view.

You have successfully centered the title page text. Next, you turn your attention to inserting a header with a descriptive name for the report and the page number at the top of every page in section 2.

Adding Headers

The report guidelines at Tyger Networks require a short report title and the page number to be printed at the top of every page except the title page. Text that is printed at the top of every page is called a **header**. For example, the information printed at the top of the page you are reading is a header. Similarly, a **footer** is text that is printed at the bottom of every page. (You'll have a chance to work with footers in the Case Problems at the end of this tutorial.)

When you insert a header or footer into a document, you switch to Header and Footer view. The Header and Footer toolbar is displayed, and the insertion point moves to the top of the document, where the header will appear. The document text is dimmed, indicating that it cannot be edited until you return to Normal or Print Layout view.

You'll create a header for the main body of the report (section 2) that prints "Options for Establishing a Wide Area Network" at the left margin and the page number at the right margin.

To insert a header for section 2:

1. Click anywhere after the section break so that the insertion point is located in section 2 and not in section 1. Refer to the status bar to verify that the insertion point is in section 2.

2. Click **View** on the menu bar, and then click **Header and Footer**. The Word window changes to Header and Footer view, and the Header and Footer toolbar appears. The header area is located in the top margin of your document, surrounded by a dashed line, and displays the words "Header -Section 2-." See Figure 3-11. (If the Header and Footer toolbar covers the header area, drag the toolbar below the header area, similar to its position in Figure 3-11.) Currently, the header is set up so that any text you type in the section 2 header will also appear in the section 1 header. In other words, the headers for sections 1 and 2 are linked. In order to create separate headers for the two sections, you need to deselect the Link to Previous button in the Header and Footer toolbar. You'll do that in the next step.

Creating a header   ◀ **Figure 3-11**

Trouble? If the header area displays "Header -Section 1-," click the Show Next button 🖹 on the Header and Footer toolbar until the header area displays "Header -Section 2-."

Trouble? If the text of the document doesn't appear on the screen, click the Show/Hide Document Text button 🖳 on the Header and Footer toolbar, and continue with Step 3.

3. Click the **Link to Previous** button 🔲 on the Header and Footer toolbar to deselect it. When Link to Previous is selected, Word automatically inserts the header text you create in one section in the previous section. You deselected it to ensure that the header text you create in section 2 applies only to the current section (section 2), and not to the previous section (section 1).

4. Type **Options for Establishing a Wide Area Network**. The title is automatically aligned on the left. See Figure 3-12.

Figure 3-12 ▶ **Header text**

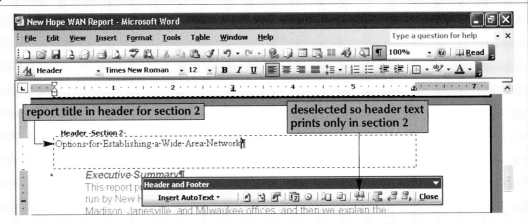

5. Press the **Tab** key to move the insertion point to the next available tab stop, on the right margin of the header area. (Notice that by default the header contains Center and Right tab stops.)

6. Type the word **Page**, and then press the **spacebar** once.

7. Click the **Insert Page Number** button 📄 on the Header and Footer toolbar. The page number "2" appears at the right-aligned tab. The page number in the header looks like you simply typed the number 2, but you actually inserted a special instruction telling Word to insert the correct page number on each page. Now consecutive page numbers will print on each page of the header within this section.

8. Click the **Close** button on the Header and Footer toolbar to return to Normal view, and then save your changes.

Trouble? If your document is not displayed in Normal view, switch to Normal view now.

Notice that you can't see the header in Normal view. To see exactly how the header will appear on the printed page, you need to switch to the Print Preview window or to Print Layout view.

To view the header and margins in Print Preview:

1. Click the **Print Preview button** on the Standard toolbar. The three pages of the document are displayed as they were earlier in the Print Preview window, although this time you can see a line of text at the top of pages 2 and 3. To read the header text, you need to increase the magnification.

2. Verify that the **Magnifier** button on the Print Preview toolbar is selected.

3. Move the pointer over the second page of the document, and then click the header text at the top of the page. The Print Preview window zooms in on the header text for page 2, as shown in Figure 3-13.

Header text for page 2 in Print Preview   **Figure 3-13**

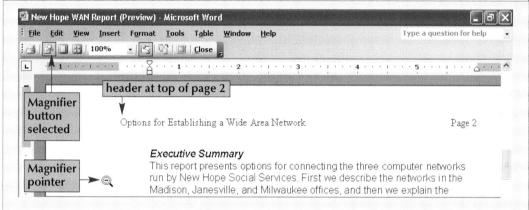

4. Use the vertical scroll bar to scroll down until you can see the header for page 3.

5. Scroll up until you can see the top of page 1. Notice that the header appears only on pages 2 and 3. The header does not appear on the title page because the title page is in a different section of the document. The correct page numbers appear on pages 2 and 3.

6. Use the **Multiple Pages** button to display all three pages of the document again.

7. Click the **Close** button on the Print Preview toolbar to return to Normal view.

8. Save your work.

The report now has the required header. You have formatted Caitlyn's report so that the results are professional-looking, presented clearly, and easy to read. Next, you will add a table that summarizes the costs of the various WAN options.

Inserting Tables

Using Word, you can quickly organize data and arrange text in an easy-to-read table format. A **table** is information arranged in horizontal rows and vertical columns. As shown in Figure 3-14, table rows are commonly referred to by number (row 1, row 2, and so forth), while columns are commonly referred to by letter (column A on the far left, then column B, and so forth). However, you do not see row and column numbers on the screen. The area where a row and column intersect is called a **cell**. Each cell is identified by a column and row label. For example, the cell in the upper-left corner of a table is cell A1 (column A, row 1), the cell to the right of that is cell B1, the cell below cell A1 is A2, and so forth. The table's structure is shown by **gridlines**, which are light gray lines that define the rows and columns. By default, gridlines do not appear on the printed page. You can emphasize specific parts of a table on the printed page by adding a **border**, which is a line that prints along the side of a table cell.

Figure 3-14 Elements of a Word table

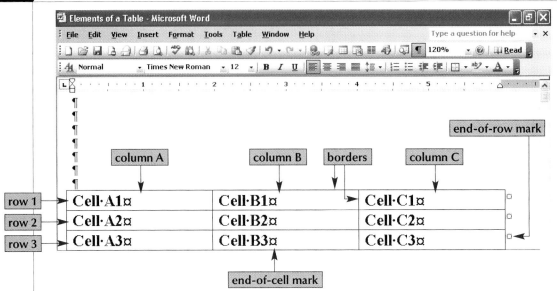

Depending on your needs, you can create a blank table and then insert information into it (as you'll do next), or you can convert existing text into a table (as you'll do in the Case Problems at the end of this tutorial).

You may be wondering why you would use a table instead of tabs to align text in columns. Tabs work well for smaller amounts of information, such as two columns with three or four rows, but tabs and columns become tedious and difficult to work with when you need to organize a larger amount of more complex information. The Word Table feature allows you to organize data quickly and to place text and graphics in a more legible format.

Creating a Table

You can create a table with equal column widths quickly by using the Insert Table button on the Standard toolbar. (You will use this technique to create the table Caitlyn requested.) You also can create a table by dragging the Draw Table pointer to draw the table structure you want. (You'll practice this method in the Case Problems.) However you create a table, you can modify it by using commands on the Table menu or the buttons on the Tables and Borders toolbar.

Caitlyn wants you to create a table that summarizes information in the Tyger Networks report. Figure 3-15 shows a sketch of what Caitlyn wants the table to look like. The table will allow the members of the New Hope board of directors to see at a glance the cost of each option. The top row of the table, called the **heading row**, identifies the type of information in each column.

Figure 3-15 Table sketch

Type of Connection	Monthly Charge
ISDN	$50 to $60
DSL	$80
T1	$1000 to $2000

Inserting a Page Break

Before you begin creating the table, you need to insert a page break because you want the table to appear on a separate page.

To insert a page break:

1. Verify that the document is displayed in Normal view.
2. Press **Ctrl+End** to position the insertion point at the end of the report.
3. Press **Ctrl+Enter**. A dotted line with the words "Page Break" appears in the document window. *Note*: You also can add a page break using the Break dialog box (the same dialog box you used earlier to insert a section break).

   Trouble? If you do not see the words "Page Break," check to make sure the document is displayed in Normal view.
4. Scroll down until the page break is positioned near the top of the document window.

   The insertion point is now at the beginning of a new page, where you want to insert the table.

Inserting a Blank Table

You'll use the Insert Table button to insert a blank table structure into the new page. Then you can type the necessary information directly into the table.

To create a blank table using the Insert Table button:

1. Click the **Insert Table** button on the Standard toolbar. A drop-down grid resembling a miniature table appears below the Insert Table button. The grid opens with four rows and five columns for the table. You can drag the pointer to select as many rows and columns as you need. In this case, you need four rows and two columns.
2. Position the pointer in the upper-left cell of the grid, and then drag the pointer down and across the grid until you highlight four rows and two columns. As you drag the pointer across the grid, Word indicates the size of the table (rows by columns) at the bottom of the grid.
3. When the table size is 4 × 2, click the mouse button. An empty table, four rows by two columns, appears in your document with the insertion point blinking in the upper-left corner (cell A1). The two columns are of equal width. Each cell contains an end-of-cell mark, and each row contains an end-of-row mark. See Figure 3-16.

Empty table in Normal view | Figure 3-16

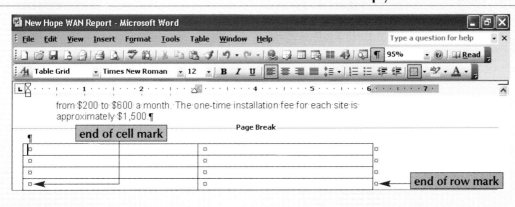

Trouble? If your table is displayed in Print Layout view, switch to Normal view and then compare your table to Figure 3-16.

Trouble? If you don't see the end-of-cell and end-of-row marks, you need to show non-printing characters. Click the Show/Hide ¶ button ¶ on the Standard toolbar to show nonprinting characters.

Trouble? If you see the Tables and Borders toolbar displayed along with the new blank table, close it. You will learn how to use the Tables and Borders toolbar later in this tutorial.

When working with tables and graphics, it's helpful to switch to Print Layout view, which allows you to get a better sense of the overall layout of the page, including the headers. Also, some special table features are only available in Print Layout view. You'll switch to Print Layout view in the following steps.

To display the table structure in Print Layout view:

▶ **1.** Click the **Print Layout View** button ▣. Note that a Zoom setting of 100% or greater should make it easy for you to see the entire table on the screen. The table is displayed in Print Layout view, where you can see the column widths indicated on the horizontal ruler. Also, notice that the document header is visible in Print Layout view.

▶ **2.** Move the mouse pointer over the empty table. The Table Move handle appears in the table's upper-left corner, and the Table Resize handle appears in the lower-right corner. See Figure 3-17. You don't need to use either of these handles now, but you should under-stand their function. To select the entire table quickly, you can click the Table Move handle. Then you can move the entire table by dragging the Table Move handle. To change the size of the entire table, you could drag the Table Resize handle.

Figure 3-17 ▶ Empty table in Print Layout view

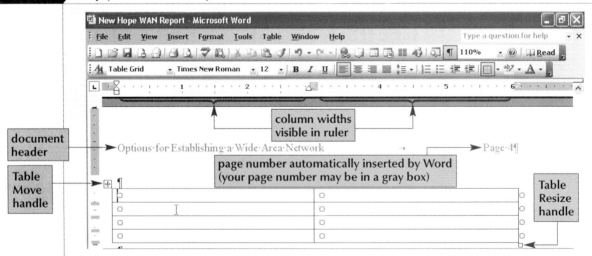

Entering Text in a Table

You can enter text in a table by moving the insertion point to a cell and typing. If the text takes up more than one line in the cell, Word automatically wraps the text to the next line and increases the height of that cell and all the cells in that row. To move the insertion point to another cell in the table, you can either click in that cell or use the Tab key. Figure 3-18 summarizes the keystrokes for moving the insertion point within a table.

Keystrokes for moving around a table ◀ **Figure 3-18**

Press	To move the insertion point
Tab or →	One cell to the right, or to the first cell in the next row
Shift+Tab or ←	One cell to the left, or to the last cell in the previous row
Alt+Home	To the first cell of the current row
Alt+End	To the last cell of the current row
Alt+PageUp	To the top cell of the current column
Alt+PageDown	To the bottom cell of the current column
↑	One cell up in the current column
↓	One cell down in the current column

Now you are ready to insert information into the table.

To insert data into the table:

▶ **1.** Verify that the insertion point is located in cell **A1** (in the upper-left corner).

▶ **2.** Type the heading **Type of Connection**.

▶ **3.** Press the **Tab** key to move to cell B1. See Figure 3-19.

Entering text in the table ◀ **Figure 3-19**

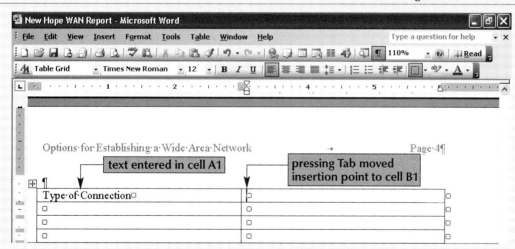

Trouble? If Word created a new paragraph in cell A1 rather than moving the insertion point to cell B1, you pressed the Enter key instead of the Tab key. Press the Backspace key to remove the paragraph mark, and then press the Tab key to move to cell B1.

▶ **4.** Type **Monthly Charge**, and then press the **Tab** key to move to cell A2. Notice that when you press the Tab key in the last column of the table, the insertion point moves to the first column in the next row.

You have finished entering the heading row, the row that identifies the information in each column. Now you can enter the information about the various WAN options.

To continue entering information in the table:

▶ **1.** Type **ISDN**, and then press the **Tab** key to move to cell B2.

▶ **2.** Type **$50 to $60**, and then press the **Tab** key to move the insertion point to cell A3.

▶ **3.** Type the remaining information for the table, as shown in Figure 3-20, pressing the **Tab** key to move from cell to cell. You'll change the column widths in the next session.

| Figure 3-20 | Table with completed information |

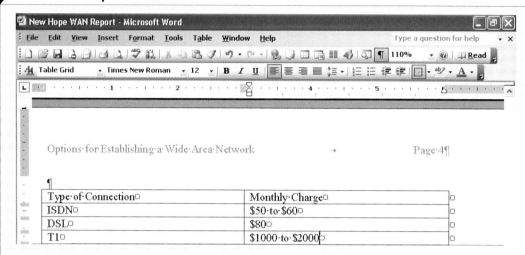

Trouble? If a new row (row 5) appeared at the bottom of your table, you pressed the Tab key when the insertion point was in cell B4, the last cell in the table. Click the Undo button ⟲ on the Standard toolbar to remove row 5 from the table.

▶ **4.** Save your work.

Keep in mind that many document-editing features, such as the Backspace key, the copy-and-paste feature, the Undo button, and the AutoCorrect feature, work the same way in a table as they do in the rest of the document. You will edit and format this table in the next session.

| Review |

Session 3.1 Quick Check

1. Define the following in your own words:
   a. section break
   b. cell
   c. table
   d. header
   e. tab stop
2. Explain how to insert a new tab stop.
3. Describe a situation in which you would want to divide a document into sections.
4. Explain how to center the title page vertically between the top and bottom margins.
5. What is the difference between a header and a footer?
6. How do you insert the page number in a header?
7. Describe how to insert a blank table consisting of three columns and two rows.
8. How do you move the insertion point from one row to the next in a table?
9. Describe a situation in which it would be better to use a table rather than tab stops.
10. Explain how to select an entire table.

Session 3.2

Displaying the Tables and Borders Toolbar

The **Tables and Borders toolbar** contains a number of useful buttons that simplify the process of working with tables. You'll display the Tables and Borders toolbar in the following steps.

To open the Tables and Borders toolbar:

1. If you took a break after the previous session, make sure Word is running and that the New Hope WAN Report document is open. Check that the nonprinting characters are displayed, that the document is displayed in Print Layout view, and that the document is scrolled so that the table is visible.

2. Click the **Tables and Borders** button [icon] on the Standard toolbar. The Tables and Borders toolbar appears.

3. Move the mouse pointer over the table. The Draw Table pointer [icon] appears. You can use this pointer to add new rows or columns in a table, and to add borders between cells. You'll have a chance to practice using this pointer in the Case Problems at the end of this tutorial. For now you'll turn it off.

4. Click the **Draw Table** button [icon] on the Tables and Borders toolbar. The pointer changes to an I-beam pointer [icon].

5. If necessary, drag the Tables and Borders toolbar down and to the right, so that it doesn't block your view of the table, as shown in Figure 3-21.

Positioning the Tables and Borders toolbar ◄ **Figure 3-21**

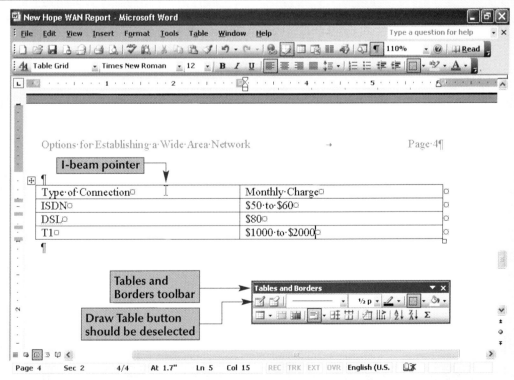

▶ **6.** Move the mouse pointer over the buttons on the Tables and Borders toolbar and read the name of each button as it is displayed in a ScreenTip. In particular, notice the Merge Cells button, which you can use to combine multiple cells into one cell; the Split Cells button, which you can use to divide one cell into multiple cells; and the AutoSum button, which you can use to total a column of numbers. You'll have a chance to practice using these buttons in the Case Problems at the end of this tutorial. Notice also the two Sort buttons, which you can use to rearrange the rows in a table. You will use the Sort Ascending button in the next section.

Sorting Rows in a Table

The term **sort** refers to the process of rearranging information in alphabetical, numerical, or chronological order. When you sort a table, you arrange the rows based on the contents of one of the columns. For example, you could sort the table you just created based on the contents of the Type of Connection column—either in ascending alphabetical order (from *A* to *Z*) or in descending alphabetical order (from *Z* to *A*). Alternately, you could sort the table based on the contents of the Monthly Charge column—either in ascending numerical order (lowest to highest) or in descending numerical order (highest to lowest). When you sort table data, Word usually does not sort the heading row along with the other information; instead, the heading row remains unsorted at the top of the table.

Caitlyn would like you to sort the table in ascending alphabetical order, based on the contents of the Type of Connection column. You start by positioning the insertion point in that column.

To sort the information in the table:

▶ **1.** Click cell **A2** (which contains the text "ISDN"). The insertion point is now located in the Type of Connection column.

▶ **2.** Click the **Sort Ascending** button 🔽 on the Tables and Borders toolbar. Rows 2 through 4 are now arranged alphabetically according to the text in the Type of Connection column. When you sort a table, all the items in a row move together as one entity. This ensures that the type of connection and the associated monthly charge don't become separated during the sort process. Also note that Word did not sort the header row along with the other rows. The header row remains in its original position at the top of the table. See Figure 3-22.

Table after being sorted | Figure 3-22

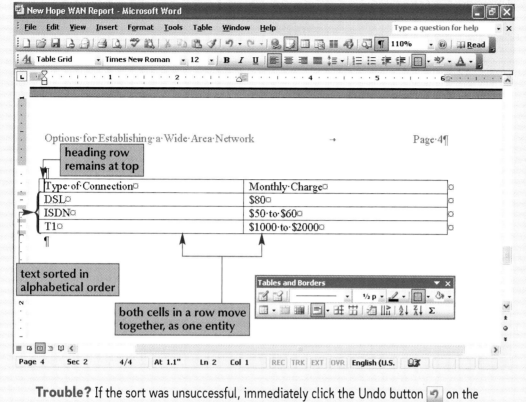

Trouble? If the sort was unsuccessful, immediately click the Undo button ↻ on the Standard toolbar, and then repeat Steps 1 and 2.

Caitlyn stops by and asks you to add an "Installation Charge" column. She also would like you to insert a new row with information about a Fractional T1 connection.

Modifying an Existing Table Structure

You will often need to modify a table structure by adding or deleting rows and columns. When you select part of a table, new buttons sometimes appear on the Standard toolbar to help you modify the table structure. For instance, when you select a column, the Insert Columns button appears to help you insert a new column in the table. In most cases, however, you'll find it easiest to use menu commands to add and delete rows and columns, because the menu commands allow you to specify exactly how you want to modify the table. For instance, by using a menu command, you can indicate whether you want to insert a column to the right or left of the selected column. By contrast, the Insert Columns button always inserts a new column to the left of the selected column.

Figure 3-23 summarizes ways to insert or delete rows and columns in a table.

Figure 3-23 Ways to insert or delete table rows and columns

To	Do this
Insert a row within a table	Select the row above or below where you want the row added, click Table on the menu bar, point to Insert, and then click Rows Above or Rows Below.
	Select the row below where you want the row added, and then click the Insert Rows button on the Standard toolbar.
Insert a row at the end of a table	Position the insertion point in the cell at the far right of the bottom row, then press the Tab key.
Insert a column within a table	Select the column to the right or left of where you want the column added, click Table on the menu bar, point to Insert, then click Columns to the Left or Columns to the Right.
	Select the column to the right of where you want the column added, then click the Insert Columns button on the Standard toolbar.
Insert a column at the end of a table	Select the rightmost column in the table, click Table on the menu bar, point to Insert, and then click Columns to the Right.
	Select the end-of-row markers to the right of the table, and then click the Insert Columns button on the Standard toolbar.
Delete a row	Select the row or rows to be deleted including the end-of-row marker(s), click Table on the menu bar, point to Delete, and then click Rows.
Delete a column	Select the column or columns to be deleted, click Table on the menu bar, point to Delete, and then click Columns.

Inserting Columns in a Table

Your first task is to insert a new column between the Type of Connection column and the Monthly Charge column. This column will contain information on the Installation Charge for each WAN option. You need to begin by selecting the column to the left of the location where you want to insert a column.

To insert a column in the table:

▶ 1. Click in cell **A1** (which contains the heading "Type of Connection"), and then drag the mouse pointer down until the entire Type of Connection column is selected.

▶ 2. Click **Table** on the menu bar, point to **Insert**, and then click **Columns to the Right**. A new column is inserted in the table to the right of the Type of Connection column.

   Note: Word inserts the same number of new columns as are selected. For example, if you had selected two columns in Step 1, Word would have inserted two new columns in the table.

▶ 3. Click in the new cell **B1** (the blank cell at the top of the new column), and then enter the **Installation Charge** heading and data shown in Figure 3-24.

Figure 3-24

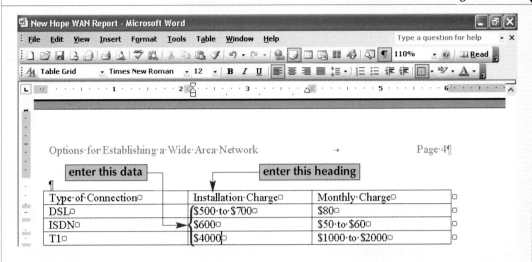

Inserting Rows in a Table

Next, you need to insert a row with information on a more economical type of T1 connection, called a fractional T1 connection. You could insert this row in its alphabetical position in the table (below the DSL row). But it's quicker to add the row to the end of the table, and then resort the table.

To insert a row at the bottom of the table:

1. Click the last cell in the Monthly Charge column (which contains "$1000 to $2000"). The insertion point is now located in the last cell in the table.

2. Press the **Tab** key. A blank row is added to the bottom of the table.

   Trouble? If a blank row is not added to the bottom of the table, click the Undo button on the Standard toolbar. Check to make sure the insertion point is in the rightmost cell of the bottom row, and then press the Tab key.

3. Enter the following information in the new row:
   Type of Connection: **Fractional T1**
   Installation Charge: **$1500**
   Monthly Charge: **$200 to $600**

4. Click anywhere in the Type of Connection column, and then click the **Sort Ascending** button on the Tables and Borders toolbar. The table rows are rearranged in alphabetical order, with the Fractional T1 row positioned below the DSL row, as shown in Figure 3-25.

Figure 3-25 Sorted table with new row

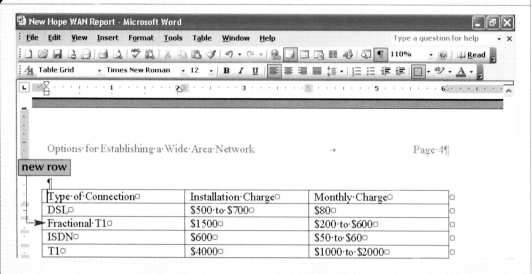

5. Save your work.

After reviewing the table, Caitlyn decides not to include the information on the full T1 connection, because it is far too expensive for New Hope's current budget. She asks you to delete the T1 row.

Deleting Rows and Columns in a Table

With Word, you can delete either the contents of table cells or the structure of the cells themselves. To delete the contents only, you select one or more cells and then press the Delete key. However, to delete both the contents and structure of a selected row or column from the table entirely, you must use one of the methods described earlier in Figure 3-23. Right now you'll use a menu command to delete the T1 row.

To delete a row using the Table menu:

1. Click the selection bar next to the T1 row, at the bottom of the table. The entire T1 row including the end-of-row marker is selected. (Take care to select the T1 row, at the bottom of the table, *not* the Fractional T1 row.)

2. Click **Table** on the menu bar, point to **Delete**, and then click **Rows**. The selected row is deleted from the table. See Figure 3-26.

Table after deleting row Figure 3-26

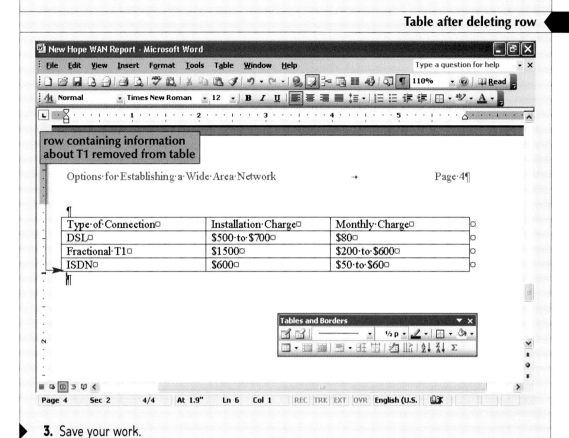

3. Save your work.

Formatting Tables

Word provides a variety of ways to enhance the appearance of the tables you create. You can alter the width of the columns and the height of the rows, or change the alignment of text within the cells or the alignment of the table between the document's left and right margins. You can change the appearance of the table borders, and add a shaded background. You can format an entire table at once using the **Table AutoFormat command** on the Table menu. (You'll have a chance to practice using this command in the Case Problems at the end of this tutorial.) In general, however, making formatting changes individually (using the mouse pointer along with various toolbar buttons and menu commands) gives you more options and more flexibility.

Changing Column Width and Row Height

Sometimes you'll want to adjust the column widths in a table to make the text easier to read. If you want to specify an exact width for a column, you should use the Table Properties command on the Table menu. However, it's usually easiest to drag the column's right border to a new position. Alternately, you can double-click a column border to make the column width adjust automatically to accommodate the widest entry in the column.

The columns in the table you have been working with are too wide for the information they contain. You'll change these widths by dragging the column borders, using the ruler as a guide. Keep in mind that to change the width of a column, you need to drag the column's right border.

To change the width of columns by dragging the borders:

1. Verify that the table is displayed in Print Layout view, and then click anywhere within the table. Verify that no part of the table is selected.

2. Move the pointer over the border between columns A and B (in other words, over the right border of column A, the "Type of Connection" column). The pointer changes to +‖+.

3. Press and hold down the **Alt** key and the mouse button. The column widths are displayed in the ruler, as shown in Figure 3-27. (The widths on your computer might differ slightly.)

   Trouble? If the Research task pane opens after you perform Step 3, leave it open until you complete Step 4 and then close it.

Figure 3-27 Column widths displayed in ruler

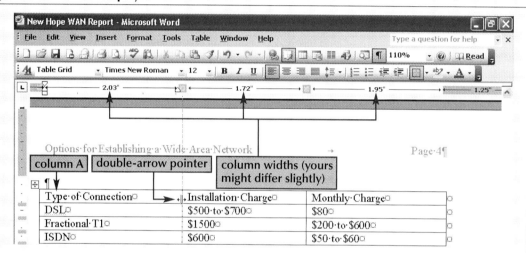

4. While holding down the **Alt** key and the mouse button, drag the pointer to the left until column A is about **1.4** inches wide, and then release the mouse button and the Alt key. As the width of column A decreases, the width of column B (the Installation Charge column) increases. The overall width of the table does not change.

   Trouble? If you can't adjust the column width to exactly 1.4 inches, make it as close to that width as possible.

Now you need to adjust the width of both columns B and C. You could do this by dragging the column border, as you did for column A. But it's much faster to double-click the right border of each column.

To change the width of columns B and C:

1. Position the mouse pointer over the right border of column B until the pointer changes to +‖+, and then double-click the right border of column B (the Installation Charge column). The column shrinks, leaving just enough room for the widest entry in the column (the column heading "Installation Charge").

2. Repeat this procedure to adjust the width of column C (the Monthly Charge column). All three columns in the table are now just wide enough to accommodate the column headings.

You can change the height of rows by dragging a border. You'll make row 1 (the header row) taller so it is more prominent.

To change the height of row 1:

1. Position the pointer over the bottom border of the header row. The pointer changes to ⬍.

2. Press and hold down the **Alt** key and the mouse button. The row heights are displayed in the vertical ruler.

3. While holding down the **Alt** key, drag the pointer down until row 1 is about **0.45** inches high, then release the mouse button and the Alt key. Notice that the height of the other rows in the table is not affected by this change. See Figure 3-28.

   Trouble? If the Research task pane opens, close it.

Table with narrower columns and a wider heading row — Figure 3-28

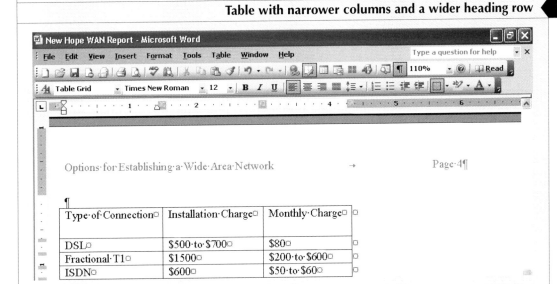

Aligning Text Within Cells

Aligning the text within the cells of a table makes the information easier to read. For example, aligning a column of numbers or percentages along the right margin helps the reader to compare the values quickly. At the same time, centering a row of headings makes a table more visually appealing. You can align text within the active cell the same way you do other text—with the alignment buttons on the Formatting toolbar. However, the Alignment buttons on the Tables and Borders toolbar provide more options.

Caitlyn would like you to align the data in the Installation Charge and Monthly Charge columns along the right side of the columns. The table also would look better with the headings centered. You'll begin by selecting and formatting all of columns B and C. For simple left and right alignment, you can use the Align buttons on the Formatting toolbar. For more sophisticated options, such as centering text horizontally and vertically in a cell, use the Align button on the Tables and Borders toolbar.

To right-align the numerical data and center the headings:

▶ **1.** Move the pointer to the top of column B until the pointer changes to ↓. Press and hold the left mouse button, and then drag right to select columns B and C.

▶ **2.** Click the **Align Right** button ▤ on the Formatting toolbar. The column heads and numbers line up along the right edges of the cells.

Notice that in the process of formatting columns B and C, you right-aligned two of the headings ("Installation Charge" and "Monthly Charge"). You will reformat those headings in the next three steps when you center the text in row 1 both horizontally and vertically in each cell.

▶ **3.** Click the selection bar next to row 1. All of row 1 is selected.

▶ **4.** Click the **Align** list arrow ▤ ▾ on the Tables and Borders toolbar to display a palette of nine alignment options.

▶ **5.** Click the **Align Center** button ▤ in the middle of the palette. The text is centered both horizontally and vertically in the row.

▶ **6.** Click anywhere in the table to deselect the row, and then save your work. See Figure 3-29.

Figure 3-29 ▶ **Table with newly aligned text**

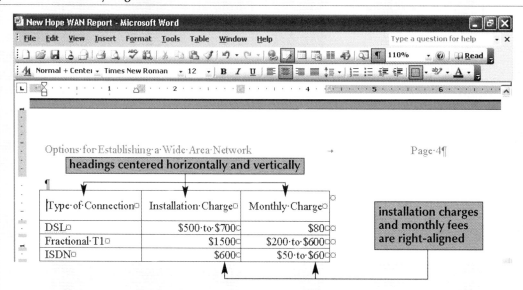

Trouble? If more than just the heading row is centered, click the Undo button ⤺ on the Standard toolbar, and then repeat Steps 3 through 6.

Changing Borders

While gridlines and borders may seem to be the same things, they are different elements of a table. Gridlines are light gray lines that indicate the structure of the table on the screen but do not show on the printed page. Borders are darker lines overlaying the gridlines, which do show on the printed page. When you create a table using the Insert Table button, Word automatically applies a thin black border, so you can't actually see the underlying gridlines.

After you have created a table, you can add new borders or erase existing borders by using the buttons on the Tables and Borders toolbar. You can modify an existing border by changing its **line weight** (its thickness). You can also choose a different **line style**—for instance, you can change a single straight-line border to a triple dotted line. If you prefer, you can create a table without any borders at all. You can also turn off the underlying gridlines by using the Hide Gridlines command on the Table menu. (Depending on how your computer is set up, gridlines might be hidden by default.)

Altering Table Borders

Reference Window

- Select the cell (or cells) whose borders you want to change.
- Click the Line Weight list arrow on the Tables and Borders toolbar, and then select a line weight.
- Click the Line Style list arrow on the Tables and Borders toolbar, and then select a line style.
- Click the Borders list arrow on the Tables and Borders toolbar, and then select a position for the new border.

or

- Use the Draw Table pointer to click the parts of the table that you want formatted with the selected line weight and line style.

To modify the table's borders:

1. Click the selection bar to the left of row 1 to select the heading row.
2. Click the **Line Weight** list arrow ½ on the Tables and Borders toolbar, and then click **2 ¼ pt**. Next, you will examine the options available in the Line Style list. Currently, a single straight-line border is selected.
3. Click the **Line Style** list arrow on the Tables and Borders toolbar, and then scroll to view the various options. Note that you can remove borders (without removing the underlying gridlines) by selecting the No Border option. Caitlyn prefers a simple border, so you decide not to change the current selection.

   Trouble? If a single, straight-line border is not selected in the Line Style list, click the first line style under "No Border" now.

4. Press the **Esc** key. The Line Style list closes. You have selected a single straight-line border, with a thickness of 2 ¼ points.
5. Click the **Outside Border** list arrow on the Tables and Borders toolbar. (The exact name shown in the ScreenTip for this list arrow will vary, depending on what option is currently selected in the list. For example, it may currently be called the All Borders list arrow instead of the Outside Border list arrow.) A palette of options appears. You want to insert a thick border at the bottom of Row 1, so you need to use the Bottom Border option.
6. Click the **Bottom Border** option (in the bottom row of the Borders palette, third from the left). The new border style is applied to the bottom border of row 1.
7. Click anywhere in the table to deselect the row. See Figure 3-30.

Figure 3-30 ▶ **Row 1 with new border**

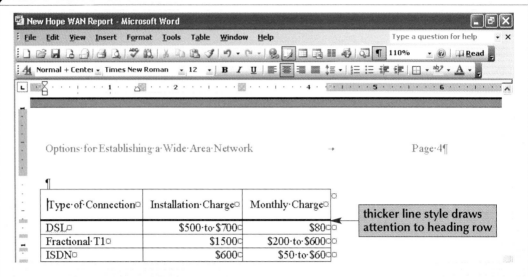

8. Save your work.

Changing the borders has made the table more attractive. You'll finish formatting the table by adding shading to the cells containing the headings.

Adding Shading

Adding **shading** (a gray or colored background) is useful in tables when you want to emphasize headings, totals, or other important items. Generally, when you add shading to a table, you also need to bold the shaded text to make it easier to read.

You will now add a light gray shading to the heading row and then format the headings in bold.

To add shading to the heading row and change the headings to bold:

▶ **1.** Click the selection bar to the left of row 1 to select the heading row.

▶ **2.** Click the **Shading Color** list arrow ⬚ ▾ on the Tables and Borders toolbar. A palette of shading options opens.

▶ **3.** Point to the fifth gray square from the left, in the top row. The ScreenTip "Gray-15%" appears.

▶ **4.** Click the **Gray-15%** square. A light gray background appears in the heading row. Now you need to format the text in bold to make the headings stand out from the shading.

▶ **5.** Click the **Bold** button **B** on the Formatting toolbar to make the headings bold. The wider letters take up more space, so Word breaks one or more of the headings into two lines within row 1.

Trouble? If any of the headings break incorrectly (for example, if the last "n" in "Installation" moves to the next line), you might need to widen columns to accommodate the bold letters. Drag the column borders as necessary to adjust the column widths so no word is split incorrectly.

6. Click in the table to deselect row 1. Your table should look like Figure 3-31, although the line breaks in your heading row may differ.

Row with shading and bold headings | **Figure 3-31**

7. Save your changes.

Centering a Table

If a table doesn't fill the entire page width, you can center it between the left and right margins. The Center button on the Formatting toolbar centers only text within each selected cell. It does not center the entire table across the page. To center a table across the page (between the left and right margins), you need to use the Table Properties command.

Caitlyn thinks the table would look better if it was centered between the left and right margins.

To center the table across the page:

1. Click anywhere in the table, click **Table** on the menu bar, and then click **Table Properties**. The Table Properties dialog box opens.

2. Click the **Table** tab, if necessary.

3. In the Alignment section, click the **Center** option. See Figure 3-32.

Figure 3-32 **Table Tab of the Table Properties dialog box**

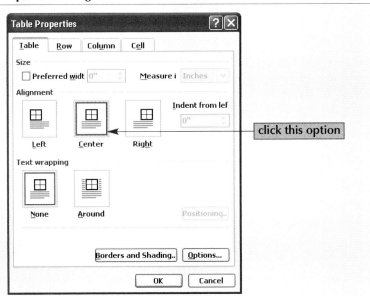

4. Click the **OK** button. The table centers between the left and right margins.

5. Save your work, and then close the Tables and Borders toolbar.

Now that you're finished with the table, you need to review the entire report quickly to make sure it requires no further work. To do that, you'll use Reading Layout view.

Reviewing a Document in Reading Layout View

As you've already seen, when you need to check the overall formatting in a document, it's useful to use the Whole Page zoom setting in Print Layout view, or the Print Preview window. But when you are only interested in the content of the document—that is, the text, tables and graphics, regardless of how they are laid out on the page—it's best to use **Reading Layout view**. This view allows you to peruse a document quickly, displaying the entire content of a page in a single screen, in a font that is large enough to read easily. Reading Layout view is designed to let you review a document online, without paying attention to margins and other page layout issues. When you're ready to concern yourself again with the document layout and formatting, you should return to Print Layout view.

Caitlyn asks you to skim the report now in Reading Layout view, to ensure that the document is completely finished.

To review the report in Reading Layout view:

▶ **1.** Click the **Reading Layout** button 📖 in the lower-left corner of the document window, just to the left of the horizontal scroll bar. Exactly what you see in Reading Layout view will depend on the choices made by the last person to use Reading Layout view on your computer, though you should see the Reading Layout toolbar below the menu bar. You will probably see the Reviewing toolbar too.

▶ **2.** Scroll up to display the top of the document, click the **Allow Multiple Pages** button 🔲 to select it (if it is not already selected), and then verify that the **Actual Page** button 📄 is *not* selected. (If it is selected, click it to deselect it now.) Finally, verify that the **Thumbnails** button is *not* selected. (If it is selected, click it to deselect it now.) Your screen should resemble Figure 3-33. Note that instead of dividing a document into pages, Reading Layout view divides a document into screens. The content of the report fills up multiple screens. Only the first two of these screens are currently displayed.

Report Displayed in Reading Layout view ◀ Figure 3-33

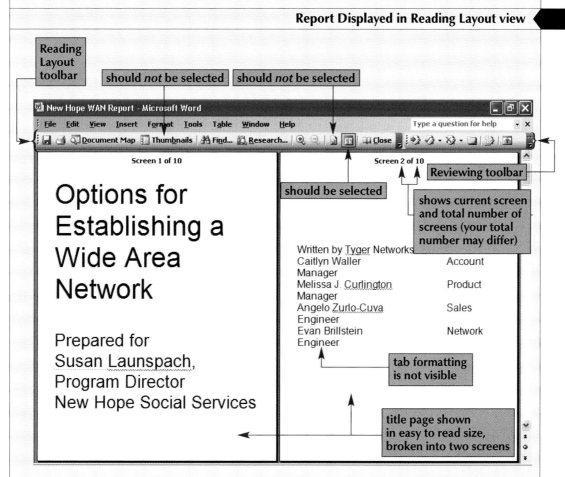

▶ **3.** Click the **down arrow** button ▾ on the vertical scroll bar. Screen 2 is now displayed on the left, with screen 3 on the right.

▶ **4.** Continue scrolling through the document until you have reviewed all the screens, and then return to the beginning of the document.

▶ **5.** Click screen 1 to move the insertion point there.

▶ **6.** Click the **Increase Text Size** button 🔍 on the Reading Layout toolbar three times. Notice how the text increases in size, making it easier to read. The line breaks change to accommodate the larger sized text. These changes affect only how the text is displayed on the screen. When you return to Print Layout view later, you will see that the document has retained its original formatting.

▶ **7.** Click the **Decrease Text Size** button 🔍 on the Reading Layout toolbar three times to reverse the change made in Step 6. When you finish, the Decrease Text Size button should be a light shade of blue, indicating that the text cannot be made any smaller.

▶ **8.** Click the **Close** button on the Reading Layout toolbar. The document returns to Print Layout view.

▶ **9.** Scroll down and verify that the document's formatting has not changed.

To verify that the document's page layout settings haven't changed, you can review the document in the Print Preview window. You'll do that next, and then print a copy of the full report for Caitlyn.

To preview and print the report:

▶ **1.** Click the **Print Preview** button 🔍 on the Standard toolbar to open the Print Preview window.

▶ **2.** Use the **Multiple Pages** button 🔳 on the Print Preview toolbar to display all four pages of the report. Verify that the table is centered horizontally on the page, and that the title page is centered vertically on the page.

▶ **3.** Click the **Print** button 🖨 on the Print Preview toolbar to print the report, and then close the document.

You now have a hard copy of the New Hope report including the table, which summarizes the costs for creating a WAN. Your four-page report should look like Figure 3-34. You give the report to Caitlyn, so that she can add a brief introduction to the table.

New Hope WAN report ◀ **Figure 3-34**

Options for Establishing a Wide Area Network

Prepared for
Susan Launspach, Program Director
New Hope Social Services

Written by Tyger Networks:
Caitilyn Waller	Account Manager
Melissa J. Curlington	Product Manager
Angelo Zurlo-Cuva	Sales Engineer
Evan Brillstein	Network Engineer

Executive Summary

This report presents options for connecting the three computer networks run by New Hope Social Services. First we describe the networks in the Madison, Janesville, and Milwaukee offices, and then we explain the options for integrating these networks into a larger structure, known as a Wide Area Network (WAN). Finally, in a table at the end of this report, we summarize the costs for implementing various WAN connections.

New Hope's Existing LANs

The term Local Area Network (LAN) refers to a network of computers and other devices (such as printers) that are geographically close to each other (for example, on the same floor of a building). A LAN is managed via a special computer known as a server. The majority of the computers on the three New Hope LANs are used to run Microsoft Office applications. The network operating system on the Janesville and Madison servers has been upgraded to Windows XP, while the Milwaukee server continues to run Windows 2000 Server. Because the three LANs are separate, a social worker in one office cannot directly access data stored on a computer in one of the other two offices.

WAN Technology

To allow interoffice data access, we propose connecting the three LANs, thereby creating a Wide Area Network (WAN). A WAN is a network that spans a geographical distance (between buildings, cities, or even countries). Strictly speaking, a WAN consists of one link between two points. It does not usually connect one site to several other sites in the way that a LAN connects multiple computers. Thus, to connect the three New Hope LANs, we would need to establish multiple WAN links. The following sections describe various options for creating these links. The options differ greatly in cost, ease of implementation, and throughput (that is, the rate at which data can be transferred).

Public Switched Telephone Network (PSTN)

The term Public Switched Telephone Network (PSTN) refers to the network of telephone lines that services residential neighborhoods and businesses. Originally, the PSTN was composed of analog lines that were developed to carry voice signals. These days, the majority of PSTN lines provide faster digital transmission. The New Hope LANs currently use the PSTN system for occasional dial-up connections to the Internet.

Integrated Services Digital Network (ISDN)

In an Integrated Services Digital Network (ISDN) connection, data travels over digital lines maintained by the local telephone carrier. Typically, an ISDN connection is a dial-up connection, rather than a continuously available connection. Because digital lines can carry voice and data

---

signals simultaneously, connecting the three New Hope offices via ISDN lines would make it unnecessary to pay for separate phone lines to support faxes, modems, and voice calls. Two types of ISDN connections are commonly used: Basic Rate ISDN (BRI) and Primary Rate ISDN (PRI). The cost of using BRI at the Madison and Janesville office is $50 per month, while the cost for the Milwaukee office is $60 per month. An additional, one-time installation fee for each site would range between $400 and $600. PRI connections are much faster BRI, but are significantly more expensive.

Digital Subscriber Lines (DSL)

Digital Subscriber Lines (DSL) is a type of connection that uses advanced data techniques to achieve even greater throughput than ISDN. DSL runs on leased lines that are maintained by the local telephone carrier. DSL uses a continuously available connection, known as a dedicated line. Unlike ISDN, DSL is offered by New Hope's current carrier. DSL generally costs more than ISDN, but less than T1 lines (described below). A high-speed DSL connection costs approximately $80 a month. In addition, each New Hope site would have to purchase or rent a DSL modem. The major drawback to DSL is the time it takes for the telephone carrier to establish service. The current waiting time is at least six months. The one-time installation fee for each site is approximately $500 to $700.

T-Carrier Line

Like DSL, a T-Carrier line is a permanent dedicated connection that is maintained by the local telephone carrier. T-carrier transmission uses a technology called multiplexing, which makes it possible to carry multiple channels of voice, data, video, or other signals. The most common type of T-carrier connection for medium to small organizations is a T1 line. Such a connection provides excellent throughput and security. Compared to the other options, a T1 connection is extremely expensive, costing as much as $4000 to install, plus an additional monthly fee of $1000 to $2000. However, a fractional T1 lease, which uses a few channels on a T1 line, is a more economical alternative. Monthly fees for a fractional lease range from $200 to $600 a month. The one-time installation fee for each site is approximately $1,500.

Type of Connection	Installation Charge	Monthly Charge
DSL	$500 to $700	$80
Fractional T1	$1500	$200 to $600
ISDN	$600	$50 to $60

Review

Session 3.2 Quick Check

1. Define the following terms in your own words:
   a. line weight
   b. line style
   c. gridline
   d. shading
2. In what order would the following numbers appear in a table if you sorted them in ascending numerical order: 26, 12, 65, 44?
3. Explain how to add a row to the bottom of a table.
4. What's the fastest way to modify a column to accommodate the widest entry in the column?
5. Explain how to adjust the height of a row in a table.
6. Explain how to alter the border on the bottom of a heading row.
7. How do you center a table between the left and right margins?

Review

Tutorial Summary

In this tutorial you learned how to set tab stops, divide a document into sections, center text on a page between the top and bottom margins, create a header, and create a table. You also learned how to display the Tables and Borders toolbar and how to sort the rows of a table. Finally, you learned how to add and delete rows and columns, how to format a table to improve its appearance, and how to review a document in Reading Layout view.

Key Terms

Bar tab	heading row	shading
border	Left tab	sort
cell	line style	tab
Center tab	line weight	tab stop
Decimal tab	page break	table
First Line Indent tab	Reading Layout view	Table AutoFormat command
footer	Right tab	Tables and Borders toolbar
gridlines	section	tab-stop alignment style
Hanging Indent tab	section break	vertical alignment
header		

Practice

Apply the skills you learned in the tutorial using the same case scenario.

Review Assignments

Data File needed for the Review Assignments: Trouble.doc

Susan Launspach, the program director at New Hope Social Services, has contacted Caitlyn Waller about another issue related to the agency's local area networks (LANs). Since last January, employees at the Madison office have experienced a number of problems, including malfunctioning printers and difficulty retrieving e-mail. Susan would like to hire Tyger Networks to resolve the network problems, a process known as troubleshooting. To secure the necessary funding, she needs a report outlining the basic issues, which she can then distribute to New Hope's board of directors. Working with a task force at

Tyger Networks, Caitlyn has completed a draft of this report. It's your job to format the report and add a table at the end. When you're finished, she would like you to create a separate document that lists only the new equipment recommended by Tyger Networks. Complete the following:

1. Open the file **Trouble** located in the Tutorial.03\Review folder included with your Data Files, and then save it as **Troubleshooting Report** in the same folder.
2. Check your screen to make sure your settings match those in the tutorial. Display nonprinting characters as necessary and switch to Print Layout view.
3. Select the list of task force members and their titles, and then insert a left tab stop 2.5 inches from the left margin.
4. Replace "Evan Brillstein" with your name.
5. Divide the document into two sections. Insert a section break so that the executive summary begins on a new page.
6. Vertically align the first section of the document using the Center alignment option, and view the results in Print Preview.
7. Create a header for section 2 that aligns your name at the left margin and centers the page number preceded by the word "Page." Don't forget to deselect the Link to Previous button. (*Hint*: To center the page number, use the second tab stop.) Close the Header and Footer toolbar, and then save your work.
8. Insert a page break at the end of the document.
9. Create the table shown in Figure 3-35.

Figure 3-35

Troubleshooting Option	Explanation	Cost
Cable Checker	3 devices for each office, at $225 a piece	$675
Onsite Troubleshooting	40 hours of onsite troubleshooting, at $120 an hour	$4800
Cable Tester	1 device to be shared among the three offices	$1400

10. Display the Tables and Borders toolbar.
11. Sort the table by the contents of the Troubleshooting Option column in ascending order.
12. Insert a new row just below the Cable Tester row, and then enter the following information into the new row:
    Troubleshooting option: Onsite Training
    Explanation: Informational seminar for all Madison employees
    Cost: $300
13. Modify the widths of columns A and C to accommodate only the widest entry in each, and then right-align the data in the Cost column.
14. Increase the height of the heading row and format it appropriately using shading and boldface. Center the headings vertically and horizontally in their cells.
15. Select the entire table, select the 2 ¼ pt line weight, select the single line style, and then use the Outside Border option in the Borders list box. Select the heading row and add a double ½-point border at the bottom of the heading row.
16. Center the table between the page's left and right margins and then save your work.

17. Use the Table Move handle to select the entire table. Copy the table, open a new, blank document, and paste a copy of the table into the new document. Use the Delete command on the Table menu to delete the Onsite Training and Onsite Troubleshooting rows. Adjust border formatting as needed. Save the document as **Equipment List** in the Tutorial.03\Review folder. Close the document.
18. Close the Tables and Borders toolbar.
19. Save your work, review it in Reading Layout view, preview the report, and then print it.
20. Close the document.

Case Problem 1

Data File needed for this Case Problem: SunRep.doc

Sun Porch Bookstore Annual Report As manager of Sun Porch Bookstore in San Diego, California, you must submit an annual report to the board of directors. Complete the following:

1. Open the file **SunRep** located in the Tutorial.03\Cases folder included with your Data Files, and then save it as **Sun Porch Report** in the same folder.
2. Check your screen to make sure your settings match those in the tutorials. Switch to Print Layout view.
3. Divide the document into two sections. Begin section 2 with the introduction on a new page.
4. Format the title ("Annual Report") and the subtitle ("Sun Porch Bookstore") using the font and font size of your choice. Center the first section vertically. Select the title and subtitle, and center them horizontally. Note that you can combine horizontal and vertical alignment styles. Use the Print Preview window to check your work.
5. Create a header for section 2 that aligns your name to the left margin, and "Sun Porch Annual Report" to the right margin. Click the Link to Previous button to deselect it.

6. While in Header and Footer view, click the Switch between Header and Footer button to switch to the footer area for section 2. Press the Tab key to move the insertion point to the center tab stop, and then type the word "Page" followed by a space and the page number (using the Insert Page Number button on the Header and Footer toolbar). Insert a space, type the word "of", insert another space, and then click the Insert Number of Pages button on the Header and Footer toolbar to insert the total number of pages in the document. Click the Link to Previous button to deselect it, if necessary. Close Header and Footer view when you are finished.

7. Select the list of members under the heading "Board of Directors," click Format on the menu bar, and then click Tabs. To insert a tab stop with a dot leader at the 4-inch mark, type 4 in the Tab stop position text box, verify that the Left option button is selected in the Alignment section, and then click the 2..... option button in the Leader section. Click Set. Notice the Clear button, which you can use to clear the tab stop you just set, and the Clear All button, which you can use to clear all the custom tab stops (that is, tab stops other than the default ones) from a document. Click OK to close the Tabs dialog box.
8. Insert a page break at the end of the document, and then insert a table consisting of four rows and three columns.
9. Insert the headings "Name," "Title," and "Duties." Fill in the rows with the relevant information about the store personnel who are mentioned by name in the "Store Management and Personnel" section. Add new rows as needed.
10. Adjust the table column widths so the information is presented attractively.

11. Increase the height of the heading row, use the Tables and Borders toolbar to center the column headings horizontally and vertically, and then bold them.
12. Insert a row in the middle of the table, add your name to the list as another assistant manager, and then assign yourself some duties. Adjust the column widths as needed.
13. Format the heading row with a light gray shading of your choice, and then change the outside border of the table to a single 2 ¼-point line weight.
14. Center the table on the page.
15. Save and preview the document. Close the Tables and Borders toolbar. Review the document in Reading Layout view, print it, and then close the document.

Case Problem 2

Data File needed for this Case Problem: Tour.doc

Apply

Apply skills you learned to create a report summarizing information on a European tour.

Top Flight Travel's "Masterpiece Tour" Report   Each year Top Flight Travel sponsors a "Masterpiece" tour, which shepherds travelers through a two-week, whirlwind tour of the artistic masterpieces of Europe. The tour director has just completed a report summarizing the most recent tour. It's your job to format the report, which includes one table. Complete the following:

1. Open the file named **Tour** located in the Tutorial.03\Cases folder included with your Data Files, and then save it as **Masterpiece Tour Report** in the same folder.
2. Check your screen to make sure your settings match those in the tutorials. Switch to Print Layout view.
3. Replace "Your Name" in the first page with your first and last name.
4. Divide the document into two sections. Begin the second section on a new page, with the summary that starts "This report summarizes and evaluates."
5. Vertically align the first section using the Center alignment option.
6. Create a header for section 2 only that contains the centered text "Top Flight Travel." (*Hint*: To center text in the header, use the second tab stop. If necessary, deselect the Link to Previous button before you begin.) Format the header text using italic and the font size of your choice.

Explore

7. On the Header and Footer toolbar, click the Switch Between Header and Footer button to move to the footer area of the document. Using the same techniques you used to create a header in the tutorial, create a footer for section 2 only that aligns "Evaluation Report" to the left margin and the date to the right margin. (*Hint*: Deselect the Link to Previous button if necessary, and then use the Insert Date button on the Header and Footer toolbar to insert the date.) Close Header and Footer view.

Explore

8. Display the Tables and Borders toolbar, and turn off the Draw Table pointer if it is active. In the table, select the text in column A (the left column), bold the text, and then click the Change Text Direction button (on the Tables and Borders toolbar) twice so that text is formatted vertically (that is, the text reads from bottom to top). Adjust the width of column A to accommodate the newly rotated text.
9. Adjust the other column width so it is approximately 5" wide.
10. Delete the blank row 2.
11. Format column A with a light colored shading of your choice.
12. Change the border around column A to 2 ¼-point line weight. Adjust the row heights, if necessary, to display each row heading in one line.
13. Save and preview the document. Close the Tables and Borders toolbar.
14. Review the document in Reading Layout view, print it, and then close the document.

Challenge

Go beyond what you've learned to convert text into a table and then use other advanced table commands to enhance the table.

Case Problem 3

Data Files needed for this Case Problem: Contacts.doc and Budget.doc

Contact List for Flower Box Bakery   Ken Yamamoto recently opened Flower Box Bakery, a wholesale bakery catering to upscale cafes and tea shops in suburban St. Louis. He has just acquired a list of potential sales contacts from the local chamber of commerce via e-mail. The information consists of names, phone numbers, and managers for a number of new cafes and restaurants in the St. Louis area. The information is formatted as simple text, with the pieces of information separated by commas. Ken asks you to convert this text into a table and then format the table to make it easy to read. When you're finished, he needs you to sum a column of numbers in his Advertising Budget table. Complete the following:

1. Open the file named **Contacts** located in the Tutorial.03\Cases folder included with your Data Files, and then save it as **Sales Contacts** in the same folder. Check your screen to make sure your settings match those in the tutorials.

Explore

2. Select the entire document, click Table on the menu bar, point to Convert, and then click Text to Table. In the Convert Text to Table dialog box, make sure the settings indicate that the table should have three columns. Select the AutoFit to contents option button to ensure that columns are sized appropriately, select the Commas option button, and then click the OK button. Word converts the list into a table.

3. Replace the name "Enrique Mendoza" with your first and last name.

4. Insert a new row at the top of the table, and then insert appropriate column headings.

Explore

5. When you need to format a table quickly, you can allow Word's AutoFormat command to do the work for you. Click anywhere in the table, click Table on the menu bar, and then click Table AutoFormat to open the Table AutoFormat dialog box. Scroll down the Table styles list box to see the available options. Click options that interest you, and observe the sample tables in the Preview box. Note that you can deselect the check boxes in the "Apply special formats to" section to remove boldface or shading from columns or rows that don't require it. Select a table style that you think is appropriate for the Contacts table, deselect check boxes as you see fit, and then click the Apply button.

6. Sort the table alphabetically by column A.

Explore

7. Place the pointer over the Table Resize handle, just outside the lower-right corner of the table. Drag the double-arrow pointer to increase the height and width of each cell to a size of your choice. Notice that all the parts of the table increase proportionally.

8. Save your work, preview the table, print it, and then close the document.

9. Open the file **Budget** located in the Tutorial.03\Cases folder included with your Data Files, and then save it as **Advertising Budget** in the same folder. If necessary, open the Tables and Borders toolbar.

Explore

10. Select the cell containing the word "Total" and the blank cell to its right. Click the Merge Cells button on the Tables and Borders toolbar. The two cells are merged into one. Format the word "Total" so that it aligns on the right side of the new, larger cell.

Explore

11. Click the blank cell to the right of the Total cell, and then click the AutoSum button on the Tables and Borders toolbar. Word automatically sums the costs in the third column and displays the total ($400.00) in the selected cell.

Explore

12. Change the cost of the Missouri Monthly advertisement to $250, click the cell containing the total ($400.00), and then click the AutoSum button again. Word updates the total.

13. Save your work, preview the document, and then close it.

Create

Use your table skills to create the camp brochure shown in Figure 3-36.

Case Problem 4

There are no Data Files needed for this Case Problem.

Brochure for Camp Winnemac Angela Freedman is the publicity director for Camp Winnemac, a sleep-away camp for girls located in Northern Michigan. She asks you to create an informational brochure announcing the dates for Camp Winnemac's two summer sessions. She gives you the sketch in Figure 3-36. In the following steps, use Word table features to structure the information in the sketch:

Figure 3-36

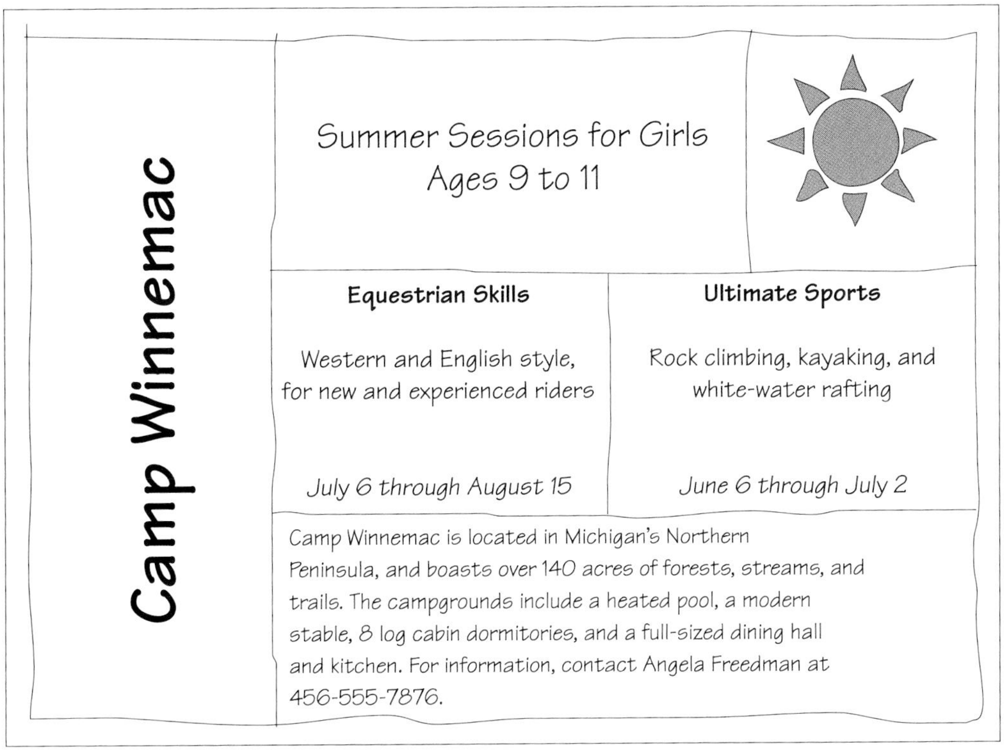

1. Open a new, blank document, and save it as **Camp Winnemac** in the Tutorial.03\Cases folder included with your Data Files.
2. If necessary, switch to Print Layout view, display rulers, and then open the Tables and Borders toolbar.

Explore

3. Click the Draw Table button on the Tables and Borders toolbar, if necessary, to select the button and change the pointer to the Draw Table pointer. Select a single-line line style, with a line weight of 1 1/2 points. Click in the upper-left corner of the document (near the paragraph mark), and then drag down and to the right to draw a rectangle about 5.5 inches wide and 3.5 inches high.

Explore

4. Continue to use the Draw Table pointer to draw the columns and rows shown in Figure 3-36. For example, to draw the column border for the "Camp Winnemac" column, click at the top of the rectangle, where you want the column to begin, and drag down to the bottom of the rectangle. Use the same technique to draw rows. If you make a mistake, use the Undo button. To delete a border, click the Eraser button on the Tables and Borders toolbar, click the border you want to erase, and then click the Eraser button again to turn it off. Don't expect to draw the table perfectly the first time. You may have to practice a while until you become comfortable with the Draw Table pointer, but once you can use it well, you will find it a helpful tool for creating complex tables. Click the Draw Table button on the toolbar again to turn off the Draw Table pointer.

Explore

5. In the left column, type the text "Camp Winnemac". With the pointer still in that cell, click the Change Text Direction button (on the Tables and Borders toolbar) twice to position the text vertically. Format the text in 26-point Times New Roman, and then center it in the cell using the Align Center option on the Tables and Borders toolbar. (*Hint*: You will probably have to adjust and readjust the row and column borders throughout this project, until all the elements of the table are positioned properly.)

6. Type the remaining text, as shown in Figure 3-36. Replace the name "Angela Freedman" with your own name. Use bold and italic as shown in Figure 3-36 to draw attention to key elements. Use the font styles, font sizes, and alignment options you think appropriate.

Explore

7. Click the Drawing button on the Standard toolbar to display the Drawing toolbar. Now you can insert the Camp Winnemac logo in the upper-right cell, using one of the tools on the Drawing toolbar. Click the upper-right cell, which at this point should be blank. Click the AutoShapes button on the Drawing toolbar, point to Basic Shapes, and then click the Sun shape. A box appears in the cell with the text "Create your drawing here." If the Drawing Canvas toolbar opens, close it. Click anywhere within the upper-right cell. The sun shape is inserted in the cell or somewhere nearby. The sun is selected, as indicated by the small circles, called selection handles, that surround it. If necessary, drag the sun to position it neatly within the cell. If the sun is not the right size, click the lower-right selection handle, and drag up or down to adjust the size of the sun so that it fits within the cell borders more precisely. With the sun still selected, click the Fill Color list arrow on the Drawing toolbar, and then click a light pink square in the color palette.

8. Adjust column widths and row heights so that the table is attractive and easy to read.

Explore

9. Now that you have organized the information using the Word table tools, you can remove the borders so that the printed flier doesn't look like a table. Click the Table Move handle to select the entire table, click Table on the menu bar, click Table Properties, click the Table tab if it is not already selected, click the Borders and Shading button, click the Borders tab if it is not already selected, click the None option, click the OK button, and then click the OK button again. The borders are removed from the flier; gridlines will not be visible on the printed page. (Depending on how your computer is set up, they may not be visible on your screen, either. If gridlines are not displayed, click Table on the menu bar, and then click Show Gridlines.)

10. Save your work, preview the flier, make any necessary adjustments, print it, and then close the document.

Research

Go to the Web to find information you can use to create documents.

Internet Assignments

The purpose of the Internet Assignments is to challenge you to find information on the Internet that you can use to work effectively with this software. The actual assignments are updated and maintained on the Course Technology Web site. Log on to the Internet and use your Web browser to go to the Student Online Companion for New Perspectives Office 2003 at **www.course.com/np/office2003.** Click the Internet Assignments link, and then navigate to the assignments for this tutorial.

Assess

SAM Assessment and Training

If you have a SAM user profile, you may have access to hands-on instruction, practice, and assessment of the skills covered in this tutorial. Log in to your SAM account and go to your assignments page to see what your instructor has assigned.

Review

Quick Check Answers

Session 3.1

1. a. in Normal view, a dotted line with the words "Section Break" that marks the point at which one section ends and another begins
   b. the intersection of a row and a column in a table
   c. information arranged in horizontal rows and vertical columns
   d. text entered one time but that is printed at the top of every page
   e. the location where text moves when you press the Tab key
2. Select the text whose tab alignment you want to change, click the tab alignment selector on the far left of the horizontal ruler until the appropriate tab stop alignment style appears, and then click in the horizontal ruler where you want to set the new tab stop.
3. You could divide a document into sections if you wanted to center only part of the document between the top and bottom margins.
4. Insert a section break, move the insertion point within the section you want to align, click File, click Page Setup, click the Layout tab, select Center in the Vertical alignment list box, make sure "This section" is selected in the Apply to list box, and then click OK.
5. A header appears at the top of a page, whereas a footer appears at the bottom of a page.
6. Click View on the menu bar, click Header and Footer, verify that the insertion point is located in the Header area, press Tab to move the insertion point to where you want the page number to appear, and then click the Insert Page Number button on the Header and Footer toolbar.
7. Move the insertion point to the location where you want the table to appear. Click the Insert Table button on the Standard toolbar. In the grid, click and drag to select three columns and two rows, and then release the mouse button.
8. If the insertion point is in the cell at the far right in a row, press the Tab key. Otherwise, press the ↓ key.

9. It's better to use a table rather than tab stops when you need to organize more than a few columns of information.

10. Click the Table Move handle.

Session 3.2

1. a. the thickness of the line used to create a border
   b. the style of the line used to create a border
   c. the outline of a row, cell, column, or table, which is hidden when the document is printed
   d. a gray or colored background used to highlight parts of a table

2. 12, 26, 44, 65

3. Click the cell at the far right in the bottom row of the table, and then press the Tab key.

4. Double-click the column's right-hand border.

5. Drag the bottom border of the row to a new position.

6. Select the row. Click the Line Style list arrow on the Tables and Borders toolbar, and select a line style. Click the Line Weight list arrow on the Tables and Borders toolbar, and select a line weight. Click the Borders list arrow on the Tables and Borders toolbar, and then click the Bottom Border option.

7. Click anywhere in the table, click Table on the menu bar, click Table Properties, click the Table tab, click Center, and then click OK.

Objectives

Session 4.1
- Identify desktop-publishing features
- Create a title with WordArt
- Work with hyperlinks
- Create newspaper-style columns

Session 4.2
- Insert and edit graphics
- Wrap text around a graphic
- Incorporate drop caps
- Use symbols and special typographic characters
- Add a page border
- Perform a mail merge

Desktop Publishing and Mail Merge

Creating a Newsletter and Cover Letter

Case

Wide World Travel, Inc.

Wide World Travel, Inc. hosts international tours for travelers of all ages. Recently, the company has expanded its business by selling clothes and shoes specifically designed for the frequent traveler. Max Stephenson, one of the Wide World tour guides, has taken on the job of managing this new retail venture. In order to generate business, he wants to create an informational newsletter. He has asked you to help him create the newsletter, as well as the form letter that will accompany each copy of the newsletter.

Max has already written the text of the newsletter, which describes some of the most popular items sold by Wide World Travel. Now Max wants you to transform this text into a publication that is neat, organized, and professional-looking. He would like the newsletter to contain headings (so the customers can scan it quickly for interesting items) as well as a headline that will give the newsletter a memorable look. He wants you to include a picture that will reinforce the newsletter content.

In this tutorial, you'll plan the layout of the newsletter and then add some information about the Wide World Travel Web site. Then you'll get acquainted with some desktop-publishing features available in Word that you'll use to create the newsletter. You'll format the title using an eye-catching design and divide the document into newspaper-style columns to make it easier to read. To add interest and focus to the text, you'll include a piece of art. You'll then fine-tune the newsletter layout, give it a more professional appearance with typographic characters, and put a border around the page to give the newsletter a finished look.

After you create the newsletter, you will use Word's mail merge feature to insert personalized information into the cover letter that will accompany the newsletter.

Student Data Files

▼**Tutorial.04**

▽ **Tutorial folder**

Addresses.doc
Clothes.doc
Letter.doc

▽ **Review folder**

Addresses.doc
Highlights.doc
Travel.doc

▽ **Cases folder**

Convert.doc
Grains.doc
Knight.bmp
Movers.doc

Session 4.1

Planning the Newsletter Document

The newsletter will provide a brief overview of some popular items sold by Wide World Travel. Like most newsletters, it will be written in an informal style that conveys information quickly. The newsletter title will help readers quickly identify the document. The newsletter text will be split into two columns to make it easier to read, and headings will help readers scan the information quickly. A picture will add interest and illustrate the newsletter's content. Drop caps and other desktop-publishing elements will help draw readers' attention to certain information and make the newsletter design attractive and professional.

Elements of Desktop Publishing

Desktop publishing is the production of commercial-quality printed material using a desktop computer system from which you can enter and edit text, create graphics, compose or lay out pages, and print documents. In addition to newsletters, you can desktop publish brochures, posters, and other documents that include text and graphics. In the Case Problems, you'll have the chance to create a brochure. The following elements are commonly associated with desktop publishing:

- High-quality printing. A laser printer or high-resolution inkjet printer produces final output.
- Multiple fonts. Two or three font types and sizes provide visual interest, guide the reader through the text, and convey the tone of the document.
- Graphics. Graphics, such as horizontal or vertical lines (called rules), boxes, electronic art, and digitized photographs help illustrate a concept or product, draw a reader's attention to the document, and make the text visually appealing.
- Typographic characters. For example, long dashes, called em dashes (—), are used in place of double hyphens (--) to separate dependent clauses; typographic medium-width dashes, called en dashes (–), are used in place of hyphens (-) as minus signs and in ranges of numbers; and typographic bullets (•) are used to draw attention to items in a list.
- Columns and other formatting features. Columns of text, pull quotes (small portions of text pulled out of the main text and enlarged), page borders, and other special formatting features that you don't frequently see in letters and other documents distinguish desktop-published documents.

Professional desktop publishers use software specially designed for desktop-publishing tasks. You can, however, use Word to create simple desktop-published documents. You'll incorporate many of the desktop-publishing elements listed above to produce the newsletter shown in Figure 4-1.

Travel in Style!

Wide World Travel Clothes

After countless trips abroad, our tour leaders have mastered the art of traveling light. The secret, they explain, is to pack a few well-made, light-weight items that you can wash in a sink and dry overnight on a line. Unless you lived in a large city with numerous specialty stores, finding good traveling clothes used to be nearly impossible. But now you can purchase everything you need for a fast-paced Wide World tour at the Wide World Web site. This newsletter describes a few of our most popular items. To learn more about other Wide World products, call us at 555-281-9010 or visit our Web site at www.wide-world-travel.com.

Travel Time Knitware

Unbelievably versatile, these knit garments are so adaptable that you can wear them from the train station to the outdoor market to the theater with just a change of accessories. They combine the softness of cotton with the suppleness of Flexistyle®, a wrinkle-resistant synthetic fabric.

The cardigan has side vents for a graceful drape and looks great layered over the knit shell. The pants have comfortable elasticized waistbands and side-seam pockets. Available in Midnight Black, Azure, and Coffee. Sizes: XS, S, M, L, and XL.

Pack It Straw Hat

If you're planning a trip to sunny climes, bring along this eminently packable broad-brimmed hat. Crunch it in a ball and stuff it into your suitcase. When you unpack, the hat will spring back to its original, elegant shape—guaranteed! Available in Cream and Taupe. Sizes: S, M, L, and XL.

Comfort Trekkers

These amazingly supportive walking shoes combine the comfort of hiking boots with the style of light-weight athletic shoes, giving your feet both stability and support. Wear them to explore a mysterious medieval city in the morning, and then hike a mountain trail after lunch. Available in Antique Black and Desert Brown, in whole and half sizes.

Prepared by Student Name 10/16/2006

Working with Hyperlinks

Web pages often include special text called **hyperlinks** (or simply **links**) that you can click to display other Web pages. You can also use hyperlinks in Word documents that will be read online (that is, on a computer). For example, if you type an e-mail address and then press the Enter key, Word automatically formats the e-mail address as a hyperlink. Hyperlink text is usually formatted in blue with an underline. When you press Ctrl and click an e-mail hyperlink, an e-mail program opens automatically, ready for you to type a message. If you completed the Case Problems for Tutorial 2, you already have experience using e-mail hyperlinks.

In addition to e-mail addresses, Word also automatically formats Web page addresses, or **URLs**, as hyperlinks. (One example of a Web address is *www.microsoft.com*.) When you press Ctrl and click a Web page address that has been formatted as a hyperlink, your computer's browser opens automatically and attempts to display that Web page. The browser may not actually be able to display the Web page if your computer is not currently connected to the Internet, or if the Web page is unavailable for some other reason.

Including hyperlinks in a Word document is very useful when you plan to distribute the document via e-mail so others can read it online. For instance, if you include your e-mail address in a memo to a potential customer, the customer can click the e-mail address to begin typing an e-mail message to you in reply. However, when you know that your document will only be distributed on paper, it's a good idea to remove any hyperlinks so that the e-mail address or Web address is formatted without the underline, in the same color font as the surrounding text. To remove a hyperlink, right-click the hyperlink, and then click Remove Hyperlink in the shortcut menu. Once you remove the hyperlink, the Web address or e-mail address remains in the document, but is no longer formatted in blue with an underline.

Max would like you to complete the newsletter text by adding a reference to the Wide World Travel Web site. He does not want the company's Web address formatted as a hyperlink, so you will have to remove the hyperlink after typing the Web address. He has saved the newsletter text in a document named Clothes. You'll begin by opening the document that contains the unformatted text, often called copy, that will serve as the content for your desktop-published document.

To open the newsletter document and add the Web address:

1. Start Word, and make sure your screen matches the figures in this tutorial. In particular, be sure to display nonprinting characters.

2. Open the file **Clothes** from the Tutorial.04\Tutorial folder included with your Data Files.

3. To avoid altering the original file, save the document as **Travel Clothes** in the same folder.

4. If necessary, change the Zoom setting on the Standard toolbar to **100%** and switch to Normal view.

5. Read the document to preview its content.

6. Click to the right of the phone number (at the end of the first main paragraph), press the **spacebar**, and then type the following: **or visit our Web site at www.wide-world-travel.com**

7. Type a period at the end of the Web address, and then press the **Enter** key. The Web address is formatted as a hyperlink, in a blue font with an underline.

8. Move the mouse pointer over the hyperlink. A ScreenTip appears, with the complete URL (including some extra characters that a browser needs to display the Web page). The ScreenTip also displays instructions for displaying the Wide World Travel Web site. See Figure 4-2.

Figure 4-2 **Hyperlink with ScreenTip**

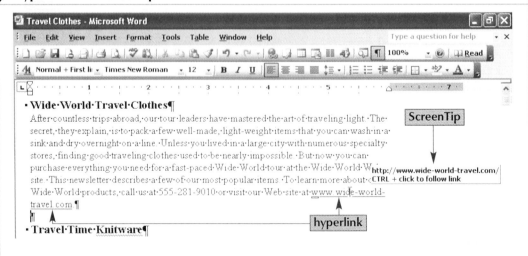

Max tells you that users will be viewing the document in printed form only. He asks you to remove the hyperlink. This will ensure that the format of the Web address matches the rest of the paragraph.

To remove the hyperlink:

▶ **1.** Right-click the text **www.wide-world-travel.com**. A shortcut menu opens.

▶ **2.** Click **Remove Hyperlink**. The shortcut menu closes, and the text is now formatted in black to match the rest of the paragraph.

You have finished adding the information about the company's Web site to the newsletter. Now that the newsletter contains all the necessary details, you can turn your attention to your first desktop-publishing task, adding a headline.

Using WordArt to Create a Headline

Max wants the title of the newsletter, "Travel in Style," to be eye-catching and dramatic. **WordArt** is a Word feature that allows you to insert specially formatted text into a document. WordArt provides great flexibility in designing text with special effects that express the image or mood you want to convey in your printed documents. With WordArt, you can apply color and shading, as well as alter the shape and size of the text.

You begin creating WordArt text by clicking a button on the Drawing toolbar. When you first display the Drawing toolbar, Word switches to Print Layout view. As a rule, Print Layout view is the most appropriate view to use when you are desktop publishing because it shows you exactly how the text and graphics fit on the page. The vertical ruler in Print Layout view helps you position graphical elements more precisely.

Creating Special Text Effects Using WordArt

Reference Window

- Click the Drawing button on the Standard toolbar to display the Drawing toolbar.
- Click the Insert WordArt button on the Drawing toolbar.
- Click the style of text you want to insert, and then click the OK button.
- Type the text you want in the Edit WordArt Text dialog box.
- Click the Font and Size list arrows to select the font and font size you want.
- If you want, click the Bold or Italic button, or both.
- Click the OK button.
- Click the WordArt to select it, and then drag any handle to resize and reshape it. To avoid altering the WordArt's proportions, press and hold down the Shift key while you drag a handle.

You're ready to use WordArt to create the newsletter title. First you will display the Drawing toolbar. Then you will choose a WordArt style and type the headline text.

To create the title of the newsletter using WordArt:

▶ 1. Press **Ctrl+Home** to move the insertion point to the beginning of the document.

▶ 2. Click the **Drawing** button 🔅 on the Standard toolbar. The Drawing toolbar appears at the bottom of the screen. Word switches to Print Layout view.

   Trouble? If the Drawing toolbar is not positioned at the bottom of the Document window, drag it there by its title bar. If you do not see the Drawing toolbar anywhere, right-click the Standard toolbar, and then click Drawing on the shortcut menu.

▶ 3. If necessary, click **View** on the menu bar, click **Ruler** to display the vertical and horizontal rulers, type **90** in the Zoom text box, and then press the Enter key to change the Zoom setting to 90%. This Zoom setting should allow you to see the entire width of the newsletter. Throughout this tutorial, feel free to zoom in or zoom out if you prefer to see more or less of the newsletter.

▶ 4. Click the **Insert WordArt** button 🔷 on the Drawing toolbar. The WordArt Gallery dialog box opens, displaying 30 different WordArt styles.

▶ 5. Click the WordArt style in the second row from the top, second column from the right, as shown in Figure 4-3.

Figure 4-3 | WordArt styles

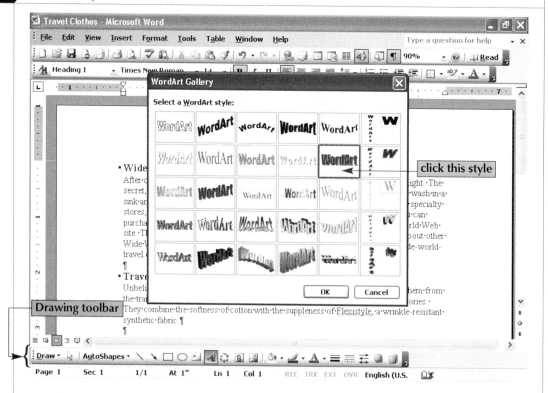

▶ 6. Click the **OK** button. The Edit WordArt Text dialog box opens, displaying the default text "Your Text Here," which you will replace with the newsletter title. Note that you can also select text in the document that you want to format as WordArt before you click the Insert WordArt button. In that case, the text you selected is displayed in the Edit WordArt Text dialog box instead of the default text "Your Text Here."

7. Type **Travel in Style** to replace the default text with the newsletter title. Notice the toolbar at the top of the Edit WordArt Text dialog box, which you can use to apply bold and italic, or to change the font or font style. You don't need to use these options now, but you might choose to when creating headlines for other documents.

8. Click the **OK** button. The Edit WordArt Text dialog box closes, and the WordArt image is inserted at the beginning of the newsletter. The "Wide World Travel Clothes" heading moves to the right to accommodate the new headline. See Figure 4-4.

WordArt headline inserted into document ◄ **Figure 4-4**

Trouble? If you see a border around the headline, the WordArt is currently selected. Click anywhere outside of the border to deselect the WordArt.

Eventually, you will position the headline so that it appears at the very top of the document, stretching from margin to margin. But for now, you can leave it in its current position.

Selecting a WordArt Object

The WordArt image you have created is not regular text. You cannot edit it as you would other text, that is, by moving the insertion point to it and typing new letters or by selecting part of it and using the buttons on the Formatting toolbar. Unlike regular text, a WordArt headline is considered an **object**—that is, something that you can manipulate independently of the text. You can think of the WordArt object as a thing that lies on top of, or next to, the text in a document. To edit a WordArt object in Word, you must first click it to select it. Then you can make changes using special toolbar buttons and dialog boxes, or by dragging it with the mouse.

Max would like you to make several changes to the newsletter headline. Before you can do this, you need to select it.

To select the WordArt headline:

1. Click the WordArt headline. The headline is surrounded by a black border with eight small black squares (called **sizing handles**). The WordArt toolbar also appears. The black sizing handles indicate that the WordArt is an **inline graphic**, that is, a graphic that is part of the line of text in which it was inserted. See Figure 4-5.

Figure 4-5 > **Selected headline**

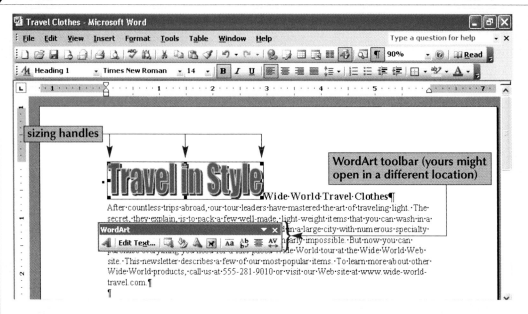

Editing a WordArt Object

Now that the WordArt object is selected, you can modify its appearance (color, shape, size, and so forth) using the buttons on the Drawing toolbar or the WordArt toolbar. First of all, Max would like you to edit the WordArt by adding an exclamation point at the end of the headline. While you're making that change, he would like you to format the headline in italic.

To change the font and formatting of the WordArt object:

▶ **1.** Verify that the WordArt object is selected, as indicated by the sizing handles.

▶ **2.** Click the **Edit Text** button on the WordArt toolbar. The Edit WordArt Text dialog box opens. As you recall, you used this dialog box earlier when you first created the WordArt headline.

▶ **3.** Click at the end of the headline (after the "e" in Style"), and then type **!** (an exclamation point).

▶ **4.** Click the **Italic** button *I* in the Edit WordArt Text dialog box. The headline in the Text box is now formatted in italic, with an exclamation point at the end.

▶ **5.** Click the **OK** button. The Edit WordArt Text dialog box closes, allowing you to see the edited headline in the document.

Changing the Shape of a WordArt Object

You can quickly change the shape of a WordArt object using the **WordArt Shape** button on the WordArt toolbar. Right now, the WordArt headline has a straight shape, without any curve to it. Max wants to use an arched shape.

To change the shape of the WordArt object:

▶ **1.** Verify that the WordArt headline is selected, and then click the **WordArt Shape** button 📐 on the WordArt toolbar. A palette of shape options opens.

▶ **2.** Move the mouse pointer over each option in the palette to display a ScreenTip with the name of each shape. As you can see, the Plain Text shape (a straight line) is currently selected.

▶ **3.** Point to the **Inflate Top** shape (fourth row down, fifth column from the left), as shown in Figure 4-6.

WordArt shapes | **Figure 4-6**

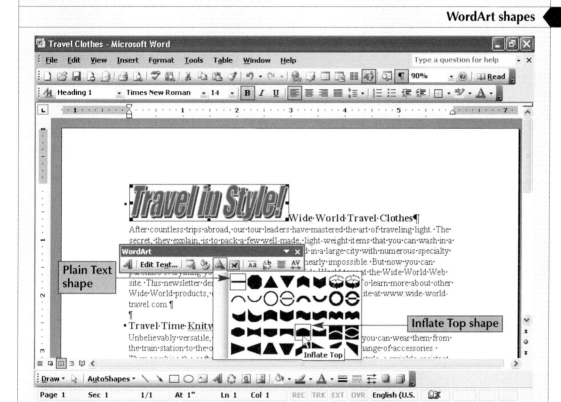

▶ **4.** Click the **Inflate Top** shape. The newsletter title is formatted in the new WordArt shape.

The headline has the shape you want. Now you can take care of positioning the WordArt object above the newsletter text.

Wrapping Text Below the WordArt Object

At this point, the WordArt object is on the same line as the heading "Wide World Travel Clothes." Max would like you to set the WordArt on its own line at the top of the document. To do this, you need to change the way the text flows, or **wraps**, around the WordArt object.

You can wrap text around objects many different ways in Word. For example, you can have the text wrap above and below the object, through it, or so the text follows the shape of the object, even if it has an irregular shape. Text wrapping is often used in newsletters to prevent text and graphics from overlapping, to add interest, and to prevent excessive open areas, called **white space**, from appearing on the page. The Text Wrapping button on the WordArt or Picture toolbar provides some basic choices, whereas the Layout tab of the Format WordArt dialog box provides more advanced options. (To open the Format WordArt dialog box, click the Format WordArt button on the WordArt toolbar.) Because you want to use a relatively simple option—wrapping text so that it flows below the WordArt headline—you'll use the Text Wrapping button on the WordArt toolbar. You'll have a chance to use the Format WordArt dialog box in the Case Problems at the end of this tutorial.

To wrap the newsletter text below the WordArt headline:

1. With the WordArt object selected, click the **Text Wrapping** button ⊠ on the WordArt toolbar. A menu of text wrapping options opens.

2. Click **Top and Bottom**. The text drops below the newsletter title. The WordArt is still selected, but instead of black sizing handles, you see small white circles. Like the black squares, the white circles are sizing handles. The white sizing handles indicate that the graphic object is a **floating graphic**, which means the graphic can be moved independently of the surrounding text. A number of other items appear around the WordArt object, as shown in Figure 4-7. You can use the sizing handles shown in Figure 4-7 to change the size and position of the WordArt object. You'll learn the meaning of the anchor symbol shortly. Don't be concerned if your WordArt object is not in the same position as the one in Figure 4-7.

Figure 4-7 ▶ **WordArt after wrapping text**

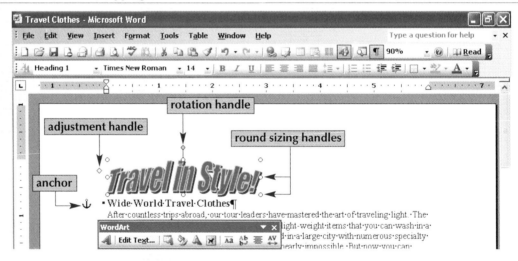

Trouble? If you can't see the anchor symbol, your Zoom setting is probably too high. Change it to 90%.

Positioning and Sizing the WordArt Object

After you choose a text wrapping style for a WordArt object, you can adjust its size and position in the document. To position a WordArt object, click it and drag it with the mouse pointer. To widen any WordArt object, drag one of its sizing handles. To keep the object the same proportion as the original, hold down the Shift key as you drag the sizing handle. This prevents "stretching" the object more in one direction than the other.

Max asks you to widen the headline so it fits neatly within the newsletter margins. As you enlarge the headline, you can practice dragging the WordArt object to a new position.

To position and enlarge the WordArt object:

1. Move the mouse pointer over the headline.

2. Use the 🔭 pointer to drag the WordArt object to the right, until it is centered below the 3-inch mark in the horizontal ruler, over the top of the newsletter.

3. Click the **Undo** button 🔄 on the Standard toolbar to undo the move. The headline returns to its original position, aligned along the left margin. Note that you can use this same technique to drag a WordArt object to any location in a document. (You'll learn more about dragging objects later in this tutorial, when you insert a picture into the newsletter.)

4. With the WordArt object still selected, position the pointer over the lower-right sizing handle. The pointer changes to 🔍.

5. Press and hold the **Shift** key while you drag the sizing handle to the right margin, using the horizontal ruler as a guide. As you drag the handle, the pointer changes to ╂ and a dotted outline appears to show you how big the WordArt will be when you release the mouse button. See Figure 4-8.

Resizing the WordArt Object **Figure 4-8**

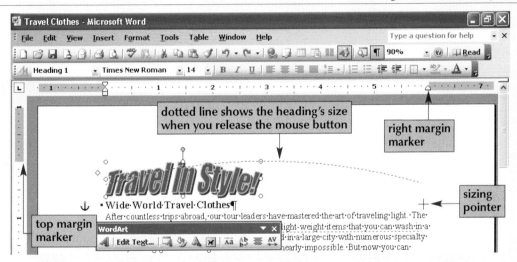

6. Release the mouse button when the dotted horizontal line stretches from the left to the right margin. The WordArt heading should be about six inches wide and a little less than 1.5 inches high at its tallest. If necessary, repeat the procedure to make the exclamation point line up with the right margin.

   Trouble? If the WordArt heading spans the margins, but is not tall enough to read easily, you probably didn't hold down the Shift key when you dragged the mouse pointer. Undo the change and begin again with Step 4.

7. If necessary, drag the headline down slightly, so that the top of the headline does not extend into the top margin, as shown in Figure 4-9. Notice that when you drag the headline down, the newsletter text also moves down to accommodate the headline.

   Trouble? If the headline jumps to the middle of the first paragraph of text, you dragged it too far. Click the Undo button 🔄, and then repeat Step 7.

In addition to moving and resizing the WordArt headline, you can drag the rotation handle to rotate the headline. You can also use the adjustment handle to increase or decrease the arch at the top of the headline. Right now you need to turn your attention to the WordArt object anchor symbol.

Anchoring the WordArt Object

After you wrap text around a WordArt object, you need to make sure the WordArt object is properly positioned within the document as a whole—a process known as anchoring. The process draws its name from the anchor symbol in the left margin, which indicates the position of the WordArt relative to the text. The anchor symbol is only visible after you wrap text around the document and when nonprinting characters are displayed. To ensure that changes to the text (such as section breaks) do not affect the WordArt, you need to anchor the WordArt to a blank paragraph before the text. At this point, the WordArt anchor symbol is probably located to the left of the first paragraph (the heading "Wide World Travel Clothes"). However, yours may be in a different position (for instance, it might be positioned above and to the left of the WordArt). In the next set of steps, you will move the anchor to a new, blank paragraph at the beginning of the document.

To anchor the WordArt object to a blank paragraph:

1. Press **Ctrl+Home**. The insertion point moves to the beginning of the newsletter text (that is, to the left of the first "W" in the heading "Wide World Travel Clothes"). The WordArt object is no longer selected; you cannot see the anchor at this point.

2. Press the **Enter** key. A new paragraph symbol is inserted either above or below the Word-Art object.

3. If the new paragraph symbol is inserted above the WordArt heading, drag the WordArt heading up slightly until the paragraph mark moves below the WordArt heading.

4. Click the WordArt object. The selection handles and the anchor symbol appear. The anchor symbol is probably positioned to the left of the "Wide World Travel Clothes" heading, though it might be located to the left of the new blank paragraph instead.

5. Click the anchor and drag it up to position it to the left of the new, blank paragraph as shown in Figure 4-9, if it is not already positioned there.

Figure 4-9   **Properly anchored WordArt**

Trouble? If your WordArt headline is positioned below the new paragraph symbol, drag it up slightly to position it above the new paragraph symbol. If you notice any other differences between your headline and the one shown in Figure 4-9, edit the headline to make it match the figure. For example, you may need to drag the WordArt left or right slightly, or you may need to adjust its size by dragging one of its sizing handles.

6. Click anywhere in the newsletter to deselect the WordArt, and then save your work.

Your WordArt is now finished. Max congratulates you on your excellent work. The headline will definitely draw attention to the newsletter, encouraging potential customers to read the entire document.

Formatting Text in Newspaper-Style Columns

Because newsletters are meant for quick reading, they are usually laid out in newspaper-style columns. In **newspaper-style columns**, a page is divided into two or more vertical blocks, or columns. Text flows down one column, continues at the top of the next column, flows down that column, and so forth. The narrow columns and small type size allow the eye to take in a lot of text, thus allowing a reader to scan a newspaper quickly for interesting information.

When formatting a document in columns, you can click where you want the columns to begin and then click the Columns button on the Formatting toolbar. However, the Columns command on the Formatting menu offers more options. Using the Columns command, you can insert a vertical line between columns. The Columns command also gives you more control over exactly what part of the document will be formatted in columns.

Max wants you to divide the text below the title into two columns and add a vertical line between them.

To apply newspaper-style columns to the body of the newsletter:

▶ **1.** Position the insertion point at the beginning of the second paragraph (to the left of the first "W" in "Wide World Travel Clothes").

▶ **2.** Click **Format** on the menu bar, and then click **Columns**. The Columns dialog box opens.

▶ **3.** In the Presets section, click the **Two** icon.

▶ **4.** Click the **Line between** check box to select it. The text in the Preview box changes to a two-column format with a vertical rule between the columns.

You want these changes to affect only the paragraphs after the WordArt headline, so you'll need to insert a section break and apply the column formatting to the text after the insertion point.

▶ **5.** Click the **Apply to** list arrow, and then click **This point forward** to have Word automatically insert a section break at the insertion point. See Figure 4-10.

Completed Columns dialog box ◀ **Figure 4-10**

- places a line between columns
- creates two columns of the same width
- shows how columns will look with current settings
- adds section break at insertion point

6. Click the **OK** button to return to the Document window. A continuous section break appears below the WordArt title. The word "continuous" indicates that the new section continues on the same page as the preceding text—in other words, the WordArt title and the newsletter text will print on the same page, even though they are in different sections of the newsletter. The text in Section 2 is formatted in two columns. The insertion point is in Section 2 as indicated by the information displayed in the status bar.

To get a good look at the columns, you need to change the Zoom setting so you can see the entire page at one time.

To zoom out to display the whole page:

1. Click the **Zoom** list arrow on the Standard toolbar, and then click **Whole Page**. Word displays the entire page of the newsletter so that you can see how the two-column format looks on the page. See Figure 4-11. Note that the Whole Page Zoom setting is only available in Print Layout view. You should use it whenever you want to have the entire page displayed as you edit it. Some details, such as the line between the columns, are not visible in the Whole Page Zoom setting.

Figure 4-11 ▶ **Whole Page view showing two columns**

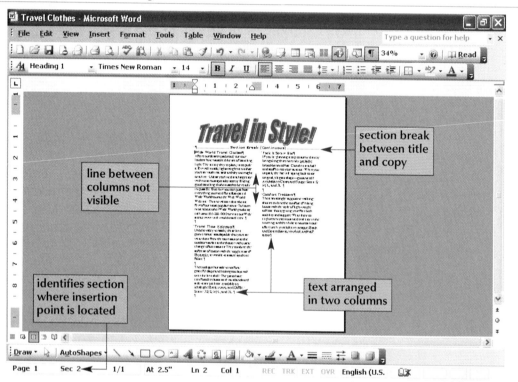

Trouble? Your columns may break at a slightly different line from those shown in the figure. This is not a problem; just continue with the tutorial.

The newsletter headline is centered on the page, and the copy is in a two-column format. The text fills the left column but not the right column. You'll fix this later, after you add a graphic and format some of the text.

2. Click the **Zoom** list arrow again, and then click **Page Width**. The Page Width option changes the Zoom setting enough to make the page span the width of the document window. Now you can read the text again.

3. Save your work.

Keep in mind that you can modify the structure of columns in a document by reformatting the document with three or more columns, or return the document to its original format by formatting it as one column. You can also insert column breaks to force text to move from one column to the next. You'll have a chance to practice modifying the columns in the Case Problems at the end of this tutorial.

Session 4.1 Quick Check

Review

1. Describe four elements commonly associated with desktop publishing.
2. True or False: When using Word's desktop-publishing features, you should display your document in Print Layout view.
3. In your own words, define the following terms:
   a. desktop publishing
   b. WordArt
   c. copy
   d. anchor
4. True or False: You can edit WordArt just as you would edit any other text in Word.
5. How do you change the text of a WordArt object after you have inserted it into a Word document?
6. What is the purpose of the WordArt Shape button on the WordArt toolbar?
7. True or False: When you first format a document into newspaper-style columns, the columns will necessarily be of equal length.

Session 4.2

Inserting Graphics

Graphics, which can include drawings, paintings, photographs, charts, tables, designs, or even designed text such as WordArt, add variety to documents and are especially appropriate for newsletters. You can use the buttons on Word's Drawing toolbar to draw pictures in your document. However, it's usually easier to create a picture in a special graphics program and then save the picture as an electronic file. (You may already be familiar with one graphics program, **Paint**, which is included as part of the Windows operating system.)

Instead of creating your own art in a graphics program, you can take a piece of art on a piece of paper (such as a photograph) and scan it—that is, run it through a special machine called a scanner. A **scanner** is similar to a copy machine except that it saves a copy of the image as an electronic file, instead of reproducing it on a piece of paper. (As you may know, many modern copy machines also function as scanners.) You can also use a digital camera to take a photograph that is then stored as an electronic file.

Electronic files come in several types, many of which were developed for use in Web pages. In desktop publishing, you will often work with **bitmaps**—a type of file that stores an image as a collection of tiny dots, which, when displayed on a computer monitor or printed on a page, make up a picture. There are several types of bitmap files, the most common of which are:

- BMP: Used by Microsoft Paint, and other graphics programs, to store graphics you create. These files, which have the .bmp file extension, tend to be very large.
- GIF: Suitable for most types of simple art. A GIF file is compressed, so it doesn't take up much room on your computer. A GIF file has the file extension .gif.
- JPEG: Suitable for photographs and drawings. Files stored using the JPEG format are even more compressed than GIF files. A JPEG file has the file extension .jpg.
- TIFF: Commonly used for photographs or scanned images. TIFF files have the file extension .tif and are usually much larger than GIF or JPEG files, but smaller than BMP files.

Once you have stored a piece of art as an electronic file, you can insert it into a document using the Picture command options on the Insert menu. You'll have a chance to explore some of these options in the Case Problems at the end of this tutorial.

If you don't have time to prepare your own art work, you can take advantage of **clip art**—a collection of ready-made images. A number of clip art selections are stored on your computer when you install Microsoft Word. You can also download additional clip art from the Web. (You'll have a chance to look for clip art on the Web in the Case Problems at the end of this tutorial.) You begin inserting clip art by opening the Clip Art task pane. From there you can search for images that are stored on your computer or on the Web. Then you copy an image to the Clipboard, and paste the image into the document.

To add visual appeal to the Travel in Style newsletter, you will insert a piece of clip art. Max wants you to use a clip art object that reflects the newsletter content.

To insert the clip art image of an airplane into the newsletter:

1. If you took a break after the previous session, make sure Word is still running, the file Travel Clothes is open, the document is in Print Layout view, and the nonprinting characters are displayed. Also verify that the Drawing toolbar is displayed.

2. Click the **Insert Clip Art** button on the Drawing toolbar. The Clip Art task pane opens, as shown in Figure 4-12. You use the top part of the Clip Art task pane to search for graphics related to a specific topic. You can click the Organize clips option (near the bottom) to open the Clip Organizer window, where you can browse among the various clip art images stored on your computer. You'll use the Clip Organizer to insert an image into the newsletter. You'll have a chance to try the Search for option in the Case Problems at the end of this tutorial. If someone recently used your Clip Art task pane to search for graphics, you may see the search topic in the Search for text box.

Figure 4-12 | **Clip Art task pane**

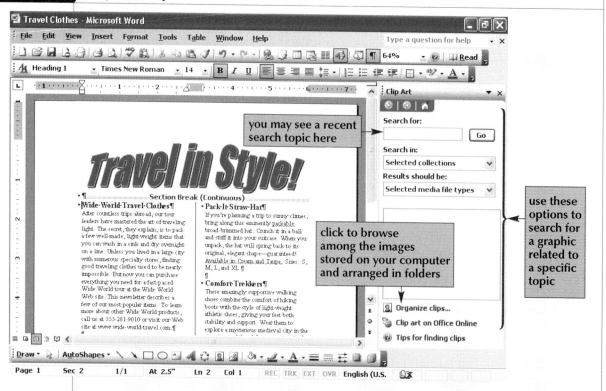

3. Click **Organize clips** near the bottom of the Clip Art task pane. The Favorites - Microsoft Clip Organizer window opens. This window is similar to Windows Explorer. For example, you click the plus sign next to a folder to display its subfolders. You select a subfolder to display its contents in the right pane. The default Microsoft Office clip art is stored in subfolders within the Office Collections folder. See Figure 4-13. You might see different folders from those shown in Figure 4-13, but you should see the Office Collections folder.

Trouble? If you see the Add Clips to Organizer dialog box, click Now. This will organize the clip art installed on your computer into folders, so that you can then use the Clip Organizer dialog box to select a piece of clip art. The Add Clips to Organizer dialog box appears the first time you attempt to use clip art on your computer. After the clip organizing process concludes, continue with Step 4.

Microsoft Clip Organizer | **Figure 4-13**

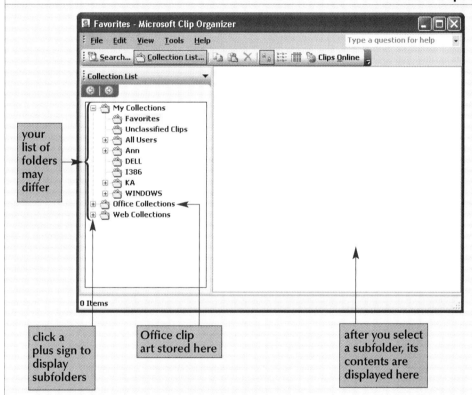

4. Scroll as needed to view the Office Collections folder, and then click the plus sign next to the **Office Collections** folder. A list of subfolders within the Office Collections folder appears. This list of folders, which is created when you install Word, organizes clip art images into related categories. The folders with plus signs next to them contain subfolders or clip art images.

5. Scroll down and examine the list of folders. Click any plus signs to open subfolders, and then click folders to display clip art images in the right pane.

6. Click the plus sign next to the **Transportation** folder to display its subfolders, and then click the **Transportation** folder to select it. Three images stored in the Transportation folder are displayed in the right pane.

Trouble? If you don't see any images in the Transportation folder, click the Travel folder to select it and display an image of an airplane in a blue circle.

7. Move the pointer over the image of the airplane in the blue circle. An arrow button appears on the right side of the image.

8. Click the arrow button. A menu of options opens, as shown in Figure 4-14.

Figure 4-14 ▶ **Image in Transportation folder selected**

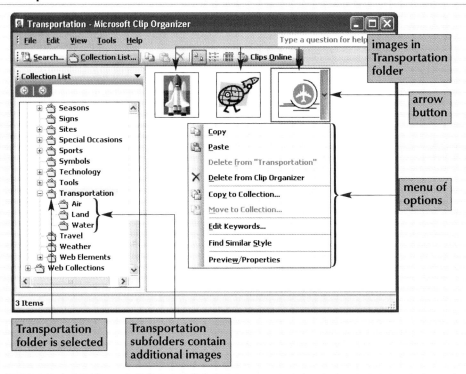

9. Click **Copy** in the menu. The image is copied to the Clipboard.

Now that you have copied the image to the Clipboard, you can paste it into the document at the insertion point. Max asks you to insert the graphic in the paragraph below the heading "Wide World Travel Clothes." Before you insert the image, you will close the Clip Art task pane.

To paste the clip art into the document:

1. Click the **Close** button ☒ in the Microsoft Clip Organizer title bar, and then click **Yes** when you see a dialog box asking if you want the item to remain on the Clipboard. You return to the Document window.

2. Click the **Close** button ☒ on the Clip Art task pane.

3. Position the insertion point to the left of the word "After" in the beginning of the first paragraph below the heading "Wide World Travel Clothes."

4. Click the **Paste** button 🗃 on the Standard toolbar. The image is inserted into the document at the insertion point. The image nearly fills the left column.

5. Save the document.

6. Click the airplane image to select it. Like the WordArt object you worked with earlier, the clip art image is a graphic object with sizing handles that you can use to change its size. The Picture toolbar appears whenever a graphic object is selected. See Figure 4-15.

Newsletter with the Clip Art object inserted ◀ **Figure 4-15**

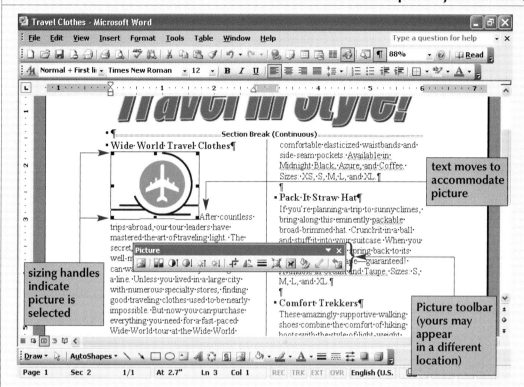

Trouble? If the Picture toolbar does not appear when you click the airplane image, right-click any toolbar, and then click Picture.

Max would like the image to be smaller so it doesn't divert attention from the text. You'll make that change in the next section.

Resizing a Graphic

It's often necessary to change the size of a graphic to make it fit into a document. This is called **scaling** the image. You can resize a graphic either by dragging its sizing handles or, for more precise control, by using the Format Picture button on the Picture toolbar.

For Max's newsletter, the dragging technique will work fine.

To resize the clip art graphic:

▶ **1.** Make sure the clip art graphic is selected.

▶ **2.** Drag the lower-right sizing handle up and to the left until the dotted outline forms a rectangle slightly less than 1.5 inches wide. Remember to use the horizontal ruler as a guide. See Figure 4-16. *Note*: You don't have to hold down the Shift key, as you do with WordArt, to resize the picture proportionally.

Figure 4-16 ▶ Resizing the graphic

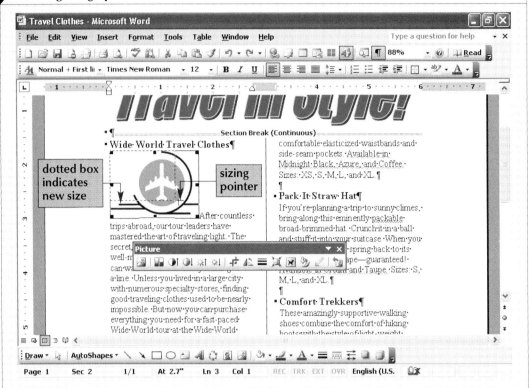

3. Release the mouse button. The airplane image is now about half as wide as the left column.

Max wonders if the graphic would look better if you deleted part of the horizontal lines on the left side of the image. You'll make that change in the next section.

Cropping a Graphic

You can **crop** the graphic—that is, cut off one or more of its edges—using either the Crop button on the Picture toolbar or the Format Picture dialog box. Once you crop a graphic, the part you cropped is hidden from view. It remains a part of the graphic image, so you can change your mind and restore a cropped graphic to its original form.

To crop the airplane graphic:

1. If necessary, click the clip art to select it. The sizing handles appear.

2. Click the **Crop** button ⊹ on the Picture toolbar. The pointer changes to ⊹. To crop the graphic, you must position this pointer over a middle handle on any side of the graphic.

3. Position the ⊹ pointer directly over the middle sizing handle on the left side of the picture.

4. Press and hold down the mouse button. The pointer changes to ⊣.

5. Drag the handle to the right. As you drag, a dotted outline appears to indicate the new shape of the graphic. Position the left border of the dotted outline along the left border of the blue circle. See Figure 4-17.

Cropping the graphic   Figure 4-17

Position the pointer over any handle and drag to crop.

6. Release the mouse button.

Max decides he prefers to display the whole airplane, so he asks you to return to the original image.

7. Click the **Undo** button ↻ on the Standard toolbar. The cropping action is reversed, and the full image reappears.

Rotating a Graphic

Max still isn't happy with the appearance of the graphic because of the amount of white space on the left side. He suggests rotating the image so that the airplane is positioned horizontally on the page. You can use the Rotate Left button on the Picture toolbar to rotate the image.

To rotate the airplane graphic:

1. If necessary, click the clip art to select it. The sizing handles appear.

2. Click the **Rotate Left 90°** button on the Picture toolbar. The graphic rotates 90 degrees to the left.

3. Click the **Rotate Left 90°** button again. The graphic rotates another 90 degrees, leaving the airplane upside down.

4. Click the **Rotate Left 90°** button again. The graphic rotates another 90 degrees. Now the airplane appears to be flying across the page from left to right. The selection handles become circles. See Figure 4-18. If you needed to rotate the image with the text wrapped around it, you could drag the rotation handle, which is the round green circle.

Figure 4-18   Rotated graphic

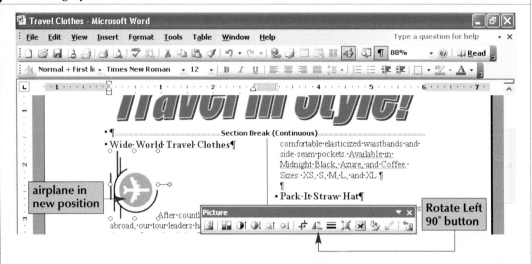

Now Max wants you to make the text wrap to the right of the graphic, making the airplane look as if it's flying into the text.

Wrapping Text Around a Graphic

For the airplane to look as though it flies into the newsletter text, you need to make the text wrap around the image. Earlier, you used Top and Bottom text wrapping to position the WordArt title above the columns of text. Now you'll apply Tight text wrapping to make the text follow the shape of the plane.

To wrap text around the airplane graphic:

1. Verify that the airplane graphic is selected.

2. Click the **Text Wrapping** button 🖼 on the Picture toolbar. A menu of text wrapping options appears.

3. Click **Tight**. The text wraps to the right of the airplane, following its shape. Your screen should look similar to Figure 4-19.

4. Click anywhere in the text to deselect the graphic, and then save the newsletter. Don't be concerned if the heading "Wide World Travel Clothes" wraps around the top of the graphic. You will move the graphic away from the heading in the next section. If the heading does not wrap around the graphic, that's fine too.

Text wrapped around graphic ◄ **Figure 4-19**

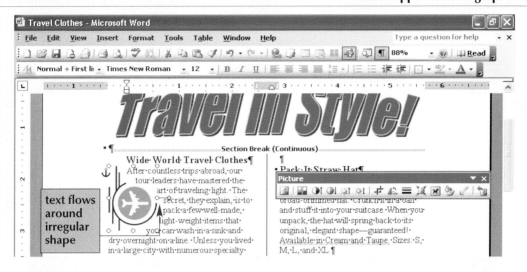

The Text Wrapping button should provide all the options you need for most situations. In some cases, however, you might want to use the more advanced options available in the Format Picture or Format WordArt dialog box. You'll have a chance to explore these options in the Case Problems at the end of this tutorial.

Moving a Graphic

Finally, Max asks you to move the graphic down to the middle of the paragraph so that it is not so close to the heading. You can do this by dragging the graphic to a new position. Like WordArt, a clip art graphic is anchored to a specific paragraph in a document. When you drag a graphic (including WordArt) to a new paragraph, the anchor symbol moves to the top of that paragraph. When you drag a graphic to a new position within the same paragraph, the anchor symbol remains in its original position and only the graphic moves. You'll see how this works when you move the airplane graphic.

To move the graphic:

1. Select the graphic. You should see an anchor symbol either within the graphic or to the left of the heading "Wide World Travel Clothes."

2. Move the mouse pointer 🕂 over the graphic.

3. Click and slowly drag the 🕂 pointer down. As you move the pointer, a dotted outline appears indicating the new position of the graphic.

4. Position the dotted outline so it is in the middle of the paragraph and aligned along the left margin, and then release the mouse button. The graphic moves to its new position, but the anchor remains at the top of the paragraph, to the left of the first line of the paragraph. Your newsletter should look similar to Figure 4-20.

Figure 4-20 ▶ **Graphic in new position**

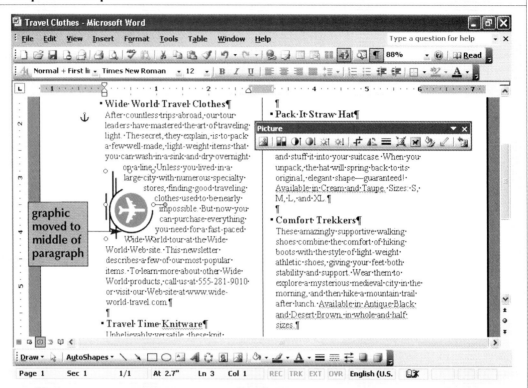

5. Click anywhere outside the graphic to deselect it.

Trouble? If paragraph text wraps to the left of the graphic, you need to drag the graphic further to the left, so that it aligns along the left margin.

The image of the airplane draws the reader's attention to the beginning of the newsletter, but the rest of the text looks plain. Max suggests adding a drop cap at the beginning of each section.

Inserting Drop Caps

A **drop cap** is a large, capital letter that highlights the beginning of the text of a newsletter, chapter, or some other document section. The drop cap usually extends from the top of the first line of the paragraph down two or three succeeding lines of the paragraph. The text of the paragraph wraps around the drop cap. Word allows you to create a drop cap for the first letter of the first word of a paragraph.

You will create a drop cap for the first paragraph following each heading in the newsletter. The drop cap will extend two lines into the paragraph.

To insert drop caps in the newsletter:

▶ **1.** If necessary, click in the paragraph below the heading "Wide World Travel Clothes" (the paragraph where you inserted the graphic).

▶ **2.** Click **Format** on the menu bar, and then click **Drop Cap**. The Drop Cap dialog box opens.

▶ **3.** In the Position section, click the **Dropped** icon.

▶ **4.** Click the **Lines to drop** down arrow once to change the setting from 3 to 2. You don't need to change the default distance from the text. See Figure 4-21.

Drop Cap dialog box ◀ **Figure 4-21**

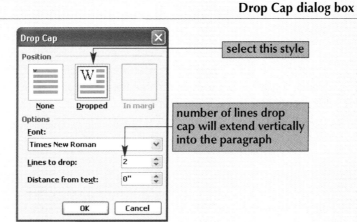

▶ **5.** Click the **OK** button to close the dialog box, and then click anywhere in the newsletter to deselect the new drop cap. Word formats the first character of the paragraph as a drop cap.

Word re-wraps the text around the graphic to accommodate the drop cap above. See Figure 4-22. If the paragraph text wraps to the left of the graphic, drag the graphic closer to the left margin.

Drop Cap begins the paragraph ◀ **Figure 4-22**

Trouble? Don't be concerned if Word now marks the "fter" of "After" as a grammatical error. Word considers drop caps to be objects, not regular text. By formatting the A in "After" as a drop cap, you essentially deleted the regular character A. Because the remaining regular characters "fter" do not appear in the Word dictionary, Word might mark it as a potential error.

▶ **6.** Position the insertion point in the paragraph following the heading "Travel Time Knitware," and then repeat Steps 2-5.

▶ **7.** Position the insertion point in the paragraph following the heading "Pack It Straw Hat," and then press the **F4** key. The F4 key repeats your previous action at the location of the insertion point.

Trouble? If something else changes when you press the F4 key, you pressed another key or performed another action after Step 6. Click the Undo button 🔄 on the Standard toolbar, position the insertion point in the paragraph following the heading "Pack It Straw Hat," and then repeat Steps 2 through 5.

▶ **8.** Use the **F4** key to add a drop cap to the paragraph following the last heading, and then click anywhere in the text to deselect the drop cap.

The newsletter looks more lively with the drop caps. Next, you turn your attention to inserting a registered trademark symbol (®) next to a registered trademark name.

Inserting Symbols and Special Characters

In printed publications, it is customary to change some of the characters available on the standard keyboard into more polished-looking characters called **typographic symbols**. For instance, while you might type two hyphens to indicate a dash, in a professionally-produced version of that document the two hyphens would be changed to one long dash (called an em dash because it is approximately as wide as the letter "m"). In the past, desktop publishers had to rely on special software to insert and print a document containing typographic symbols, but now you can let Microsoft Word do the work for you.

Word's AutoCorrect feature automatically converts some standard characters into more polished-looking typographic symbols as you type. For instance, as Max typed the information on the Pack It Straw Hat, he typed two hyphens after the words "elegant shape." As he began to type the next word "guaranteed," Word automatically converted the two hyphens into an em dash. Figure 4-23 lists some of the other characters that AutoCorrect automatically converts to typographic symbols. In most cases you need to press the space-bar and type more characters before Word will insert the appropriate symbol. You'll have a chance to practice using AutoCorrect to insert typographic symbols in the Review Assignments at the end of this tutorial.

Figure 4-23 ▶ **Common typographic symbols**

To insert this symbol or character	Type	Word converts it to
em dash	word--word	word—word
smiley	:)	☺
copyright symbol	(c)	©
registered trademark symbol	(r)	®
trademark symbol	(tm)	™
ordinal numbers	1st, 2nd, 3rd, etc.	1st, 2nd, 3rd, etc.
fractions	1/2, 1/4	½ ¼
arrows	--> or <--	→ or ←

To insert typographic symbols into a document after you've finished typing it, you can use the Symbol command on the Insert menu.

Inserting Symbols and Special Characters

- Move the insertion point to the location where you want to insert a particular symbol or special character.
- Click Insert on the menu bar, and then click Symbol to open the Symbol dialog box.
- Click the appropriate symbol, or click the name from the list on the Special Characters tab.
- Click the Insert button.
- Click the Close button.

Max noticed that he forgot to insert a registered trademark symbol (®) after "Flexistyle." He asks you to insert this symbol now, using the Symbol command on the Insert menu.

To insert the registered trademark symbol:

▶ **1.** Scroll down to display the paragraph below the heading "Travel Time Knitware," and then click to the right of the word "Flexistyle." (Take care to click between the final "e" and the comma.)

▶ **2.** Click **Insert** on the menu bar, and then click **Symbol** to open the Symbol dialog box.

▶ **3.** If necessary, click the **Special Characters** tab. See Figure 4-24.

Inserting a typographic symbol ◀ Figure 4-24

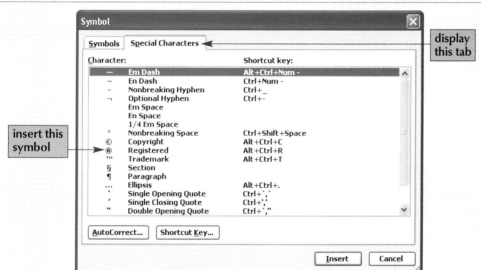

▶ **4.** Click **Registered** to select it, and then click the **Insert** button.

▶ **5.** Close the Symbol dialog box. Word inserts an ® immediately after the word "Flexistyle." Finally, you need to format the symbol as superscript, so that it is raised slightly above the surrounding text.

▶ **6.** Select the symbol, click **Format** on the menu bar, click **Font**, verify that the Font tab is selected, click the **Superscript** check box to insert a check (in the Effects section of the Font dialog box), and then click **OK.** The registered trademark symbol is now smaller and raised slightly above the surrounding text.

Next, you need to adjust the columns of text so they are approximately the same length.

Balancing the Columns

You can shift text from one column to another by adding blank paragraphs to move the text into the next column or by deleting blank paragraphs to shorten the text so it will fit into one column. The problem with this approach is that any edits you make could throw off the balance. Instead, Word can automatically **balance** the columns, or make them of equal length. You'll balance the columns in the newsletter next.

To balance the columns:

1. Position the insertion point at the end of the text in the right column, just after the period following the word "sizes."

   Next, you need to change the zoom to Whole Page so you can see the full effect of the change.

2. Click the **Zoom** list arrow on the Standard toolbar, and then click **Whole Page**.

3. Click **Insert** on the menu bar, and then click **Break**. The Break dialog box opens.

4. Below "Section break types," click the **Continuous** option button.

5. Click the **OK** button. Word inserts a continuous section break at the end of the text. As shown in Figure 4-25, Word balances the text between the two section breaks.

Figure 4-25 ▶ **Newsletter with balanced columns**

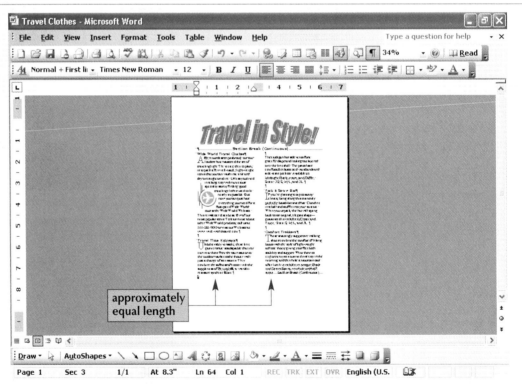

Drawing a Border Around the Page

You can add definition to a paragraph or an entire page by adding a border. You can also emphasize individual paragraphs within a document by putting a border around one or more paragraphs and by adding shading. Right now, Max wants to add a border around the entire newsletter page. (In the Case Problems at the end of this tutorial, you'll have a chance to add a border around individual paragraphs.)

To draw a border around the newsletter:

1. Make sure the document is in Print Layout view and that the Zoom setting is set to Whole Page so that you can see the entire newsletter.

2. Click **Format** on the menu bar, and then click **Borders and Shading**. The Borders and Shading dialog box opens.

3. Click the **Page Border** tab. You use the Setting options on the left side to specify the type of border you want. In this case, you want a simple box.

4. In the Setting section, click the **Box** option. Now that you have selected the type of border you want, you can choose the style of line that will be used to create the border.

5. In the Style list box, scroll down and select the ninth style down from the top (the thick line with the thin line underneath), and then verify that the Apply to option is set to **Whole document**. See Figure 4-26. (While the Borders and Shading dialog box is open, notice the Shading tab, which you can use to add a colored background to a page. You'll have a chance to use this tab in the Case Problems at the end of this tutorial.)

Adding a border to the newsletter   **Figure 4-26**

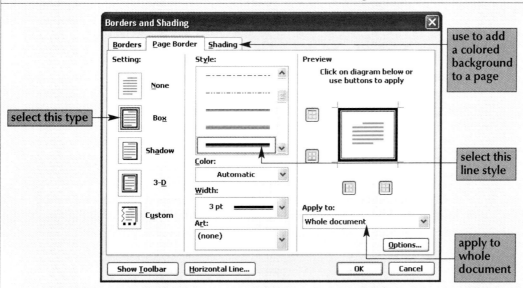

6. Click the **Options** button in the lower-right corner of the Borders and Shading dialog box. The Border and Shading Options dialog box opens. See Figure 4-27. Here you can change settings that control where the border is positioned on the page. Currently, the border is positioned 24 points from the edge of the page. To ensure that your printer will print the entire border, you need to change the Measure from setting so that it is positioned relative to the outside edge of the text rather than the edge of the page.

Figure 4-27 Border and Shading Options dialog box

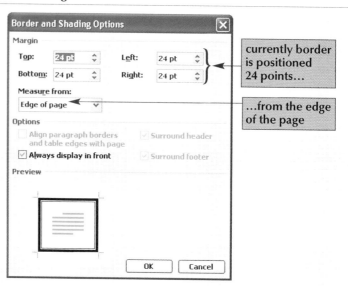

7. Click the **Measure from** list arrow, and then click **Text.** The settings in the Top and Bottom boxes change to 1 pt, and the settings in the Left and Right boxes change to 4 pts, indicating the border's position relative to the edge of the text.

8. Click the **OK** button in the Border and Shading Options dialog box, click **OK** in the Borders and Shading dialog box, and then save your work. The newsletter is now surrounded by an attractive border, as shown earlier in Figure 4-1.

9. Switch to Header and Footer view, change the Zoom setting to Page Width, create a footer that centers **Prepared by your name** and the current date at the bottom of the document. (Be sure to replace "your name" with your first and last name.) Format the footer in a small font to make it as unobtrusive as possible.

10. Close Header and Footer view to return to Print Layout view. Change the Zoom setting to Whole Page. Note that with the Whole Page Zoom setting selected in Print Layout view, there's no need to switch to the Print Preview window. (The Print Preview window provides a fast way to see how the entire document will look at one glance, but does not include the editing tools found in Print Layout or Normal view. By contrast, the Whole Page Zoom setting in Print Layout view allows you to view one page at a time while still providing access to the usual Word editing tools.)

11. Print the newsletter, close the Drawing toolbar, and then close the document but keep Word open, saving the document if prompted to do so. Unless you have a color printer, the WordArt headline and the airplane will print in black and white.

You give the printed newsletter to Max, along with a copy on disk. He thinks it looks great and thanks you for your help. He'll print it later on a high-quality color printer (to get the best resolution for printing multiple copies).

Now that the newsletter is finished, you need to create an accompanying cover letter. Max would like to use Word's mail merge feature to insert customer names and addresses into a form letter.

Understanding the Merge Process

The term **mail merge** refers to the process of combining information from two separate documents to create many final documents, each containing customized information. The two separate documents are called a main document and a data source.

A **main document** is a document (such as a letter) that contains standard text and placeholders (called **merge fields**) that tell Word where to insert variable information (such as a name or an address). You can distinguish merge fields from the other text of the main document, because each merge field name is enclosed by pairs of angled brackets—like this: << >>.

Max's main document is a letter that contains the text shown in Figure 4-28. You will replace the text in brackets with merge fields.

Max's main document **Figure 4-28**

May 25, 2006

[insert address]

Dear [insert first name]:

Enclosed you'll find a newsletter describing Wide World Travel's exciting new Web site, where you can purchase travel clothes selected by our in-house travel experts. From now on, when you are looking for practical and elegant travel attire, think of Wide World Travel. This publication describes just a few of our most popular items. For more information, visit our Web site at www.wide-world-travel.com.

Sincerely,

Max Stephenson
Senior Travel Guide

A **data source** is a document that contains information, such as clients' names and addresses, which will be inserted into the main document. Max plans to send the newsletter to a small test group of clients for starters. His data source is a table in a Word document that contains the names and addresses of five Wide World Travel clients. This table is shown in Figure 4-29. The header row in the table contains the names of the merge fields. Each row in the table contains information about an individual client and, in mail merge terminology, is called a **record**.

Max's data source **Figure 4-29**

a merge field name | header row includes all merge field names for this data source

First Name	Last Name	Street Address	City	State	ZIP
Deborah	Browne	3519 Olbrich Avenue	Hartford	CT	06115
Tom	Finnegan	634 Bay View Court	Hartford	CT	06114
Nikki	Nijhawan	2276 Fairlawn Avenue	Good Hope	CT	06117
Alessandra	Ramirez	1 West Main Street	Hartford	CT	06115
Melissa	Sobek	654 State Street	Newark	DE	19716

record for individual client

During a mail merge, the merge fields in the main document instruct Word to retrieve information from the data source. For example, one merge field in the main document might retrieve a first name from the data source; another merge field might retrieve a street address. For each record in the data source, Word will create a separate letter in the final document, which is called the **merged document**. Thus, if the data source contains five sets of client names and addresses, the merged document will contain five separate letters, each one containing a different client name and address in the appropriate places.

Using the Mail Merge Task Pane

Word's Mail Merge task pane walks you through the steps involved in merging documents. When you first open the Mail Merge task pane, the steps you see described there will vary, depending on what document you have open in the main Word window. To ensure that you see the same thing in the Mail Merge task pane each time, it's helpful to open a new, blank document before you open the Mail Merge task pane. Max asks you to start the mail merge process now.

To begin the mail merge process:

1. Click the **New Blank Document** button ⌐ on the Standard toolbar to open a blank document. Verify that Print Layout view is selected and change the Zoom setting to 100%.

2. Click **Tools** on the menu bar, point to **Letters and Mailings**, and then click **Mail Merge**. The Mail Merge task pane opens. Depending on how your computer is set up, you might also see the Mail Merge toolbar. If you do see the Mail Merge toolbar, close it. See Figure 4-30.

Figure 4-30 ▶ Mail Merge task pane

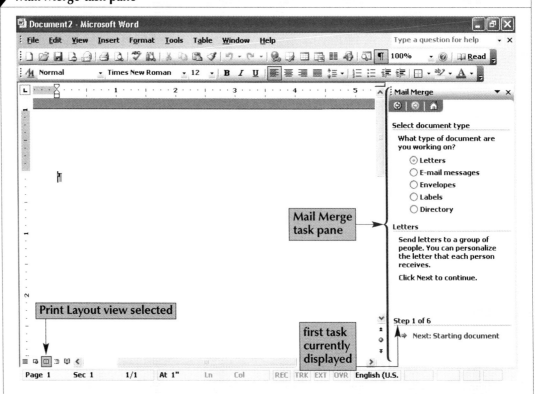

The Mail Merge task pane currently shows the first of six tasks related to completing a mail merge. Your first task is to specify the type of main document you want to use for the merge.

3. Verify that the **Letters** option button is selected in the Mail Merge task pane.

4. At the bottom of the Mail Merge task pane, click **Next: Starting document**. The Mail Merge task pane displays information and options that you can use to select a starting document—that is, to select a main document. In this case, you want to start from an existing document. Specifically, you want to use the Letter document included with your Data Files.

5. Click the **Start from existing document** option button. The task pane displays options for opening an existing document.

6. Verify that **(More files...)** is selected, click the **Open** button on the task pane, and then use the Open dialog box to select and open the file **Letter** located in the Tutorial.04\Tutorial folder. Word inserts the text of the Letter file into the new, blank document, leaving the original Letter file untouched.

7. Check your screen to make sure your document window is in Print Layout view at 100% zoom and with nonprinting characters displayed.

8. Save the document as **Cover Letter** in the Tutorial.04\Tutorial folder, and then scroll down if necessary to display the entire letter. Close the rulers if they are open.

When he first typed the letter, Max included the text in brackets as placeholder text. You will replace the bracketed text with merge fields. First, you need to tell Word where to find the list of recipients for Max's letter.

Selecting a Data Source

You can use many kinds of files as data sources for a mail merge including Word tables, Excel worksheets, Access databases, or a special file designed to store addresses for Microsoft Office applications. You can select a pre-existing file, or you can create a new data source from scratch. In this situation, you will use a pre-existing document containing a simple Word table.

To select the data source:

1. In the bottom of the Mail Merge task pane, click **Next: Select recipients**, and then verify that the **Use an existing list** option button in the task pane is selected.

2. Click **Browse** in the Mail Merge task pane. The Select Data Source dialog box opens. This dialog box is similar to Word's Open dialog box, which you've already used many times.

3. Use the Look in list arrow to open the Tutorial.04\Tutorial folder, select the **Addresses** document, and then click the **Open** button. The table from the Addresses document is displayed in the Mail Merge Recipients dialog box.

4. Click the **OK** button. The Mail Merge Recipients dialog box closes, and you return to the Cover Letter document with the Mail Merge task pane open. Under "Use an existing list," you see the name of the file selected as the data source. (Depending on where you store your Data Files, you may see only the beginning of a directory path, which identifies the location where the data source file is stored.)

5. Click **Next: Write your letter** at the bottom of the Mail Merge task pane. The task pane displays options related to inserting merge fields in the main document.

Inserting Merge Fields

Max's letter is a standard business letter, so you'll place the client's name and address below the date. You could insert individual merge fields for the client's first name, last name, address, city, and ZIP code. But it's easier to use the Address block link in the Mail Merge task pane, which inserts a merge field for the entire address at one click.

To insert an Address Block merge field:

▶ **1.** Select the text **[insert address]**, and then delete it. Remember to delete the opening and closing brackets. Do not delete the paragraph mark following the text.

▶ **2.** Verify that there are four blank paragraphs between the date and the salutation, and that the insertion point is positioned in the third blank paragraph below the date.

▶ **3.** Click **Address block** in the Mail Merge task pane. The Insert Address Block dialog box opens. See Figure 4-31. The options in this dialog box allow you to fine-tune the way the address will be inserted in the letter.

Figure 4-31   **Insert Address Block dialog box**

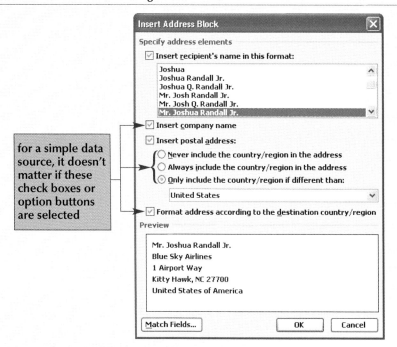

▶ **4.** Verify that the **Insert recipient's name in this format** check box is selected, and then click **Joshua Randall Jr.** in the list box to ensure that Word will insert each recipient's first and last name. (The other options in this list are only useful with more complicated data sources.)

▶ **5.** Verify that the **Insert postal address** check box is selected. It doesn't matter whether any of the other check boxes and option buttons are selected. (These options are only useful with more complicated data sources.)

▶ **6.** Click the **OK** button. An Address Block merge field is inserted in the letter. See Figure 4-32. Depending on how your computer is set up, you might see a gray background behind the merge field. Notice the angled brackets that surround the merge field. The angled brackets are automatically inserted when you insert a merge field. It is important to note that you cannot type the angled brackets and merge field information—you must enter it via a dialog box selection.

Address Block merge field in letter | Figure 4-32

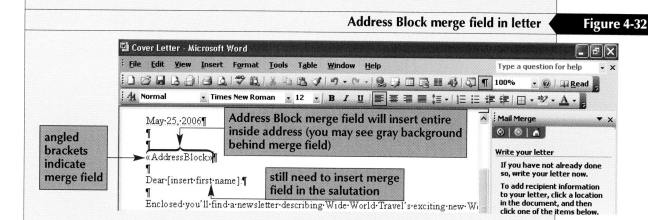

Later, when you merge the main document with the data source, Word will replace the Address Block merge field with information from the data source. Your next job is to insert a merge field that will include each client's first name in the salutation. To insert individual merge codes (rather than a code for the entire address), you need to use the More items option in the Mail Merge task pane.

To insert the merge field for the salutation:

▶ 1. Select and delete **[insert first name]** in the salutation. Remember to delete the opening and closing brackets. Do not delete the colon.

▶ 2. If necessary, insert a space to the left of the colon. When you finish, the insertion point should be positioned between the space and the colon.

▶ 3. Click **More items** in the Mail Merge task pane. The Insert Merge Field dialog box opens. The Fields list shows all the merge fields in the data source. See Figure 4-33. Note that merge fields cannot contain spaces, so Word replaces any spaces in the merge field names with underlines. You want to insert the client's first name into the main document, so you need to make sure the First_Name merge field is selected.

Insert Merge Field dialog box | Figure 4-33

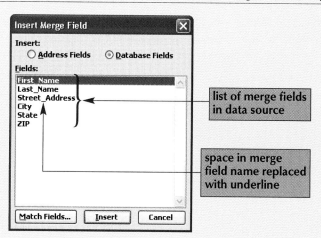

▶ 4. Verify that **First_Name** is selected, click the **Insert** button, and then close the Insert Merge Field dialog box. The First_Name merge field is inserted in the document. See Figure 4-34.

Figure 4-34 **First_Name merge field inserted in document**

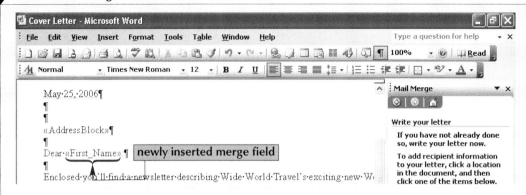

Trouble? If you make a mistake and insert the wrong merge field, click the Undo button 🔄 on the Standard toolbar, and then repeat Steps 3 and 4.

5. Save your changes to the main document.

The main document now contains all the necessary merge fields, but not the data. To include data, you merge the main document and the data source. First, however, you should preview the merged document.

Previewing the Merged Document

When you preview the merged document, you can check one last time for any missing spaces between the merge codes and the surrounding text. You can also look for any other formatting problems, and, if necessary, make final changes to the main document.

To preview the merged document:

1. In the Mail Merge task pane, click **Next: Preview your letters**. The data for the first client in the data source (Deborah Browne) replaces the merge fields in the form letter. See Figure 4-35. Carefully check the letter to make sure the text and formatting are correct. In particular, check to make sure that the spacing before and after the first name in the salutation is correct because it is easy to omit spaces or add extra spaces around merge fields. Finally, notice that the task pane indicates which record is currently displayed in the document.

Previewing the merge document ◄ Figure 4-35

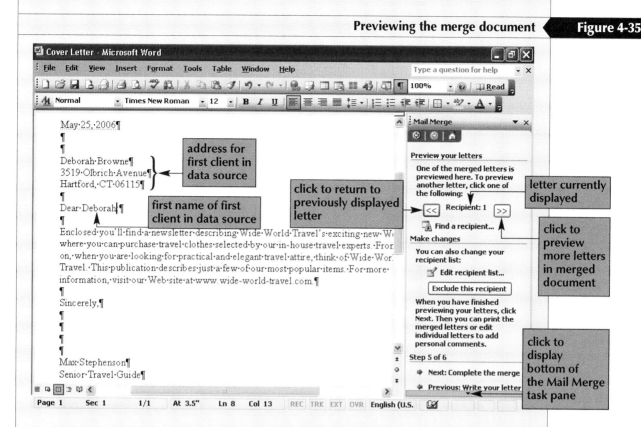

Trouble? If you need to make any changes to the form letter, click the down arrow at the bottom of the Mail Merge task pane to scroll to the bottom of the task pane, click Previous: Write your letter in the task pane, edit the document, save your changes, and then click Next: Preview your letters in the task pane. When you are finished, your screen should look like Figure 4-35.

You are ready for the final step, completing the merge.

Merging the Main Document and Data Source

Now that you've previewed the merge, you're ready to complete the merge between the main document and the data source. The result will be personalized letters to Wide World Travel clients. Because the data source consists of five records, you'll create a merged document with five pages, one letter per page.

To complete the mail merge:

1. In the Mail Merge task pane, click **Next: Complete the merge**. The task pane displays options related to merging the main document and the data source. You can use the Print option to have Word print the customized letters immediately, without displaying them on the screen. Instead, you'll use the Edit individual letters option to merge to a new document.

2. Click **Edit individual letters** in the Mail Merge task pane. The Merge to New Document dialog box opens. Here, you need to specify which records you want to include in the merge. You want to include all the records in the data source.

3. Verify that the **All** option button is selected, click the **OK** button, and then scroll as needed to display the entire first letter. Word creates a new document called Letters1, which contains five pages, one for each record in the data source. Each letter is separated from the one that follows it by a section break. See Figure 4-36. The main document with the merge fields (Cover Letter) remains open, as indicated by its button in the taskbar.

Figure 4-36 ▶ **Newly merged document with customized letters**

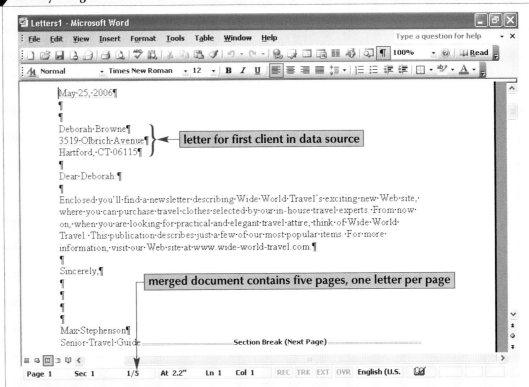

4. Save the merged document in the Tutorial.04\Tutorial folder, using the filename **Merged Cover Letters**. You saved this merged document because it is a small one. However, there's usually no need to waste disk space by saving large merged documents. Typically, you would just print the merged document and close it without saving it. If you need another copy of the merged document later, you can simply merge the data source and main document again.

5. Scroll down and review the five letters. Note the different address and salutation in each.

6. Close the Merged Cover Letters document. The document named Cover Letter reappears, along with the Mail Merge task pane.

7. Close the document and the task pane, and then click the **Yes** button if you are asked to save changes.

You have completed a mail merge and generated a merged document. Max will send the cover letters out with five sample copies of his newsletter right away.

Review

Session 4.2 Quick Check

1. Define the following in your own words:
   a. drop cap
   b. scaling
   c. clip art
   d. main document
   e. data source
2. Explain how to insert a clip art graphic in Word.
3. True or False: When inserting a drop cap, you cannot specify the number of lines you want the drop cap to extend into the document vertically.
4. Describe two different methods for inserting the registered trademark symbol in a document.
5. Describe the process for drawing a border around a page.
6. Describe the steps involved in performing a mail merge.

Review

Tutorial Summary

In this tutorial you planned a newsletter and learned about the elements of desktop publishing. You worked with hyperlinks, created a WordArt headline, anchored a WordArt object, and formatted text in newspaper-style columns. You also inserted a graphic into a document, edited the graphic, inserted drop caps, and inserted symbols and special characters. Finally, you balanced the newsletter columns, drew a border around the page, and used mail merge to create customized cover letters to accompany the newsletter.

Key Terms

balance	links	scanner
bitmap	mail merge	sizing handle
clip art	main document	typographic symbols
crop	merge fields	URL
data source	merged document	Web page
drop cap	newspaper-style column	white space
floating graphic	object	WordArt
graphics	Paint	WordArt Shape button
hyperlinks	record	wrap
inline graphic	scaling	

Practice

Apply the skills you learned in the tutorial using the same case scenario.

Review Assignments

Data Files needed for the Review Assignments: Travel.doc, Highlights.doc, and Addresses.doc

Max's Wide World Travel newsletter was a success; the sales for the advertised items were brisk. Now he has been asked to create a newsletter describing the highlights of some recent Wide World Travel tours. Max has already written the text of the newsletter and asks you to transform it into a professional-looking newsletter. He asks you to create an accompanying cover letter using Word's mail merge feature. Complete the following:

1. Open the file **Travel** from the Tutorial.04\Review folder included with your Data Files, and then check your screen to make sure your Word document is displayed in Print Layout view at 100% zoom, that the nonprinting characters are displayed, and that the Drawing toolbar is open.
2. Save the document as **Travel Highlights** in the same folder.
3. In the first paragraph, replace "YOUR NAME" with your first and last name.
4. Insert "or visit our Web site at www.wide-world-travel.com" at the end of the first paragraph, immediately after the phone number (do not include the quotation marks). Add a period to complete the sentence. Then insert a blank line and remove the hyperlink from the Web address.
5. At the top of the document, create the headline "Wide World Highlights" using WordArt. In the WordArt Gallery, choose the fourth style from the left in the third row down from the top (the rainbow style with the shadow).
6. Change the shape of the WordArt object to Triangle Up, and then italicize the WordArt text.
7. Apply the Top and Bottom wrapping style to the WordArt object.
8. Insert a blank paragraph at the beginning of the document, anchor the WordArt headline to the new paragraph, and then save your work. If the WordArt moves below the new paragraph symbol, drag it up above the new paragraph. When you are finished, the anchor symbol should be positioned to the left of the new paragraph symbol, with the WordArt object positioned above the new paragraph symbol.
9. If necessary, enlarge the WordArt object to span the entire width of the page. Be sure to hold down the Shift key while you drag. When you are finished, the WordArt object should be approximately .5 inches high on the left end, and about 1 inch tall at the center.
10. Position the insertion point to the left of the first word in the paragraph (which begins "Wide World Travel, Inc."), and then format the newsletter text in two columns using the Columns dialog box. Insert a section break so that the two-column formatting is applied to the part of the newsletter after the insertion point. Do not insert a line between columns. View the new columns in Print Layout view, using the Whole Page Zoom setting.
11. Switch to Page Width zoom, and then click to the left of the paragraph that begins "We prefaced our adventure . . . "
12. Insert the clip art graphic of the Eiffel Tower from the Buildings folder in the Office Collections folder.
13. Select and resize the graphic so it is approximately 1.5 inches square.
14. Crop the image vertically about .25" on both the left and right so that, when you are finished, the image is approximately 1 inch wide.
15. Wrap text around the graphic using Tight text wrapping
16. Create a drop cap in the first paragraph under each heading, including the first paragraph below the WordArt headline, using the default settings for the Dropped position.

the insertion point to the top of the column, and click the Text Box button on the Drawing toolbar. A gray box called a drawing canvas appears at the top of the middle column. The drawing canvas contains the text "Create your drawing here." Drag the mouse pointer inside the drawing canvas to draw a rectangle about 1.5 inches wide and one inch tall (using the rulers as a guide), and then release the mouse button. Type "Learn about the advantages of membership!" (without the quotation marks). Select the text in the text box and format it in 14-point Times New Roman, italic, bold. Use the Center Align button to center the text in the text box, and then click anywhere outside the drawing canvas to deselect the text box and the drawing canvas. Switch the Zoom setting to Whole Page and adjust the text box size and the position of the graphic as needed so that the content of the center column fits nicely on the page. Save your work.

Explore

15. To print the brochure, you need to print the first page and then print the second page on the reverse side. Click File on the menu bar, click Print, click the Pages option button, type 1, and then click OK. Retrieve the printed page, and then insert it into your printer's paper tray so that "WHY JOIN?" prints on the reverse side of the list of member benefits; likewise, "WILD GRAINS" should print on the reverse side of the "Welcome to Wild Grains" text. Whether you should place the printed page upside down or right-side up depends on your printer. You may have to print a few test pages until you get it right. When you finish, you should be able to turn page 1 (the page with the heading "Welcome to Wild Grains") face up, and then fold it inward in thirds, along the two column borders. Fold the brochure so that the "WILD GRAINS" column lies on top. *Note*: Ask your instructor if you should print the brochure before doing so.

16. Close the document.

Create

Create the table shown in Figure 4-38, and then use it as the data source for a mail merge resulting in cover letters and envelopes for your own job search.

Case Problem 4

There are no Data Files needed for this Case Problem.

Job Search Cover Letters You're ready to start looking for a job, and plan to use Word's mail merge feature to create customized cover letters to accompany your resume. You'll start by creating the table shown in Figure 4-38 and filling it with address information for potential employers. Then you'll create a cover letter to use as a main document, and customize it by inserting the appropriate mail merge fields.

Figure 4-38

First Name	Last Name	Company Name	Street Address	City	State	ZIP

Complete these steps:

1. Open a new, blank document, and then save it as **Job Search Data Source** in the Tutorial.04\Cases folder included with your Data Files.

2. Create the table shown in Figure 4-38, and then enter information for three potential employers. The information can be real or fictitious. For the First Name and Last Name columns, use the name of an appropriate contact at each company. Save your work and close the document.

3. Open a new, blank document and save it as **Job Search Cover Letter** in the Tutorial.04\Cases folder.
4. Create a cover letter that introduces yourself and describes your experience and education. Instead of an inside address, include the placeholder text "[Inside Address]". For the salutation, use "Dear Ms. [Last Name]". (You'll have a chance to change "Ms." to "Mr." where necessary when you edit the individual merged letters.) Refer the reader to your resume for more information. Use the correct business letter style for your cover letter. Include a sentence in the cover letter that mentions the company name. Use the placeholder "[Company Name]" to remind you to insert the appropriate merge field later. Save your work and close the document.
5. Open a new, blank document, open the Mail Merge task pane, and follow the steps outlined in the Mail Merge task pane. Use the Job Search Cover Letter document as the main document, and select the **Job Search Data Source** file as the data source. Use the Address block merge field for the inside address (and verify that the Insert company name check box is selected in the Insert Address Block dialog box). Add a merge field for the last name in the salutation of the letter, and add a merge field to replace the Company Name placeholder text in the body of the letter. Save your changes to the main document before completing the merge.
6. Preview your letters, and then complete the merge (choosing the Edit individual letters option). Review the letters, and edit them as necessary to use Ms. or Mr. appropriately in the salutation. Save the merged document as **Job Search Cover Letter Merged** in the Tutorial.04\Cases folder, close it, and close the Mail Merge task pane.
7. Print your main document, and then close it.
8. Open a new, blank document, and then save it as **Job Search Envelopes** in the Tutorial.04\Cases folder.

Explore

9. Open the Mail Merge task pane, click the Envelopes option button under Select document type, click Next: Starting document, click Envelope options, and then click OK in the Envelope Options dialog box to select the default settings. The document layout changes to resemble a business size envelope.
10. Continue with the steps in the Mail Merge task pane, selecting the **Job Search Data Source** file as the data source.

Explore

11. Click Next: Arrange your envelope, and then type your name and address as the return address. Notice that the insertion point is positioned in the return address, ready for you to begin typing. (Change the Zoom setting if necessary to make the text easier to read.) Click the paragraph mark in the center of the document and insert an Address block merge field. Save your work.
12. Preview the envelopes, and complete the merge (choosing the Edit individual envelopes option). Save the merged document as **Job Search Envelopes Merged** in the Tutorial.04\Cases folder, and then close it. If your computer is connected to a printer that is stocked with envelopes, print the main document. Close the main document and the Mail Merge task pane.

Research

Go to the Web to find information you can use to create documents.

Internet Assignments

The purpose of the Internet Assignments is to challenge you to find information on the Internet that you can use to work effectively with this software. The actual assignments are updated and maintained on the Course Technology Web site. Log on to the Internet and use your Web browser to go to the Student Online Companion for New Perspectives Office 2003 at **www.course.com/np/office2003**. Click the Internet Assignments link, and then navigate to the assignments for this tutorial.

Assess

SAM Assessment and Training

If you have a SAM user profile, you may have access to hands-on instruction, practice, and assessment of the skills covered in this tutorial. Log in to your SAM account and go to your assignments page to see what your instructor has assigned.

Review

Quick Check Answers

Session 4.1

1. List any four of the following: The document uses multiple fonts; the document incorporates graphics; the document uses typographic symbols; the document uses columns and other special formatting features; the printing is of high-quality.
2. True
3. a. using a desktop computer system to produce commercial-quality printed material; with desktop publishing, you can enter and edit text, create graphics, lay out pages, and print documents
   b. a Word feature that allows you to insert specially formatted text into a document.
   c. unformatted text
   d. a symbol that appears in the left margin, which shows a WordArt object's position in relation to the text
4. False
5. To change the text of a WordArt object, click the object to select it, click the Edit Text button on the WordArt toolbar, edit the text in the Edit WordArt Text dialog box, and then click OK.
6. The WordArt Shape button allows you to change the basic shape of a WordArt object.
7. False

Session 4.2

1. a. a large, uppercase letter that highlights the beginning of the text of a newsletter, chapter, or some other document section
   b. resizing an image to fit a document better
   c. premade artwork that you can insert into your document
   d. a document (such as a letter) that contains standard text and placeholders (called merge fields) that tell Word where to insert variable information (such as a name or an address)
   e. a document that contains information, such as clients' names and addresses, which will be inserted into the main document

2. Position the insertion point at the location where you want to insert the image, click the Insert Clip Art button on the Drawing toolbar, click Organize clips in the Clip Art task pane, open the folder containing the image you want, click the arrow button on the image, click Copy, and then close the Clip Organizer. Finally, paste the graphic into the document.

3. False

4. Click where you want to insert the symbol in the document, click Insert on the menu bar, click Symbol, click the Special Characters tab in the Symbol dialog box, click Registered Trademark in the list, click the Insert button, and then click the Close button. Another option is to type "(r)" and press the spacebar.

5. Click Format on the menu bar, click Borders and Shading, click the Page Border tab in the Borders and Shading dialog box, select the border type you want in the Setting section, choose a line style from the Style list box, make sure Whole document appears in the Apply to list box, and then click OK.

6. Select or create a main document. Select or create a data source. Use the Mail Merge task pane to insert merge fields into the main document. Preview the merged document. Merge the data source and the main document.

Glossary/Index

Task Reference

TASK	PAGE #	RECOMMENDED METHOD
Action, redo	WD 27	Click 🔁 or list arrow
Action, undo	WD 27	Click 🔄 or list arrow
AutoCorrect, use	WD 20	Click 🔽, click correct spelling
Boldface, add to text	WD 72	Select text, click **B**
Border, change in table	WD 119	See Reference Window: Altering Table Borders
Border, draw around page	WD 163	Click Format, click Borders and Shading, click Page Border tab, click Options, click Measure from list arrow, click Text, adjust settings in Top, Bottom, Left and Right boxes, click OK, click OK.
Bullets, add to paragraphs	WD 68	Select paragraphs, click ≔
Clip art, crop	WD 154	Click clip art, click 🔳, drag picture border to crop
Clip art, find	WD 150	Click 🔳 on Drawing toolbar, type search criteria, click Go
Clip art, insert in document	WD 150	Click 🔳 on Drawing toolbar, click Organize Clips, click picture, click Copy, click in document, click 📋
Clip art, resize	WD 153	Click clip art, drag resize handle
Clip art, rotate	WD 155	Click clip art, click 🔄 on the Picture toolbar
Clip art, wrap text around	WD 156	Click clip art, click 🔳 button on the Picture toolbar, click text wrapping option
Clipboard Task Pane, open	WD 54	Click Edit, click Office Clipboard
Clipboard Task Pane, use to cut, copy, and paste	WD 54	See Reference Window: Cutting or Copying and Pasting Text
Column, Insert in table	WD 112	Click Table, point to Insert, click Columns to Right or Columns to Left
Column width, change in table	WD 116	Double-click or drag border between columns; to see measurements, press and hold Alt while dragging
Columns, balance	WD 162	Click the end of the right-most column, click Insert, click Break, click Continuous, click OK
Columns, format text in	WD 147	Click where you want to insert columns, or select text to divide into columns, click Format, click Columns, select options, click OK
Comment, display in Normal view	WD 76	Point to comment
Comment, insert	WD 75	Click insert, click Comment
Date, insert with AutoComplete	WD 24	Start typing date, press Enter
Dictionary, create and select as default	WD 46	Click Tools, click Options, click Spelling & Grammar tab, click Custom Dictionaries, click New, type a name in the File name text box, click Save, click the name of the new dictionary, click Change Default, click OK.
Document, open	WD 43	Click 📂, select drive and folder, click filename, click open
Document, open new	WD 11	Click 🗋
Document, preview	WD 29	Click 🔍

TASK	PAGE #	RECOMMENDED METHOD
Document, save with same name	WD 19	Click 💾
Drawing toolbar, open	WD 140	Click 🔧
Drop cap, insert	WD 158	Click in paragraph, click Format, click Drop Cap, select options, click OK
Envelope, create	WD 30	Click Tools, point to Letters and Mailings, click Envelopes and Labels, click Envelopes tab, type delivery and return addresses, click Print
Find and replace text	WD 58	See Reference Window: Finding and Replacing Text
Font, select default	WD 8	Click Format, click Font, click Font tab, click font name
Font and font size, change	WD 70	See Reference Window: Changing the Font and Font Size
Font size, select default	WD 8	Click Format, click Font, click Font tab, click font size
Footer, add	WD 101	Click View, click Header and Footer, click 🔄, type footer text, click Close
Format, copy	WD 66	Select text with desired format, double-click 🖌, select paragraphs to format, click 🖌
Graphic, crop	WD 154	Click graphic, click ✛, drag to crop
Graphic, find	WD 150	Click 🖼 on Drawing toolbar, type search criteria, click Go
Graphic, resize	WD 153	Click graphic, drag resize handle
Graphic, rotate	WD 155	Click graphic, click 🔄 on the Picture toolbar
Graphic, wrap text around	WD 156	Click graphic, click 📐 button on the Picture toolbar, click text wrapping option
Header, add	WD 101	Click View, click Header and Footer, type header text, click Close
Hyperlink, add in document	WD 138	Type e-mail address or URL, press spacebar
Hyperlink, remove	WD 139	Right-click hyperlink, click Remove Hyperlink
Hyperlink, use	WD 138	Press Ctrl and click the hyperlink
Italics, add to text	WD 73	Select text, click *I*
Line spacing, change	WD 63	Select text to change, press Ctrl+1 for single spacing, Ctrl+5 for 1.5 line spacing, or Ctrl+2 for double spacing
Mail Merge, perform	WD 165	Click Tools, point to Letters and Mailings, click Mail Merge, follow steps in Mail Merge task pane
Margins, change	WD 61	Click File, click Page Setup, click Margins tab, enter margin values, click OK
Nonprinting characters, show	WD 10	Click Show/ Hide ¶
Normal view, change to	WD 7	Click ≡
Numbering, add to paragraphs	WD 69	Select paragraphs, click 🔢
Page, preview more than one	WD 99	Click 🔍, click 🖿
Page, vertically align	WD 100	Click File, click Page Setup, click Layout tab, click Vertical alignment list arrow, click Center
Page, view whole	WD 148	Click Zoom list arrow, click Whole Page
Page break, insert	WD 105	Click where you want to break the page, press Ctrl+Enter
Page number, insert	WD 102	Open header or footer, click 📄 on Header/Footer toolbar
Page orientation, change	WD 60	Click File, click Page Setup, click Margins tab, click Landscape or Portrait icon, click OK.
Paragraph, decrease indent	WD 65	Click 📑

TASK	PAGE #	RECOMMENDED METHOD
Paragraph, indent	WD 65	Click ⬚
Paste options, select	WD 53	Click ⬚
Print layout view, change to	WD 106	Click ⬚
Research task pane, open	WD 76	Click ⬚ .
Research task pane, use Books	WD 77	Connect to Internet, click ⬚ , enter text in Search for text box, verify All Reference is selected in box below Search for text box, click ⬚ .
Row, delete from table	WD 112	See Reference Window: Ways to Insert or Delete Table Rows and Columns
Row, insert in table	WD 112	See Reference Window: Ways to Insert or Delete Table Rows and Columns
Row height, change in table	WD 115	Drag divider between rows; to see measurements, press and hold Alt while dragging
Ruler, display	WD 8	Click View, click Ruler
Section, insert in document	WD 96	Click where you want to insert a section break, click Insert, click Break, click one of the Section break types option buttons, click OK
Section, vertically align	WD 99	Click File, click Page Setup, click Layout tab, click apply to list arrow, click This Section, click Vertical alignment list arrow, click Center, click OK
Shading, apply to table	WD 120	Select table area to shade, click Shading Color list arrow on Tables and Borders toolbar, click a color
Smart Tag, remove	WD 28	Click ⬚ ▾, click Remove this Smart Tag
Special character, insert	WD 160	Click Insert, click Symbol, click Special Characters tab, click special character, click Insert, click Close
Spelling, correct individual word	WD 22	Right-click misspelled word (as indicated by a wavy red line), click correctly spelled word
Spelling and grammar, check	WD 46	See Reference Window: Checking a Document for Spelling and Grammatical Errors
Symbol, insert	WD 161	Click Insert, click Symbol, click desired symbol, click Insert, click Close
Tab stop, set	WD 92	Click tab alignment selector, click ruler
Table, center on page	WD 121	Click in table, click Table, click Table Properties, click Table tab, click Center alignment option, click OK
Table, create	WD 105	Click ⬚ , drag to select columns and rows; or click ⬚ on Tables and Borders toolbar, draw columns and rows
Table, sort	WD 110	Click in the column you want to sort, click ⬚ or ⬚ on Tables and Borders toolbar
Tables and Borders toolbar, display	WD 109	Click ⬚
Task Pane, open	WD 7	Click View, click Task Pane
Text, align	WD 64	Select text, click, ⬚ , ⬚ , ⬚ , or ⬚
Text, align in table	WD 117	Click Align list arrow on Tables and Borders toolbar, click alignment option
Text, copy and paste	WD 54	Select text, click ⬚ click at target location, click ⬚
Text, delete	WD 50	Press Backspace to delete character to left of Insertion point; press Delete to delete character to the right, press Ctrl+Backspace to delete to beginning of word; press Ctrl+Delete to delete to end of word

REF 8 | New Perspectives Series

TASK	PAGE #	RECOMMENDED METHOD
Text, move by cut and paste	WD 54	Select text, click ✂ click at target location, click 📋
Text, move by drag and drop	WD 52	Select text, drag selected text to target location, release mouse button
Text, select a block of	WD 49	Click at beginning of block, press and hold Shift and click at end of block
Text, select entire document	WD 49	Press Ctrl and click in selection bar
Text, select multiple adjacent lines	WD 49	Click and drag in selection bar
Text, select multiple nonadjacent lines	WD 49	Select text, press and hold Ctrl, and select next text
Text, select multiple paragraphs	WD 49	Click and drag in selection bar
Text, select paragraph	WD 49	Double-click in selection bar next to paragraph
Text, select sentence	WD 49	Press Ctrl and click in sentence
Text, wrap around WordArt	WD 144	Click WordArt, click 📷 on the WordArt toolbar, click text wrap option
Toolbar, display	WD 7	Right-click any visible toolbar, click toolbar name
Underline, add to text	WD 73	Select text, click U
Word, start	WD 5	Click start, point to All Programs, point to Microsoft Office, click Microsoft Office Word 2003
WordArt, change shape	WD 143	Click WordArt, click A on the WordArt toolbar, click shape
WordArt, edit text	WD 142	Click WordArt, click Edit Text button on WordArt toolbar, edit text, click OK
WordArt, insert	WD 139	Click 📄, click WordArt style, click OK, type WordArt text, select font, size, and style, click OK
WordArt, wrap text	WD 144	Click WordArt, click 📷 on the WordArt toolbar, click text wrap option
Zoom setting, change	WD 8	Click Zoom list arrow, click zoom selection